When in France,
DO AS THE
FRENCH DO

The Clued-In Guide to French Life, Language, and Culture

Ross Steele

McGraw-Hill

Chicago   New York   San Francisco   Lisbon   London   Madrid   Mexico City
Milan   New Delhi   San Juan   Seoul   Singapore   Sydney   Toronto

Library of Congress Cataloging-in-Publication Data

Steele, Ross.
    When in France, do as the French do : the clued-in guide to French life,
language and culture / Ross Steele.
       p.   cm. — (When in— do as the locals do)
    Includes index.
    ISBN 0-8442-2552-5
    1. France—Civilization.   2. France—Description and travel.   3. France—
Social life and customs.   I. Title.   II. Series.

DC33.S84   2002
944—dc21   2002023529

McGraw-Hill

A Division of The McGraw·Hill Companies

1 2 3 4 5 6 7 8 9 0   LBM/LBM   0 9 8 7 6 5 4 3 2

ISBN 0-8442-2552-5 2899 8499 $11/02$

This book was set in Electra
Printed and bound by Lake Book Manufacturing

Cover design by Nick Panos
Cover photograph copyright © Corbis
Interior design by Jennifer Locke
Interior illustration by Fred Dolven
Map on page 93 by Mapping Specialists

McGraw-Hill books are available at special quantity discounts to use as premiums and
sales promotions, or for use in corporate training programs. For more information, please
write to the Director of Special Sales, Professional Publishing, McGraw-Hill, Two Penn
Plaza, New York, NY 10121-2298. Or contact your local bookstore.

This book is printed on acid-free paper.

Contents

Test Yourself Quizlinks

When in France, do you know how to adapt by doing as the French do? How aware are you of French customs and traditions? How *au fait* are you with French history, which permeates so much of modern-day France? And how *au courant* are you with contemporary daily life and the typical domestic routines of the French people?

The following quiz will test your knowledge. There are 177 questions in all, each corresponding to a specific section within the book. To discover the answer and more information about the subject, follow the quizlink to the relevant section. Alternatively, you can check the answers listed at the back.

Do as the French Do

1. To whom should you direct introductions in a business meeting? ➤50
   a. oldest man present   b. oldest woman   c. youngest woman

2. During business meals, when is the business topic generally discussed? ➤51
   a. immediately   b. over dessert   c. food and business are not mixed

3. When are business cards given out? ➤52
   a. on first introduction   b. at the end of the meeting   c. business cards are rarely used

4. How do family members and close friends greet each other? ➤54
   a. one kiss on both cheeks   b. three kisses   c. it varies according to region

5. How often do work colleagues go out on Friday nights? ➤55
   a. once a week   b. occasionally   c. very rarely

6. What is not an appropriate gift for the hostess of a dinner? ➤57
   a. wine   b. flowers   c. candy for children

7. What is usually said before a meal begins? ➤58
   a. grace   b. *Bon appétit!*   c. *Santé*

8. What is a frequent topic of conversation at the dinner table? ➤59
   a. weather   b. politics   c. money

9. How should you gesture for two beers? ➤62
   a. thumb and index finger   b. index and middle finger   c. thumb and little finger

10. How late is it acceptable to arrive for a business appointment? ➤50
    a. punctually on time   b. five minutes late   c. ten minutes late

TEST YOURSELF QUIZLINKS

11. How should personal criticism be delivered? ➤63
    a. preface it with an apology   b. in a roundabout way   c. it should be avoided

12. Which action is *not* considered to be a sign of good luck? ➤65
    a. to see a ladybug flying   b. to walk on animal   c. to cross the path of a
                                    droppings with the   black cat at night
                                    left foot

13. How should you attract the waiter's attention in a restaurant? ➤127
    a. snap your fingers   b. *"Garçon!"*   c. *"Monsieur, s'il vous
                                                          plaît!"*

14. How should you begin a formal professional letter to a Monsieur Dupont? ➤84
    a. *Cher Monsieur*   b. *Cher M. Dupont*   c. *Monsieur*

15. How do parents generally respond to their child's misbehavior in public? ➤166
    a. tolerance   b. reprimand on the spot   c. punishment when back at home

What's the Number?

1. How much French territory is agricultural? ➤41
   a. 40 to 50 percent   b. 50 to 60 percent   c. 60 to 70 percent

2. How much annual paid vacation are all salaried workers entitled to? ➤46
   a. three weeks   b. four weeks   c. five weeks

3. How many French have a garden or terrace? ➤72
   a. 58 percent   b. 76 percent   c. 93 percent

4. How much wine do the French drink per person per year? ➤78
   a. 33 liters   b. 55 liters   c. 77 liters

5. How much bread sold in France is produced by individual *boulangerie*
   shops? ➤81
   a. 40 percent   b. 60 percent   c. 75 percent

6. How much of a young person's diet is made up of hamburgers? ➤83
   a. 1 percent   b. 11 percent   c. 23 percent

7. How many French are obese? ➤97
   a. 7 percent   b. 13 percent   c. 21 percent

8. How many French soldiers died in World War I? ➤106
   a. 500,000   b. 1.5 million   c. 2.5 million

9. According to the proverb, *un point à temps* (a stitch in time) is worth how much? ➤122
   a. *deux* (2)　　　　　　　b. *cent* (100)　　　　　　c. *mille* (1,000)

10. Which of these numbers is the smallest? ➤124
    a. 3 456　　　　　　　　b. 3,456　　　　　　　　c. 3.456

11. How many French vacation abroad? ➤136
    a. less than 20 percent　b. 20 to 40 percent　　c. 40 to 60 percent

12. How many foreign tourists visit France every year? ➤138
    a. 38 million　　　　　　b. 66 million　　　　　　c. 84 million

13. How many bridges cross the Seine in Paris? ➤143
    a. 17　　　　　　　　　b. 23　　　　　　　　　c. 31

14. How much of the housework do women do, on average? ➤158
    a. 60 percent　　　　　　b. 70 percent　　　　　　c. 80 percent

15. How many couples have a civil marriage? ➤165
    a. 47 percent　　　　　　b. 67 percent　　　　　　c. 100 percent

16. How many of the most famous and powerful come from working-class homes? ➤174
    a. less than 5 percent　　b. 5 to 15 percent　　　c. more than 15 percent

17. How many French live below the poverty threshold? ➤176
    a. less than 10 percent　b. 10 to 20 percent　　c. more than 20 percent

18. How many times has Alsace changed hands over the past 150 years? ➤189
    a. two　　　　　　　　　b. three　　　　　　　　c. four

Who's Who?

1. Who is a RMIste? ➤49
   a. farmer trade unionist　b. Corsican terrorist　　c. unemployment
   　　　　　　　　　　　　　　　　　　　　　　　　　　benefit recipient

2. Who were the victims of the Saint Bartholomew's Day massacre? ➤102
   a. Jews　　　　　　　　b. Protestants　　　　　c. Catholics

3. Who are the *Immortels*? ➤118
   a. World Cup soccer stars　b. highest ranking judges　c. members of the
   　　　　　　　　　　　　　　　　　　　　　　　　　　Académie française

4. Which is the largest religious group, after Catholics (67%) and nonbelievers (23%)? ➤168
   a. Muslims   b. Jews   c. Protestants

5. Which is the largest category of male workers? ➤167
   a. professionals   b. farm workers   c. the retired

6. Who are *les gens bien*? ➤175
   a. the aristocracy   b. the new elite   c. intellectuals

Famous French

1. This famous writer became General de Gaulle's Minister of Cultural Affairs, instituting a policy of cleaning major monuments and buildings. ➤16
   a. André Gide   b. André Malraux   c. François Mauriac

2. This customs official was a self-taught naive artist who painted exotic junglescapes. ➤21
   a. Henri Matisse   b. Henri Rousseau   c. Georges Braque

3. He made operetta the most popular musical entertainment in 19th-century France. ➤28
   a. Hector Berlioz   b. Jacques Offenbach   c. Georges Bizet

4. He was France's first rock star. ➤31
   a. Georges Brassens   b. Johnny Hallyday   c. Yves Montand

5. This 16th-century monk, physician, and satirist was author of *Gargantua and Pantagruel*. ➤35
   a. François Rabelais   b. Jean de la Fontaine   c. Pierre Ronsard

6. The first woman elected to Académie française was a writer who moved permanently to Maine, in the United States. ➤37
   a. Marguerite Duras   b. Nathalie Sarraute   c. Marguerite Yourcenar

7. This ancient man was found in the Dordogne. ➤99
   a. Megalith man   b. Cro-Magnon man   c. Jurassic man

8. He led the French Resistance movement within France. ➤107
   a. Charles de Gaulle   b. Jean Moulin   c. Philippe Pétain

9. She represents the Mother Country. ➤111
   a. Marianne   b. Marie   c. Brigitte

10. He is head of the International Organization of Francophonie. ►115
    a. Valéry Giscard d'Estaing   b. Jacques Delors   c. Boutros Boutros Ghali

11. His work *Esprit des Lois* expounded the separation of power of the legislature,
    executive, and judiciary. ►149
    a. Jean-Jacques Rousseau   b. Montesquieu   c. Blaise Pascal

12. She was France's first woman prime minister. ►157
    a. Simone Veil   b. Martine Aubry   c. Edith Cresson

13. This person founded the popular benevolent association Restos du coeur. ►177
    a. an actor   b. a priest   c. a president's wife

What's My Line?

1. For what did Zizi Jeanmaire become a national idol? ►27
   a. contemporary dance   b. singing ballads   c. acting

2. For what is Olivier Messiaen known? ►29
   a. music of the whole world   b. dissonant harmonies   c. polytonality

3. What is Saint-Ouen famous for? ►71
   a. a flea market   b. a dog cemetery   c. media companies

4. Alain Ducasse is famous as . . . ►77
   a. a DNA scientist   b. a serial bank robber c. a celebrity chef

5. For which sport is Zinédine Zidane known? ►110
   a. soccer   b. cycling   c. slalom skiing

6. For what is Baron Haussmann noted? ►140
   a. first beheading by   b. modernization of Paris c. crossing the Channel
      the Revolution   by balloon

7. In which area of social science is Claude Lévi-Strauss best known? ►150
   a. psychoanalysis   b. semiotics   c. anthropology

8. In which area were Antoine Lavoisier and Joseph Gay-Lussac distinguished? ►160
   a. chemistry   b. immunology   c. electrodynamics

Organizations and Companies

1. What was the Gobelins factory famous for making? ►20
   a. tapestries   b. hunting equipment   c. porcelain

TEST YOURSELF QUIZLINKS

2. What are Bénéteau and Jeanneau known for? ➤39
   a. pharmaceuticals   b. boat construction   c. telecommunications

3. Which was the first Japanese manufacturer to build a car plant in France? ➤45
   a. Toyota   b. Mitsubishi   c. Nissan

4. Trade union membership constitutes how much of the total workforce in France? ➤48
   a. less than 20 percent   b. 20 to 50 percent   c. more than 50 percent

5. Which of these is not a champagne producer? ➤78
   a. Heidsieck   b. Clos-Vougeot   c. Veuve Cliquot

6. Which of the following organizations is not based in Paris? ➤139
   a. UNESCO   b. OECD   c. European Bank

7. Where does the Rassemblement pour la République (RPR) lie on the political spectrum? ➤154
   a. left   b. center   c. right

France and Beyond

1. Which city holds an annual opera festival? ➤17
   a. Strasbourg   b. Avignon   c. Aix-en-Provence

2. Where does *raï* music originate from? ➤31
   a. North Africa   b. Southeast Asia   c. French Polynesia

3. Where are France's nuclear reactors primarily located? ➤42
   a. Aquitaine   b. Loire and Rhône valleys   c. Picardie and Lorraine

4. Where are European Space Agency satellites launched? ➤44
   a. French Guiana   b. Martinique   c. La Réunion

5. Which region is known for foie gras, cassoulet, truffles, and goat cheese? ➤75
   a. Southwest   b. Alsace   c. Provence

6. What is the longest river in France? ➤86
   a. Loire   b. Garonne   c. Seine

7. What is the famous wildlife area in the estuary of the Rhône? ➤87
   a. Camargue   b. Cevennes   c. Massif Central

8. Which of these châteaux is *not* in Ile-de-France (the region surrounding Paris)? ➤89
   a. Chantilly   b. Fontainebleu   c. Blois

9. Which city is a major administrative and insurance center, two hours from Paris by high-speed train? ➤90
   a. Nantes   b. Lille   c. Orléans

10. Where is the popular Futuroscope theme park? ➤91
    a. Poitiers   b. Limoges   c. Clermont-Ferrand

11. Which city was the capital of Roman and Christian Gaul? ➤92
    a. Nice   b. Arles   c. Marseille

12. Which of the following territories is not a DOM (*département d'outre-mer*)? ➤94
    a. Guadeloupe   b. Corsica   c. Réunion

13. What city did Joan of Arc relieve in 1429? ➤100
    a. Rouen   b. Le Mans   c. Orléans

14. Where was Napoléon Bonaparte first buried? ➤104
    a. Elba   b. Waterloo   c. Sainte Helena

15. Which of these was never a French colony? ➤105
    a. Cambodia   b. Sierra Leone   c. Sudan

16. Where in France would you hear a twangy, nasal accent? ➤116
    a. North   b. South   c. Brittany

17. Which of these towns was founded first, judging by word origins? ➤125
    a. Aix   b. Isère   c. Honfleur

18. What is the most popular tourist destination in Europe? ➤138
    a. Eiffel Tower   b. Disneyland Paris   c. Notre Dame Cathedral

19. Which was the last region to be created, in 1976? ➤151
    a. Provence-Alpes–Côte d'Azur   b. Nord-Pas-de-Calais   c. Ile-de-France

20. Where did nationalist violence occur in the late 1990s? ➤152
    a. Corsica   b. French Pyrénées   c. Guadeloupe

21. Which of these cities does not have a Metro system? ➤182
    a. Rennes   b. Rouen   c. Toulon

TEST YOURSELF QUIZLINKS

22. The first TGV (high-speed train) line ran between Paris and where? ➤183
    a. Lille   b. Lyon   c. Bordeaux

23. What river joins the Canal du Midi to link the Atlantic Ocean with the Mediterranean? ➤184
    a. Dordogne   b. Garonne   c. Rhône

24. What international airport is situated nine miles south of Paris? ➤185
    a. Roissy–Charles de Gaulle   b. Le Bourget   c. Orly

25. Where have the French never tested nuclear weapons? ➤186
    a. French Polynesia   b. Sahara   c. New Caledonia

26. Where does the European Parliament meet? ➤187
    a. Strasbourg   b. Paris   c. Luxembourg

Know Your Way Around Paris

1. Where did the installation of sculptures in the mid-1980s cause controversy? ➤22
   a. Palais Royal   b. Champs-Elysée   c. Rodin Museum

2. Where should you *not* go to see an erotic show? ➤56
   a. Folies Bergère   b. Les Halles   c. Lido

3. What area has become the fashionable location for bars for young people? ➤85
   a. Trocadero   b. Montmartre   c. Bastille

4. Where does the president give his national address on July 14? ➤131
   a. Bastille   b. Palais de l'Elysée   c. Arc de Triomphe

5. What is held at Roland Garros every year? ➤134
   a. Formula 1 Grand Prix   b. French Open Tennis   c. final stage of the Tour de France

6. What major cultural monument was opened by President Valéry Giscard d'Estaing? ➤137
   a. Louvre pyramid   b. Bastille Opera   c. Musée d'Orsay

7. Which of these monuments is located on the left bank? ➤141
   a. Eiffel Tower   b. Notre Dame   c. Arc de Triomphe

8. Where are Voltaire, Zola, and Marie Curie buried? ➤142
   a. Père Lachaise Cemetery   b. Sacré Coeur Basilica   c. Panthéon

9. Mourners mark the death of Princess Diana by the Liberty Flame near what bridge? ➤144
   a. Pont de la Concorde   b. Pont d'Iéna   c. Pont Royal

10. Which former village in Paris contains the former houses of Renault factory workers that have become homes for office workers? ➤145
    a. Saint-Denis   b. Auteil   c. Neuilly

11. What is the huge forest and garden area situated west of the city? ➤146
    a. bois de Vincennes   b. parc de la Villette   c. bois de Boulogne

12. Which of these is not a Parisian department store? ➤147
    a. Les Galeries Lafayette   b. La Samaritaine   c. Les Trois Suisses

13. What is the science and technology museum complex in the north of Paris? ➤161
    a. Futuroscope   b. La Villette   c. Parc Asterix

14. Why is traffic stopped on Friday nights on certain routes in Paris? ➤181
    a. demonstrations   b. roller blading   c. road resurfacing program

Dates

1. When did France join the European Economic Community? ➤38
   a. 1951   b. 1957   c. 1964

2. What does *les trente glorieuses* (the 30 glorious years) refer to? ➤40
   a. military successes against the Germans   b. prime vintages from Bordeaux   c. the post–World War II boom years

3. When could women join the workforce without their husbands' consent? ➤47
   a. 1919   b. 1939   c. 1965

4. When did the first restaurant open in Paris? ➤74
   a. 1634   b. 1765   c. 1816

5. When was the *tricolore* adopted as France's flag? ➤111
   a. 1583   b. 1790   c. 1830

6. When was French made the official language of government? ➤117
   a. 7th century   b. 11th century   c. 16th century

7. When was the Minitel home computer service introduced? ➤162
   a. 1979   b. 1983   c. 1988

TEST YOURSELF QUIZLINKS

8. When did the euro replace the franc? ➤178
   a. January 2000   b. January 2001   c. January 2002

9. When did France sign the Treaty of Maastricht? ➤189
   a. 1454   b. 1815   c. 1992

A Question of Time

1. How long must young people serve in compulsory military or civil service? ➤66
   a. 1 year   b. 18 months   c. not required

2. When is an *étrenne* gift given to children by their grandparents? ➤67
   a. first communion   b. christening   c. New Year's

3. How long is the average weekday dinner? ➤68
   a. 24 minutes   b. 33 minutes   c. 46 minutes

4. When is cheese usually served? ➤80
   a. after the main course b. with dessert   c. after dessert

5. When do French-born children of immigrants become citizens? ➤110
   a. automatically at birth b. after 10 years' residence c. upon application at 18

6. How long did it take to build Notre Dame Cathedral in Paris? ➤114
   a. 40 years   b. 60 years   c. 80 years

7. When are most short messages sent by mobile phone? ➤129
   a. noon to 1:00 P.M.   b. 5:00 to 6:00 P.M.   c. 10:00 to 11:00 P.M.

8. Which holiday is the worst time to drive on the autoroutes in France? ➤130
   a. Assomption   b. Pentecôte   c. Toussaint

9. What is celebrated each year on June 21? ➤132
   a. cheese   b. music   c. technology

10. How long does the president serve? ➤153
    a. four years   b. five years   c. seven years

11. What is the key time of year for labor conflict? ➤156
    a. February   b. May   c. September

12. What is the average retirement age in France? ➤164
    a. 57   b. 59   c. 63

The Order of Things

1. Buildings in order of construction, from earliest to most recent. ➤19, 21
   a. Picasso Museum
   b. Grande Arche at La Défense
   c. Centre Georges Pompidou

2. Greetings in order of formality, from most to least. ➤53
   a. *Salut*
   b. *Bonjour*, Madame/Monsieur
   c. *Bonjour*

3. Appliances in order of ownership, from highest to lowest. ➤70
   a. microwave oven
   b. dishwasher
   c. coffeemaker

4. Pets in order of popularity, from the most to the least. ➤73
   a. dog
   b. cat
   c. fish

5. Events in the order they occur during the year. ➤133, 134
   a. French Tennis Open
   b. Six Nations Rugby
   c. Tour de France

6. Environmental concerns held by the public, from most to least. ➤155
   a. air pollution
   b. water pollution
   c. protecting countryside

7. Origin of French immigrants, from most to least. ➤163
   a. Europe
   b. Africa
   c. Asia

8. Public sector employees in order of respect, from most to least. ➤172
   a. police
   b. hospital staff
   c. postal workers

Identify This

1. What is the Comédie-Française? ➤26
   a. a theater
   b. an annual festival of humor
   c. a series of novels by Balzac

2. What is *un smoking*? ➤61
   a. overalls
   b. sport jacket
   c. tuxedo

3. What is the "national pastime" *système D*? ➤64
   a. circumventing regulations
   b. getting to the head of a line
   c. avoiding paying taxes

4. What are *cartons* and *faire-parts*? ➤128
   a. announcement cards
   b. dressmaking tools
   c. cheese packaging

5. What is a *code de la porte*? ➤170
   a. door number
   b. door number-code lock
   c. zip code

11

6. What is a *carte grise*? ➤171
   a. national identity card   b. social security card   c. car registration

7. What are Banco, Tac-O-Tac, and Millionnaire? ➤179
   a. television game shows   b. scratch lottery tickets   c. casino chains

Know What the French Know

1. In what style of architecture were the cathedrals of Reims, Amiens, and Chartres built? ➤18
   a. Romanesque   b. Gothic   c. Baroque

2. What is considered the first school of French photography? ➤23
   a. Daguerreotypes   b. Portraitistes   c. Reportage

3. What was the first film of the French film industry? ➤25
   a. *Napoléon*   b. *Voyage dans la lune*   c. *Sortie des usines Lumière*

4. What is the French equivalent of the Oscars? ➤25
   a. Palme d'Or   b. Césars   c. Lumières

5. What genre is the recent television hit "Loft Story"? ➤32
   a. soap opera   b. reality television   c. extreme game show

6. What news magazine would a political moderate purchase? ➤33
   a. *Libération*   b. *L'Equipe*   c. *L'Express*

7. What was the first Tintin story? ➤34
   a. *Le Mystère de la toison d'or*   b. *Tintin au pays des soviets*   c. *Le Temple du soleil*

8. Which of these novels forms part of Balzac's *La Comédie humaine*? ➤36
   a. *Madame Bovary*   b. *Eugénie Grandet*   c. *Le Rouge et le Noir (The Red and the Black)*

9. What is the most common credit card used in France? ➤43
   a. Carte Bleue   b. Visa   c. MasterCard

10. What is the largest cause of discomfort among retired apartment dwellers? ➤69
    a. noisy neighbors   b. dust and pollution   c. unpleasant smells

11. What does the *GaultMillau Guide* award top restaurants? ➤76
    a. chef's hats   b. stars   c. forks

12. Which of these would you order if you wanted sparkling water? ➤79
    a. Evian   b. Vitel   c. Badoit

13. What do most children eat at school? ➤82
    a. state-provided lunch b. packed lunch from home c. snacks bought in
                                school

14. What does the Bayeux Tapestry depict? ➤100
    a. coronation of   b. Norman invasion of Britain c. Renaissance
     Charlemagne   hunting scenes

15. What ended the First Republic? ➤109
    a. Napoléon's First Empire b. defeat by Germany   c. the French Revolution

16. What is the emblem worn by French sports teams? ➤111
    a. *fleur de lys*   b. *tricolore*   c. rooster

17. What do the French *not* consume more than other Europeans? ➤95
    a. wine   b. sedatives and   c. tobacco
               sleeping pills

18. What do the French suffer from least, compared with other Europeans? ➤96
    a. domestic accidents b. appendicitis   c. cardiovascular disease

19. What do French women think they need most to attract the opposite sex? ➤98
    a. a good figure   b. a pleasant personality c. intelligence

20. What was the rallying cry of the Revolution? ➤111
    a. *Egalité, Liberté, Autorité* b. *Liberté, Egalité,*   c. *Egalité, Fraternité,*
                 Fraternité   *Maternité*

21. What crisis brought Charles de Gaulle out of retirement in 1958? ➤108
    a. European Union   b. war in Algeria   c. war in Indochina

22. What does the Toubon law (1994) require? ➤117
    a. use of French in   b. disabled access to   c. listing ingredients on
     advertisements   public buildings   food labels

23. What did television presenter Bernard Pivot launch in 1985? ➤119
    a. World French Spelling b. National Lottery   c. annual television
     Competition   dance-athon

24. Which of these words does not appear in the latest edition of the *Petit Larousse*
    dictionary? ➤121
    a. *top-model*   b. *narcodollar*   c. *le supersizing* **13**

25. Which of these abbreviations has nothing to do with transportation? ➤123
    a. CRS   b. RER   c. TGV

26. What is the most common family name? ➤126
    a. Dubois   b. Dupont   c. Martin

27. What culinary movement uses authentic produce and ingredients from other
    national traditions? ➤139
    a. *la cuisine bourgeoise*   b. *la nouvelle cuisine*   c. *la cuisine mince*

28. Which of these principles is espoused in Cartesian logic? ➤148
    a. relativity   b. objectivity   c. pragmatics

29. What does the controversial PACS law (passed in 1999) concern? ➤159
    a. the legal status of   b. abortion rights   c. citizenship for
       domestic partner   immigrants
       relationships

30. What is the top score in the *baccalauréat* exam? ➤167
    a. 100   b. A+   c. 20

31. In what part of town do high-income earners usually live? ➤170
    a. downtown   b. the suburbs   c. surrounding villages

32. What does each newly elected president grant an amnesty for? ➤180
    a. speeding tickets   b. parking tickets   c. train ticket-evasion
                                                            fines

33. In what respect are France and Germany similar? ➤190
    a. theater and opera   b. shop opening hours   c. museum opening
       starting times   hours

34. What major concession did Euro Disney make to French culture? ➤191
    a. removed Main   b. staff to only speak   c. allowed serving of
       Street, USA   French   alcohol

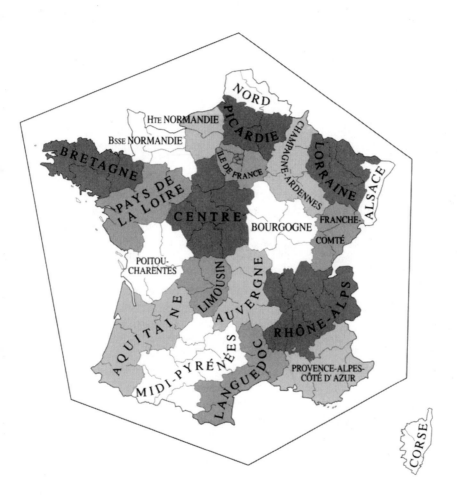

NORD

Hte NORMANDIE

Bsse NORMANDIE

PICARDIE

CHAMPAGNE-ARDENNES

LORRAINE

ALSACE

BRETAGNE

ILE DE FRANCE

PAYS DE LA LOIRE

CENTRE

BOURGOGNE

FRANCHE-COMTÉ

POITOU-CHARENTES

LIMOUSIN

AUVERGNE

RHÔNE-ALPS

AQUITAINE

MIDI-PYRÉNÉES

LANGUEDOC

PROVENCE-ALPES-CÔTÉ D'AZUR

CORSE

ARTS
Cultural Policy

The image of France is inextricably linked to that of its culture, which in the national interest has traditionally been preserved and promoted by the state. This goes back to the 16th and 17th centuries, with the creation of the Académie française in 1635 to protect the purity of French language. The French monarchy proclaimed itself "Protector of the Arts" in the 17th century and encouraged artists and writers. The Palace of Versailles and the Comédie-Française (1680) theater are monuments and institutions that still exist today and bear witness to this great cultural tradition.

In the second half of the 20th century this policy of promoting cultural heritage was reformulated. To the two objectives of encouraging art and conservation of the national heritage, a third was added, that of the diffusion of French culture throughout the world. In 1959, the Fifth Republic instituted a Ministry of Cultural Affairs, which was headed for ten years by the well-known writer, cultural historian, and politician, André Malraux. He created cultural centers for young people throughout France and introduced a state policy of cleaning major monuments and buildings that had become black with age and pollution. The cleaner white facades of Notre Dame and the Paris Opera, for example, gave them new beauty. In the 1980s, Jack Lang, the dynamic Minister for Culture who collaborated closely with President Mitterrand, continued the decentralization of culture to the regions with Arts Festivals and a Festival of Music. The French government allocates approximately 1 percent of the national budget to culture, and today French culture flowers throughout the country.

The richness of France's artistic and high cultural heritage is associated with masterpieces of architecture, painting, sculpture, and music, as well as literature, photography, and cinema. Archaeological sites, Roman monuments, and Gothic cathedrals are considered part of the national heritage. Some works of French art and sculpture have become international cultural icons, and examples of French painting, such as impressionism, are essential components of the leading art museums throughout the world. The Louvre, in Paris, the biggest art museum in the world, has a history dating back to the 16th century, when King François I began the collection by purchasing numerous Italian masterpieces, including the *Mona Lisa*. And each year, over a weekend in September, the French celebrate their cultural heritage along with appreciation of their history during the Journées du patrimoine.

Related Web links: culture.gouv.fr is the site of the Ministry of Culture and Communication (F)

Culture for the People

Summer in France is when culture goes to the streets. At no other time is French culture so visible and so accessible to both the French and tourists alike. The summer cultural festivals, especially in the south of France with its sunny climate, are the exuberant manifestation of French traditions and contemporary creations in art, music, theater, dance, and cinema. Heavily sponsored by local, regional, and national governments, these festivals occur all over France, in tiny villages and towns as well as in Paris. They often continue the popular traditions of a region or give expression to local talent in drama or music.

Since 1982, on June 21, the fête de la Musique (Festival of Music) is celebrated all over France by thousands of musicians, amateur or professional, playing anything from classical to rap. In addition, at other times certain regions have special festivals. The internationally famous theater festival, founded by the actor and director Jean Vilar in 1947, takes place in June and July in Avignon. There's a festival of opera at Aix-en-Provence, choral singing at Vaison-la-Romaine, contemporary dance at Strasbourg, and a world music festival in Arles in July.

In Paris, the Festival d'automne (from mid-September to the end of December) celebrates music, dance, and theater. It includes a religious art festival at the church of St.-Germain-des-Prés, the largest international contemporary art fair in Paris, and the Paris Jazz Festival, held throughout the city and attracting international jazz musicians. In addition, a festival of baroque music takes place at the Château of Versailles, not far from Paris. November is known as the Month of the Photo in Paris, and numerous photography shows are held in galleries and museums.

You can also find culture on television. Public television in France has always devoted a part of its programming to culture. A popular program on literature, hosted by Bernard Pivot, was initially called "Apostrophe," and then "Bouillon de culture" (A Soup of Culture). Pivot also hosted a national spelling test (*Les Dicos d'or*). Since 1992, Arte, a television chain jointly run by France and Germany and devoted entirely to cultural programs, has offered programs in both French and German. And FNAC, a popular chain of French stores dedicated to knowledge and leisure, offers a vast choice of French language books, literature, music, and videos for the general public.

Related Web links: fetedelamusique.culture.fr is the official guide to fête de la Musique (F)

Architectural Heritage

Architectural reminders of France's role in European history, as well as of the evolution of its own history, are evident throughout the country. From Paris to the smallest village, buildings and monuments from the distant past have survived. In a sense, the French live amid their history. The aqueducts, amphitheaters, and arches attest to the occupation of France by the Romans. The small Romanesque churches of the 10th and 11th centuries, with their heavy, rounded arches, and the vast Gothic cathedrals of the 12th and 13th centuries, demonstrate the growth of Christianity in France. New architectural techniques used to express the triumph of the Christian faith represent the sophistication of medieval civilization and the influence of the new social class—the clergy. The main innovations were the pointed arch, rib vaulting, and the flying buttress combined with vertical lines of tall pillars, spires, and greater height in interior spaces. The cathedrals of Notre Dame in Paris; Reims, Amiens, and Chartres in northern France; and Sainte Chapelle in Paris are all magnificent examples of Gothic architecture.

Architectural triumphs of the medieval and Renaissance periods can be seen in the fortified castles, once military strongholds, and the elegant castles such as Amboise, Blois, Chambord, Azay-le-Rideau, and Chenonceau, built along the Loire River in north-central France. These graceful residences of the kings and nobles of France combine both Gothic and Renaissance architectural features, often with Gothic exteriors, but with Italian influences dominating the interiors. King François I returned from his wars in Italy with Italian architects, craftsmen, and artists, including Leonardo da Vinci. Around the time of Louis XIII, the architecture of the castles had changed, displaying classical influences and a more sober style. King Louis XIV built the Palace of Versailles, with its magnificent gardens, designed by Le Nôtre. The main innovation of the baroque style was the dome. The Invalides in Paris, built by Louis XIV, is a surviving example. Louis XV built the Ecole Militaire in Paris and the Place de la Concorde—originally called Place Louis XV—the biggest public square in the city.

Paris underwent a major transformation in the 19th century under the Emperor Napoléon III, who commissioned his prefect, Baron Haussmann (1809–91), to refashion the city, giving it the urban layout we know today. More concerned with preventing political uprisings than obeying an architectural aesthetic, Haussmann demolished the crowded, unsanitary streets of the medieval city and created a well-ordered, well-ventilated capital with wide avenues and boulevards. He improved the water supply and laid the underground sewage system. He also created beautiful woods and parks, such as the bois de Boulogne, the bois de Vincennes, parc Monceau, and Buttes-Chaumont.

Related Web links: monum.fr for Notre Dame, Sainte Chapelle, Chambord, Azay-le-Rideau, Chenonceau (E, F); architecture.about.com (E)

Modern Architecture

Constructed during the Third Republic for the 1889 Universal Exhibition, the Eiffel Tower is the most famous icon in Paris. French engineer Gustave Eiffel (1832–1923) designed the 1,050-foot-high tower that attracts tourists from all over the world. However, during its construction a large, vociferous group of eminent citizens campaigned to have it demolished because of its ugliness! The Statue of Liberty was built around the same time. A gift from France to celebrate American independence, it was designed by the French architect Frédéric Bartholdi.

The Belle Epoque at the end of the 19th century came to be symbolized in architecture by the art nouveau style. In Nancy, where the style originated, there are many magnificent art nouveau buildings and a superb Musée d'Art Nouveau. In Paris the art nouveau style is evident in monumental buildings like the Grand Palais and the Petit Palais and in the interior of Les Galeries Lafayette, the large Parisian department store. The Paris Metro entrances (the first station opened in 1891) provide some of the most beautiful examples of art nouveau. The entrance at Porte Dauphine, for example, is the work of well-known art nouveau designer Hector Guimard (1867–1942).

The architecture of contemporary industrial society was the concern of the Swiss-born but France-based architect Le Corbusier. His functionalist approach to town planning in an industrial society was the model for many future generations of modern architects. His concept, la Ville Radieuse, developed in Marseille

(1945–50), placed buildings and open spaces with related functions in a circular formation. His most famous house in Paris, La Roche Villa, was built in the 1920s and constructed from concrete and steel with straight lines, horizontal windows, and a flat roof, a radical design for those times.

In the last two decades of the 20th century, Paris was the site of a new wave of French architecture, including the work of Bernard Zehrfuss—the UNESCO building (1958) and the Bercy Sports Stadium (1983), Adrien Fainsilber (the Géode), Christian de Portzamparc (Cité de la Musique at La Villette), Jean Nouvel (the Arab World Institute building), and Dominique Perrault (the striking four towers of the Bibliothèque Nationale François Mitterrand, 1996). Foreign architects have also left their mark on the architecture of Paris. The British and Italian architects Richard Rogers and Renzo Piano designed the Centre Georges Pompidou (1977); Chinese-American architect Ieoh Ming Pei designed the glass pyramid entrance to the Louvre (1988); and Johan Von Spreckelsen, of Denmark, designed the La Grande Arche de la Défense (1989). More recently, in 1996, Mario Botta, an Italian, designed the only new cathedral built in Europe during the 20th century, at Evry, north of Paris.

Related Web links: greatbuildings.com (E); kubos.org/AN for art nouveau (E, F); grand earche.com for Grande Arche de la Défense (F)

Painting Heritage

Christianity was the source of early French art. Jean Fouquet (1420–80), the first great French painter, produced magnificent religious paintings and portraits. Jean Clouet (1475–1541) and his son François (1520–72) excelled in portraits of Renaissance families. Artists were attracted to tapestry. The 16th-century *Lady and the Unicorn*, exhibited in the Cluny Museum near the Sorbonne, depicts the medieval idea of courtly love. Charles Le Brun (1619–90), Louis XIV's influential administrator of the arts, designed tapestries woven by the famous Gobelins factory in Paris.

Like other French painters of the time, Nicolas Poussin (1594–1665), France's greatest classical painter, spent much of his life in Rome, painting scenes from antiquity that symbolized moral precepts. In the following century, Antoine Watteau (1684–1721) and Jean Honoré Fragonard (1732–1806) abandoned classical splendor in favor of portrayals of the elegant frivolity and amorous entertainments of the aristocracy. By contrast, Jean-Baptiste Chardin (1699–1779) painted scenes from the everyday life of simple people with solid values, as well as beautiful still lifes. Louis David (1748–1825) was the leader of the neoclassical movement and the preferred painter of Napoléon Bonaparte. David's pupil, Dominique Ingres (1780–1867), continued the classical tradition with perfectly harmonious portraits.

There has been a strong connection between French art and literature. While romantic writers were reclaiming the power of the imagination over rationalism, French painters were challenging the classical tradition.

Eugène Delacroix (1798–1863), for instance, developed a highly colored and fluid style in paintings of exotic scenes and wild animals as well as in portraits of contemporaries. At the same time, Honoré Daumier (1808–79) was doing brilliant caricatures of political and social abuses. Jean-Baptiste Corot (1796–1875), Théodore Rousseau (1812–67), and Jean-François Millet (1814–75) reintroduced the theme of nature into their art, and in particular into a landscape style with cool colors and soft focus.

Gustave Courbet (1819–77), reacting against both romanticism and classicism, sought to establish a new realism based on ordinary life. His painting *Burial at Ornans*, which depicted ordinary working people gathered around a village grave, shocked art critics and the public by its "vulgarity." This break with tradition could also be observed in Edouard Manet's (1832–83) *Picnic on the Grass*, which depicted a naked woman and fully clothed men, and in *Olympia*, which also offended many with its matter-of-fact treatment of the nude body. Manet is credited with inspiring impressionism.

Related Web links: artchive.com for images of neoclassicism, romanticism, impressionism (E); **painting.about.com**

Modern Painting

When the impressionists staged their group exhibitions in reaction to the official academic painting salons, they caused a profound revolution in art. Their name comes from the title of a 1872 painting, *Impression, Sun Rising*, by Claude Monet (1848–1926). They painted in the open air and explored the effects of color and light on form. Monet's series of paintings of haystacks, cathedrals, and water lilies at different times of the day show how constantly changing patterns of light and shade evoke different aspects and moods of the landscape. Pierre-Auguste Renoir (1840–1926) excelled in depicting people enjoying themselves outdoors or in family scenes. The fame of Edgar Degas (1843–1917) is linked to his paintings of ballet dancers and modern life. Paul Cézanne (1839–1906) broke away from impressionism and revealed an interest in structure. Cézanne is considered the father of fauvism and cubism. The enjoyment of life that characterized the Belle Epoque at the end of the century is captured in the poster art of Toulouse-Lautrec (1864–1901), which immortalized the singers and dancers of the cafés and cabaret clubs of Montmartre in Paris.

Henri Rousseau (1844–1910), the *douanier* (customs official), occupies a unique position in French art as a self-taught naive artist whose subject matter ranged from Parisian life to exotic junglescapes. Henri Matisse (1869–1954) and Maurice Vlaminck (1876–1958) were leaders of the fauves (wild beasts), who expressed their feelings in an avalanche of bright color. The cubists, among them Georges Braque (1882–1963), recomposed reality into abstract forms. Pablo Picasso (1881–1973), though Spanish, spent most of his life in France, and is regarded as one of the most influential artists of the 20th century. In 1907 his revolutionary painting *Les Demoiselles d'Avignon* launched cubism. Over his lifetime, Picasso's work reflected many different styles. The Picasso Museum in Paris, which opened in 1985, exhibits his impressive range of art.

Inspired by the unconscious mind, surrealism was expressed in the literary movement led by André Breton (1896–1966), Russian-born Marc Chagall (1887–1985), Jean Arp (1887–1966), and Marcel Duchamp (1887–1968). After World War II, the Ecole de Paris designated both abstract and figurative art. Geometric abstraction was represented by Victor Vasarély (1908–97), and lyrical abstraction by Alfred Manessier (1911—93) and Pierre Soulages (1919–). Using children's drawing, graffiti, uncommon materials, and a free association of images, Jean Dubuffet (1901–1985) has acquired a vast international reputation.

After World War II, New York replaced Paris as the world center of art innovation. However, young foreign artists are still attracted to Paris, and many stay at the state-funded Cité Internationale des Arts.

Related Web links: artchive.com for images of impressionism and surrealism (E); paris.org/Musees is a guide to Paris galleries (E, F)

Sculpture

The imposing facades of the Gothic cathedrals were covered with sculpted figures standing alone or grouped in biblical scenes. Their purpose was to instruct the majority of the faithful, who were unable to read, in the teachings of the Bible. The lives of the saints were often the subject matter, as well as the serenity of life in paradise with the Holy Family, and the tortures and fires awaiting sinners in Hell. The craftsmen who sculptured beautiful figures like the *Smiling Angel* on Reims Cathedral are anonymous.

The Italian Primatrice, brought by King François I to direct the building of the castle at Fontainebleau, introduced the Italian Renaissance style. *The Fountain of Innocents* (1550), a Renaissance masterpiece sculptured by Jean Goujon (1510–64), can be seen on rue Saint-Denis in Paris. Germain Pilon (1528–90) was the predecessor to a long period of classical French sculpture. King Louis XIV employed many sculptors to decorate his palace and gardens at Versailles, including François Girardon (1628–1715) and Antoine Coysevox (1640–1720), whose *Winged Horses*, are today in the Tuileries Gardens in Paris. François Rude (1784–1855) became one of the leaders of romanticism. His celebrated *Departure of the Volunteers in 1792*, renamed *The Marseillaise*, adorns the Arc de Triomphe on the Champs-Elysées. *The Dance*, a well-known sculpture by Jean-Baptiste Carpeaux (1827–75) representing the gracefulness of classical ballet, can be seen at the Paris Opera.

The world famous sculptor, Auguste Rodin (1840–1917), continued the romantic tradition. Leaving aside the details of external appearance, he concentrated on expressing an essential truth about human nature. This new expressionist style did not please the literary society that had commissioned his sculpture of novelist Honoré de Balzac (1799–1850). *Les Bourgeois de Calais* shows six leading burghers, during the English siege of Calais in 1347, going to offer their lives in order to save the city's inhabitants from massacre. Rodin's *The Thinker*, might well be the most reproduced sculpture in the world. His *Hand of God*, in which the bodies of Adam and Eve are intertwined in a mass of unfinished marble, and *The Kiss* are other masterpieces that can be seen at the Rodin Museum in Paris. Voluminous marble sculptures of reclining women by Aristide Maillol (1861–1944) are in the Tuileries Gardens.

Examples of contemporary sculpture include *Les Nanas* (1965), bulky figures of brightly colored women, by Niki de Saint-Phalle; *Accumulations* (1985), by Arman, in front of the gare Saint-Lazare; and *Hommage to Picasso* (1966), by César, in Paris. Sculpture continues to provoke passionate reactions. Daniel Buren's installation of striped columns in the Palais Royal in the mid-1980s caused a fierce debate between critics and admirers.

Related Web links: **artchive.com**, see *Sculpture* (E); **musee-rodin.fr** for Rodin Museum (E, F)

Photography

Photography as a technique is a French invention, as is the notion of photography as art. Indeed, for the French the two are inseparable. The invention of the photo goes back to 1816, when Nicéphore Niépce (1765–1833) succeeded in obtaining negative images and then to 1822, when he was able to obtain positive images on a glass plate. This history and its aftermath are presented in the Musée Niépce, in Chalon-sur-Saône, in Burgundy. Financial difficulties forced Niépce into a partnership with Louis-Jacques Mandé-Daguerre, the proprietor of the Diorama, a theater of light-animated panoramas, very popular in Paris at that time. After Niépce died, Daguerre invented the daguerreotype, an iodized, polished, silver-plated copper plate, onto which the image was materialized. Five years later the secret of photography was revealed by François Arago, and Daguerre was forced to sell the state the rights to his invention. Soon after, other inventors throughout Europe began refining the technique.

The Daguerreotypistes (1839–60) are considered to be the first school of French photography. The Portraitistes, so called after the work of the photographer Nadar (1820–1910), endured as a school for 30 years. Nadar is particularly remembered for his portraits of famous contemporaries: the mystery of Baudelaire, the irony of Offenbach, and the humor of Rossini. Nadar took the first aerial photographs from a balloon in 1858. From the 1860s on, a third school of photography emerged, Reportage, whose subject matter was the "great wars" of Crimea and of Italy. French photographers Français de Tannyon and Charles Laongloi followed the soldiers into these battlefields. By the time the Pictorialistes, the fourth French school of photography, was forming in the 1890s, the American George Eastman, represented in France by Nadar, was selling his first films printed on paper. This last 19th-century school tried to obtain the same effects as impressionist art by using the process of clear blurredness (*flou net*), or an image enveloped in artistic blurredness (*flou artistique*).

In France in the 20th century, the relationship between documentary and creative photography has been fluid. Famous photographers like Henri Cartier-Bresson, Robert Doisneau, Jean-Loup Sieff, Jacques Lartigue, Edouard Boubat, and Guy le Querrec have captured many aspects of French life, as well as international events and cultures. One of the most famous photo clubs in Paris during the 1950s, Photo-Club du Val-de-Bièvre in rue Daguerre, still offers contemporary photographers a space to show their work and for visitors to share their enthusiasm. And each year there is a Photo Festival Paris.

Related Web links: artcyclopedia.com for links to Cartier-Bresson, Doisneau, and others (E); lartigue.org (E, F); http://gallica.bnf.fr, see *Recherche* for historic photographic collections, including monuments and geographic society collections (F)

ARTS

The "Seventh Art"

In 1995, France celebrated the centennial of the invention of the cinema by the Lumière Brothers, Louis (1864–1948) and Auguste (1862–1954). The screening of *Sortie des Usines Lumière (Going Home from the Lumière Factory)* is now celebrated as the first French film. Part of the Lumière brothers' genius was what would now be called their "marketing skills." The 50-second film was screened at Lyon on March 19, 1895; then at two different locations in Paris; then back to Lyon; and finally, on December 28, 1895, at the Grand Café in Paris. Other French pioneers of film were Georges Méliès (1861–1938) and Charles Pathé (1863–1957). Méliès invented the first special effects and made more than 500 small films between 1896 and 1913, including *Voyage dans la lune (Voyage on the Moon)*. Pathé was the first to rent films to fairgrounds for public screenings instead of selling them, thus creating the modern cinema industry.

From the beginning, France and America were rivals in the race to further the uses of film. In 1891, Thomas Edison and George Eastman patented the Kinetoscope, and in 1895 a film about a boxing match lasting four minutes was screened in New York. Throughout the 20th century there was a continual chase and overtake when it came to technological progress, the addition of sound and Technicolor, the three-dimensional screen, and special effects. Around 1930, the film market became international, and the 1946 Franco-American Blum-Byrmes accord created the basis of a screen quota system.

The real differences between the two countries concerned the nature of cinema itself. For French filmmakers, cinema was more than just entertainment, it was an art. Yet for the French public, American films have become progressively more appealing, with the French film industry often describing it as a cultural invasion. In December 1999, 63.5 percent of the total films screened in France were American and 27.4 percent were French. On television, 42 percent of films screened were American. In contrast, remakes of French films in the United States often fail given the linguistic and cultural divide between the two countries. Two exceptions, *Three Men and a Baby* and *Birdcage*, used Hollywood stars in the remakes.

The French film industry receives generous state subsidy in the form of "advances on receipts," often awarded on the basis of the artistic quality of a film's scenario. This has enabled the industry to resist the domination of American films and to continue producing between 120 and 200 films annually. The French Cinémathèque in the Musée du Cinéma at the Palais de Chaillot in Paris testifies to the artistic vitality of French cinema since 1895.

Related Web links: http://perso.magic.fr/ concept for the Lumière years (E, F); culture.fr/culture/inventai/itiinv/expo_lum.html for the Lumière brothers' villa and factory (F); sosi.cnrs.fr/ARFHC presents a photo album of stars and films (F)

Cinema

In the French *auteur* tradition, films were often better known for their directors than for the actors who appeared in them. The French director makes films in a distinctive style and has complete creative control. Compared to Hollywood, French films are more often intellectual and psychological dramas, with love relationships a frequent theme. Well-known film directors of the 1920s and 1930s include Abel Gance (*Napoléon*, 1927), René Clair (*Paris qui dort*, 1924; *Sous les toits de Paris*, 1930), Michel Carné (*Drôle de drame*, 1937; *Le jour se lève*, 1939), Marcel Pagnol (*La femme du boulanger*, 1938), and Jean Renoir (*La grande illusion*, 1937; *La bête humaine*, 1938).

Some of the most famous postwar directors were Jean Cocteau, Robert Bresson, Marcel Ophuls, and Jacques Tati, who invented a new type of film humor in *Les vacances de M. Hulot* (1953). At the end of the 1950s a new wave, or Nouvelle Vague, of young directors broke with the classical tradition. Most notable among them were Louis Malle (*Ascenseur pour l'échauffaud*, 1957), Alain Resnais (*Hiroshima mon amour*, 1958), François Truffaut (*Les 400 coups*, 1959), and Jean-Luc Godard (*A bout de souffle*, 1960). More recent directors whose films have attracted large audiences are Claude Berri, Luc Besson, Bertrand Tavernier, and, for farcial comedies, Claude Zidi.

The French equivalent of the Hollywood Oscars are the Césars, and, as in the United States, the French public avidly follows the lives of their famous actors and actresses. Among the female stars, past and present, are Isabelle Adjani, Brigitte Bardot, Juliette Binoche, Emmanuelle Béart, Catherine Deneuve, and Jeanne Moreau. Among male stars some favorites are Gérard Depardieu (now an international star), Daniel Auteuil, Jean-Paul Belmondo, Alain Delon, Philippe Noiret, and Michel Piccoli. The Cannes Film Festival, which began in 1946, attracts the world's attention every May. Its awards includes the Palme d'Or for the best film.

Going to the movies is a popular pastime in France, particularly for the young. About 60 percent of cinema tickets are purchased by people younger than 25 years old. The number of cinema complexes in France is growing each year, and most of them are controlled by three film distributors: UGC, Gaumont, and Pathé. Despite the domination of American films, French films have a loyal audience in France, in the Francophile countries of the world, and in the art-film cinemas of most Western countries. A major reason for their popularity is that they express a genuine "Frenchness" rather than trying to be international.

Related Web links: cinemathequefrancaise.com for Musée du cinema (F); **lepetitmondedesfilms francais.com** presents reviews of films, actors, directors, links (E, F); **festivale-cannes.com** has events, awards, archives (E, F); **sortir.lemonde.fr**, see *Cinéma* for reviews (F); **cinemaffiche.fr** for movie posters (E, F); **moviecovers.com** has French video and DVD covers (F)

Theater

The two great traditions of French theater—tragedy and comedy—grew from religious and popular theater respectively, both dating from around the Middle Ages. From reenactments of miracles performed in the Church came French tragedy, which reached a peak in the 17th century with Pierre Corneille (1606–54) and Jean Racine (1639–99), who made brilliant use of the three unities of time, place, and action. Corneille's heroes struggle to maintain their sense of honor when faced with conflicting emotions. Racine's *Phèdre*, a drama of love, jealousy, and death about a legendary Greek queen, is the most famous French tragedy. The satirical theater of Molière (1622–73) founded modern French comedy. Molière makes fun of religious hypocrisy (*Tartuffe*), obsession with money (*The Miser*), social ambition (*The Bourgeois Gentleman*), and the medical profession (*The Imaginary Invalid*). The comic tradition was continued throughout the 18th century by Pierre Marivaux (1688–1763) and the *Marriage of Figaro* by Beaumarchais (1732–99), which criticizes the power of the nobility prior to the French Revolution.

In the 19th century, Victor Hugo's (1802–85) play *Hernani* (1830) first broke the rules of French classic tragedy. The "boulevard comedy," whose aim was to amuse the bourgeois, began a new type of theater, one that continues to prosper in commercial theaters today. Influenced by realism and naturalism, André Antoine founded the Théâtre libre around 1880, and modern French experimental theater traces its origins to this period.

Religious faith inspired Paul Claudel (1868–1955) in his epic dramas about love and redemption. The moral dilemmas of World War II inspired the plays of Jean-Paul Sartre and Albert Camus. In the 1950s, foreign-born playwrights revolutionized theater in Paris. *The Bald Soprano* by Eugene Ionesco (1912–94) and *Waiting for Godot* by Samuel Beckett (1906–89) are examples of what has been described as avant-garde or absurd theater. The Théâtre du Soleil founded by Ariane Mnouchkine grew out of the social protest movement of May 1968. The plays *1789* and *1793* were an amazing success. Other innovative contemporary directors like Roger Planchon, Patrice Chéreau, and Antoine Vitez impose their personality on the text of the play.

Theater activity remains strong. There are 42 national centers of drama, 568 theater companies partly or fully subsidized by the state, and more than 1,000 independent companies. A policy of decentralization has removed the monopoly of Paris on theater. This process has been aided by successful summer theater festivals like the Avignon Festival, which celebrated its 55th anniversary in 2001. In Paris, the classical French theater tradition continues at the Comédie-Française.

Related Web links: site-moliere.com for biography, works, links (F); festival-avignon.com (E, F); comedie-francaise.fr (E, F); theatre-du-soleil.fr (F); sortir.lemonde.fr, see *Théâtre* for reviews (F)

Dance and Mime

Since the early 1980s there has been a spectacular development in modern dance in France, strongly supported by state subsidies. Until then dance was dominated by classical ballet by the Ballet de l'Opera de Paris, for instance, recognized as a world premier company. Its home is the Opera de Paris-Garnier, one of the largest theaters in Europe, which it shares with the National Opera Company. Begun in 1861 during the Second Empire, the opulent Opera House, designed by the French architect Charles Garnier, took 13 years to build.

The other main dance company, the Ballet National de Marseille, under the direction of the dancer/choreographer Roland Petit began to include modern dance in its program. These performances featured his wife, Zizi Jeanmaire, who became a national idol. In the 1970s the popular French dancer/choreographer Maurice Béjart was appointed director of dance at the Théâtre royal de la monnaie in Brussels. He choreographed large-scale dance spectacles for that company, which regularly visited France, where the public was attracted by Béjart's innovative ideas.

Young choreographers, who had also been influenced by the Americans Martha Graham and Merce Cunningham developed their own contemporary styles and ideas. The French Ministry of Culture subsidized the development of modern dance companies in provincial cities, and choreographers such as Jean-Claude Gallota, Dominique Bagouet, Angelin Preljocal, Philippe Decouplé, and Marie-Claude Pietragalla, who today directs the Ballet National de Marseille. Touring France and performing in summer festivals, these companies have built up a modern dance audience. However, the ultimate challenge is to succeed in front of the highly critical audiences in the Théâtre de la Ville, which was once run by the famous French actress Sarah Bernhardt (1844–1923) and has become the most important venue for modern dance in Paris. Within 20 years modern dance has become a leading art form in France, enhancing the country's international cultural reputation.

Mime is particularly associated with France. In the 19th century, in the traditions of the Italian Commedia dell'arte, the father and son Jean-Baptiste (1796–1846) and Jean Charles Deburau (1829–73) made this art form popular with their Pierrot. In the second half of the 20th century, a number of international mimes had learned their art at the Jacques Lecoq School in Paris. The most famous French mime is Marcel Marceau (1923–), who created the clown-harlequin Bip and mime sequences such as "Youth, Maturity, Old Age, and Death." In recognition of his ability to speak to all without needing language, the United Nations appointed Marceau, at the age of 78, its goodwill ambassador.

Related Web links: marceau.org, see *Biography* (E); theatredelaville-paris.com (F); frenchculture.about.com, see *Dance* (E); opera-de-paris.fr on Opera Garnier and Opera Bastille (E); sortir.lemonde.fr, see *Opéra-Danse* section for reviews (F)

Musical Heritage

French music began with religious music. Josquin des Prés (1440–1521) spent more than 20 years as a musician in the Pope's chapel in Rome before becoming King Louis XII's official musician. Des Prés composed masses and motets, and invented the polyphonic song. Clément Janequin (1485–1558) was an outstanding composer of polyphonic songs, such as "La Guerre" ("War"), "Le chant des oiseaux" ("Birdsongs"), and "Les cris de Paris" ("The Cries of Paris").

Jean-Baptiste Lully (1632–87), an Italian violinist, was the chief musician at the court of Louis XIV and established the French style of music and opera. He composed 12 dramatic operas, including *Alceste* and ballets and musical interludes for Molière's comedies, such as *Le Bourgeois gentilhomme*. Marc-Antoine Charpentier (1634–1704) today has a high reputation as a composer of masses, oratorios, and motets. François Couperin (1668–1733), known as *le grand* (the great) in a well-known family of musicians, is considered the greatest French composer for the harpsichord. He composed motets, sonatas, and *concerts royaux* (chamber music suites) for the court of Louis XIV. Jean-Philippe Rameau (1683–1764), a harpsichordist and organist who wrote an influential treatise on harmony, is famous for his 18th-century operas (*Castor et Pollux*) and opera-ballets (*Les Indes galantes*), with their subtle mixture of emotions, rhythms, and instrumental harmonies.

Music flourished in 19th-century France beginning in the romantic period with Hector Berlioz (1803–69), the founder of modern orchestration. Berlioz wrote symphonic works (*Symphonie fantastique* and *Roméo et Juliette*), dramatic cantatas (*La Damnation de Faust* and *L'Enfance du Christ*), sacred music, and operas. Another famous romantic composer claimed by both the French and the Poles is Frédéric Chopin (1810–49). A brilliant concert pianist, Chopin composed piano works of expressive lyricism and melancholy. Two talented opera composers were Charles Gounod (1818–93) and Georges Bizet (1838–75). Gounod's *Faust* and Bizet's *Carmen*, with its striking "Toreador" song, remain among the most frequently performed in the international opera repertoire. Jacques Offenbach (1819–80) made operetta the most popular musical entertainment in 19th-century France. His huge musical output of almost 90 bright and amusing operettas included *La Belle Hélène* and *La Vie parisienne*, as well as his successful opera *The Tales of Hoffman*. Camille Saint-Saëns (1835–1921) and Gabriel Fauré (1845–1924) were masters of subtle melodies and emotional refinement in their compositions for piano and orchestra. Saint-Saëns's "Carnival of the Animals" for two pianos and orchestra is a popular favorite with music lovers.

Related Web links: fredchopin.multimania.com includes musical extracts (F); france.diplomatie .fr/culture/france.musique (F); amazon.com, see *Classical Music* for recordings and 20-second samples (E)

Modern Music

Claude Debussy (1862–1918) overturned all the traditions of Western classical music. Open to all the influences of his time (the symbolist movement, ancient and Occidental music), he subtly organized rhythm, tone, harmony, and even silence to renew musical genres and piano pieces (*Estampes* and *Préludes*), a symphony (*Prélude à l'après-midi d'un faune*), a dramatic piece (*Pelléas et Mélisande*), and a ballet (*Jeux*). Debussy's innovative approach to harmony produced a type of music which was said to be similar to the atmosphere and mood evoked by the paintings of the impressionists. Another innovator of this period was Maurice Ravel (1875–1937), whose work was characterized by sensuousness of tone and rhythm. A master of orchestration, he composed passionate works such as *Daphnis et Chloé* and *Rhapsodie espagnole*, as well as the well-known *Bolero*, which was written for a ballet and first performed in 1928.

An influential group of avant-garde musicians inspired by Jean Cocteau and known as the Groupe des Six produced a collective work in 1921 called *Les mariés de la Tour Eiffel*. The group of musicians included Georges Auric (1899–1983), Francis Poulenc (1899–1963), Darius Milhaud (1892–1974), as well as Arthur Honegger (1892–1955). Auric became well-known for his film and ballet music. Poulenc, who was self-taught, composed witty and irreverent melodies and choral music. Milhaud, who lived in both France and the United States, was influenced by jazz and wrote works in chamber, orchestral, and choral music that are known for their polytonality. Honegger used dissonant harmonies to express his pessimism and anguish in symphonies and oratorios (*Le Roi David, Jeanne au bûcher*).

Electroacoustic music was developed in France in 1928 and was used by French composers like Florent Schmitt (1870–1958) and André Jolivet (1905–74). Jolivet wrote symphonies that explored African and Asian music to express his spirituality. Just after World War II, Pierre Schaeffer (1910–95) invented *la musique concrète* (concrete music), creating a completely new musical sound. The two most famous names in late 20th-century-French music are Olivier Messiaen (1908–92) and Pierre Boulez (1925–). Messiaen has been credited with introducing the Gregorian plain chant, Indian music, and other cultural influences into his compositions. His personal inspiration came largely from nature, his "greatest master," and from Catholicism. Much of his music, which is deeply spiritual and religious in character, was written for organ. Boulez was trained by Messiaen and became an ardent promoter of contemporary music. Conductor of both the BBC Symphony and the New York Philharmonic in the 1970s, in 1976 he founded IRCAM, which is a music research center based in the Pompidou Center in Paris. His music, described as "serial and expressionistic," includes works for both opera and orchestra.

Related Web links: emory.edu/MUSIC/ARNOLD /20thComposers.html for Debussy, Messiaen, Poulenc, Ravel biographies, and links (E)

Chanson (Song)

Inventors of the music hall (known as the "café concert") in the mid-19th century, the French are also the creators of a unique tradition of "literary song" (*chanson littéraire*) which may be poetic, satirical, or dramatic and whose most famous performers include Barbara, Georges Brassens, Jacques Brel, Juliette Greco, Yves Montand, Edith Piaf, and Charles Trenet. Twentieth-century chanson began with the debut of an 11-year-old boy, Maurice Chevalier, singing folk songs. Chevalier's career was to last 67 years in song, musical comedy, and film, in both France and the United States. In 1937, Edith Piaf began her career in Paris. Charles Trenet, known as *le fou chantant* (the singing madman), and whose song "Douce France" became a pseudonational anthem, celebrated 50 years of concerts in 1987.

After the Liberation of Paris in 1944, the "intellectual song" was born in the jazz cellars of St.-Germain-des-Prés and the cabarets of the Latin Quarter. Giving pride of place to the text, it was interpreted by Juliette Greco, who sung the words of Jacques Prévert and Léo Ferré, who brought poetry and protest to the streets. They were followed by the lyrical singer of poetic texts, Barbara. In the years following the war, African-American jazz musicians filled the Paris clubs with their music and were joined by French jazz musicians such as Stephane Grappelli and Django Reinhardt. The jazz scene in Paris has continued to be lively, and the city is often described as "jazz mad." Serge Gainsbourg began his career in the left-bank clubs at that time. Boris Vian wrote protest songs against war. Georges Brassens's style of chanson has continued to produce great singers such as Jean Ferrat, Yves Duteil, Serge Lama, Claude Nougaro, and Michel Sardou. In the 1970s, Jacques Higelin, whose music bridges both the chanson and rock genres, became an idol of the younger generations with his unconventional words and the reintroduction of the accordion in modern French music, paving the way for singers like Renaud, Alain Souchon, and Jean-Jacques Goldman.

As the 1950s drew to a close, French rock and roll was developing its own personality, with France's first rock star, Johnny Hallyday (1943–), capturing the hearts of a generation of French youth. He released France's first rock record in 1958. It was the start of Yéyé, the French adaptation of the Beatles' "yeah-yeah," as well as the music of other British and American pop groups.

Related Web links: paroles.net has lyrics of thousands of French songs (F); **perso.wanadoo.fr/juliette.greco** discography, photos (E, F); **little-sparrow.co.uk** for a biography of Edith Piaf (E); **http://delamargelle.free.fr /brassens** discography, pictures, lyrics (E, F); **emusic.com** has samples of Piaf, Chevalier, Montand (E); **worldmusic.about.com**, see *France* for Cabrel, Piaf, Brassens (E); **amazon.com**, see *Popular Music* for recordings and 20-second samples (E)

Rock, Contemporary, and World Music

Joining Johnny Hallyday on the early French rock scene were Eddy Mitchell, Sylvie Vartan, and Françoise Hardy. Now, more than 40 years later, Hallyday, who symbolized the revolt of his generation, has become a national icon. Continually reinventing himself and his music, he still draws huge audiences at the Palais d'Omnisports de Bercy in Paris.

Taking inspiration from the poetic and protest song tradition of Jacques Brel and Léo Ferré, as well as English and American rock, the French rock scene in the 1990s was renewed with groups such as Noir Désir, Louise Attaque, the Breton Miossec, Les Rita Mitsouko, and the singer Alain Bashung. Meanwhile, pop music also diversified, helped in 1994 by a law that set a quota of French music that radio stations were required to play. Social protest themes from the rock scene have been continued by French rap, with MC Solaar, NTM, IAM, and Assassin. Paris is today strong in techno and house music. In 1996 the album *Sacré français* of Dimitri from Paris created a stir, and in 1997 the album *Homework* by Daft Punk created a media hysteria. This success continued with the album *Air* and then the album *1999* of Cassius. The success of the "French touch" has been described as the willingness of French techno and house musicians to mix different contemporary music, and their openness to experimentation.

Paris is today a center for Western, African, Arab, Indian, and Latin American musicians. The music of France's large immigrant population from its former colonies of North Africa and Africa has become the music of the younger generation: from Algeria and Tunisia comes *raï*, a rebellion against the constraints of Islam, closely associated to the Berbers of North Africa. Traditional music from around the world is fused with techno, rap, funk, and rock to create a new world music. The Congolese group Bisso Na Bisso mixes rap and the Congolese rumba, Cheb Khaled and Rachid Taha mix *raï* with techno, while traditional African music of the savanna is fused with digitized music in the albums of Deep Forest and Manau Mangu.

Some world musicians are doing versions of famous French chansons. Egyptian singer Natacha Atlas has recorded a techno-loukoum version of the François Hardy song "Mon amie la rose," and there is a salsa version of Jacques Brel's "Ne me quitte pas" by the Colombian singer Yuri Buenaventura. Perhaps the event that most reveals the future of French music is the success of the Cheb Khaled song, "Aïcha," which crossed generational and cultural divides.

Related Web links: rfimusic.com is a French pop music station (E, F); **miditext.com/index .htm** provides words and music for karaoke (F); **france-pub.com/erap.html** has links and audio samples for rap and techno (E); **solaarpleure.net** for multimedia MC Solaar (E, F); **cheblahcen.free .fr/khaled.htm** has a Khaled biography and samples (F); **assassin-productions.fr** see *Sons for Assassin* samples (F)

Radio and Television

The French spend an average of three hours and twenty minutes a day watching television. They see television as having the positive effects of education, information, and entertainment, although 51 percent see it as having negative effects on family life. There is a big difference between the French and Americans when it comes to renting videos. The average in France is 2 video rentals per year, compared to 46 per year in the United States.

Until 1982, radio and television were both a state monopoly in France. Now, the public and private sectors are involved in both mediums. Within a year of the end of the state monopoly, 18 radio stations had been given broadcast licenses. To protect the independence of the electronic media—particularly from political pressure—an administrative body, the Conseil supérieur de l'audiovisuel (CSA), was set up to ensure that broadcasters respect the legal obligations of their licenses.

In the public sector, broadcasting is controlled by Télédiffusion de France (TDF) and there are three national television chains: France Télévision, which consists of France 2 (Paris) and France 3 (Regional), La Cinquième (Paris), and Arte (jointly French and German). Each chain specializes in different areas, with France 2 and 3 providing news and general programming; La Cinquième, knowledge and education; and Arte, high quality cultural programs. The public radio network, Radio-France, consists of six national radio and 39 regional stations as well as an international station, Radio-France International (RFI). The latter, created in 1987 and operating on a continuous news and information format, has been one of public radio's biggest successes.

On the private side in television, there are TF1 (privatized in 1987), a general chain that has 45 percent of the audience share; M6, specializing in modern music; and Canal+, an extremely popular pay television chain. French viewers can select cable or satellite, giving them ample opportunity to practice *le zapping* between channels. In privately run radio, the largest chains are Europe 1, RTL, and Radio Monte-Carlo. Under-20s can choose among stations that broadcast mainly music, like Europe 2, Fun Radio, Nostalgie, NRJ, Skyrock, RFM, and Chérie FM.

The large number of television stations gives the French public a choice of watching programs made in France, coproduced with other European countries, or made in the United States, though French voices are often dubbed over the American ones. One of the most popular long-running programs is "Les Guignols de l'info," in which lifelike puppets caricature leading political and public figures. In line with the globalization of the television market, overseas ideas are often remade for the French viewer, including the 2001 hit, "Loft Story," the first French version of reality television.

Related Web links: **francetv.fr** for France 2, France 3, and La Cinquième sites (F); **tf1.fr** for games, webcams, news, radio stations (F); **canalplus.fr**, **m6.fr** and **francetv.fr** for television channel sites (F); **radio-france.fr** (F)

Print Media

The modern press began in 19th-century France and grew rapidly, responding to the public's demand for information and entertainment. Although freedom of the press had been foreshadowed in the 1789 Declaration of the Rights of Man as "freedom of expression," it was not enshrined in law until nearly a century later, in 1881. Around 49 percent of the French read a newspaper every day, compared to 55 percent 20 years ago. The weekly press is a different story—95 percent regularly reading a magazine. Overall, there are approximately 3,100 titles, with 2,300 available on the newsstands.

The state subsidizes some of the small-circulation newspapers such as the Communist national daily, *L'Humanité*, and the Catholic daily, *La Croix*, in order to maintain a diversity of opinion in the press. The four big national dailies are *Le Figaro*, which celebrated its 170th anniversary in 1996; *Le Monde*, which turned 50 in 1995; *Le Parisien*, founded in 1944; and *Libération*, which was born out of the student revolts in May 1968. Many French dailies align themselves with a particular political point of view. *Le Figaro* offers conservative views to its large bourgeois readership, and *Le Parisien* offers similar conservative views to its popular readership, while *Libération* was founded as a left-wing newspaper, a position it adheres to today. *Le Monde* promotes itself as an intellectual paper that tries to remain independent in its presentation of a diverse range of opinions designed to stimulate debate. One of the most unusual weekly papers in France is the *Canard enchaîné*, a satirical paper that is known equally for its investigative journalism about corruption and political hypocrisy.

There are many regional dailies. The one with the greatest circulation is *Ouest-France*, which is read in Brittany, Normandy, and the Loire region. Four national weekly magazines exert considerable influence on opinions, attitudes, and tastes: the conservative *Le Point*, the moderate *L'Express*, the left-leaning *Le Nouvel Observateur*, and, finally, the bourgeois *Le Figaro Magazine*. There is a great variety of specialty magazines, including those geared toward youth, women, sports enthusiasts and followers, and those interested in economics and finance, information technology, and so on. The largest selling of all French magazines is the weekly television guide, *Télé 7 Jours*.

The French press is mainly controlled by a few large groups: Hersant, Hachette, Filipacchi, Amaury, and, more recently, Prisma Press, the French branch of a large German media group, Axel Ganz. The only international press agency is Agence France-Presse. Created in 1944, AFP is now one of the ten biggest world news agencies. It employs more than 1,200 journalists and has offices all over France and in 150 countries throughout the world. France also has three of the world's largest photo agencies: Sygma, Gamma, and Sipa.

Related Web links: lemonde.fr, liberation.fr, lefigaro.fr, leparisien.fr, lexpress.fr, lepoint.fr, nouvelobs.com (*Nouvel Observateur*), tele7jours .com (F); afp.fr for Agence France-Presse (E, F)

Les Bande-Dessinée (B.D.), the "Ninth Art"

The *bande-dessinée* (B.D.) is French for cartoon book. It is regarded as an art and an industry, and has become a feature of French cultural life. This means of expression, which is both graphic and narrative, is full of references — cultural, historical, political — to French society, past and present. Often funny, biting, or satirical, the phenomenon of the B.D. reveals the ability of the French to laugh gently at themselves. The first famous B.D. author in France, Christophe (Georges Colomb, 1856–1945), goes back to the late 19th century. He wrote *La Famille Fenouillard*, *Le Sapeur Camembert* (1890), and *Le Savant Cosinus* (1893). Pinchon and Caumery produced *Bécassine* (1905), of which new editions were still being released in 1995.

A few heroes of the B.D. have become internationally famous. Tintin and Milou were created by Hergé, and Asterix was created by Albert Uderzo (1927–) and René Goscinny (1926–77). The Belgian-born Georges Rémi (1907–83), known as Hergé, published his first Tintin cartoon book in 1929–30. It was called *Tintin in the Land of the Soviets*. Since then, Tintin and his dog Milou, known as Snowy in the English language translation, have had adventures all over the world. Tintin has been translated into more than 39 languages or dialects. There have also been film adaptations, as in 1960, *Le Mystère de la toison d'or*, and in 1964, *Les Oranges bleues*. In 1969 the animation *Le Temple du soleil* was released, followed in 1972 by *Le Lac aux requins*.

In 1999, the 40th anniversary of the creation of Asterix, the little Gaulois, ancestor of the modern French, was celebrated. The first album, *Astérix le Gaulois*, was published in 1961. Since then, 292 million copies of Asterix albums have been sold all over the world. No doubt the popularity of Asterix has something to do with its depiction of the French character. As Uderzo told a newspaper interviewer in 1999, both he and Goscinny were inspired by the modern French, and in particular, by the Parisians of their neighborhood, when creating the character and antics of Asterix. These particularly French traits were: *grand parleur, bagarreur et bon vivant* (a big talker, fighter, and an enjoyer of life). Asterix is still an extremely popular character in French cultural life. A film released in 1998, *Astérix et Obélix contre César*, starring Gérard Depardieu as Obélix, was a huge success.

Such is the popularity of the B.D. that an international convention is held during the Festival d'automne in Paris, and the Musée national de la B.D. in Angoulême, southwest of Paris, hosts an international festival each year.

Related Web links: asterix.tm.fr for characters and games (F); **tintin.be** for information and games (E, F); **france.diplomatie.ft/culture /france/biblio/folio/bd-france** presents an overview of 50 French cartoonists (F)

Literary Heritage

The birth of French literature can be traced back to Roman times and the growth of Christianity, when the lives of the saints were widely written about. The chansons, or epic poems of the Middle Ages, popularized the history of France for the people. One of the most famous is the *Chanson de Roland*, which was sung by troubadours in the fortified castles and public places of 12th-century France. With the invention of printing, Renaissance France rediscovered its taste for antiquity. One of the most famous representatives of the Renaissance humanist tradition was François Rabelais (1494–1553), a monk, physician, and satirist. His comic writings on the two imaginary giants, Gargantua and Pantagruel, mix fantasy, satire, gravity, and wisdom to express the Renaissance values of justice, respect for the individual, and a love of both physical and intellectual life. The Renaissance was also a golden age for poetry. La Pléiade, a group of seven poets led by Pierre Ronsard (1524–85) and Joachim du Bellay (1522–60), wrote a manifesto, *Défense et illustration de la langue française*, which established French as the language of literature. Du Bellay's laments for France during his stay in Rome and Ronsard's love sonnets, conveying a tragic sense of the passage of time, remain popular masterpieces. The writer Michel de Montaigne (1533–92) is well-known for his *Essais*, in which he attempted to discover universal truths about human nature by analyzing his own character.

During the second half of the 17th century, literature and the arts flourished under the personal patronage of Louis XIV. His court at Versailles became an unsurpassed center of artistic and intellectual activity. Classicism developed rules that became the basis of clear and rational expression, moderation, and harmony in all forms of the arts. Respect for these rules by writers analyzing the intricacies of human emotions and behavior produced some of the greatest works of French literature. *La princesse de Clèves* (1678), by Madame de La Fayette, established the tradition of the French novel. The witty, moral *Fables* by the poet Jean de La Fontaine (1621–95) illustrated human vanity, dishonesty, and cunning. Observation of the unities of time, place, and action created a golden age of French theater: Corneille and Racine's tragedies and Molière's comedies explored the emotional conflicts, inner contradictions, and inconsistencies of human nature.

In 18th-century Paris, literary and intellectual life centered around cafés, clubs, and salons. In the intimate atmosphere of the salons, which were hosted by powerful, aristocratic women, writers and philosophers dared to express ideas critical of the monarchy and religion. This century, mainly comprising the period known as the Enlightenment, produced the great writers and philosophers Montesquieu, Voltaire, Diderot, and Rousseau.

Related Web links: http://globegate.utm.edu /french/lit/middle.ages.html has a vast list of links to medieval French literature (E);

Literature in the 19th Century

Four artistic movements—romanticism, realism, naturalism, and symbolism—spanned the 19th century. Just as realism was a reaction against romanticism, symbolism reacted against naturalism. Romanticism could be summarized as a break with classicism and a revolt against the rationalism of the Enlightenment. Liberty is the catchword, with individualism and sensibility valued above rationality.

Romantic writers wanted to express their emotions with complete spontaneity, and poetry became a favored form. Themes such as love, melancholy, nostalgia, and life's transience inspired poets Alphonse de Lamartine (1790–1869), Alfred de Vigny (1791–1863), Alfred de Musset (1810–57), and Victor Hugo (1802–85). Hugo's poetry ranged from simple lyrics to grandiose epics. He was also a successful novelist (*Les Misérables*) and playwright (*Hernani, Ruy Blas*) revered for the richness of his language and imagery. The poetry of Charles Baudelaire (1821–67) is the transition from romanticism to symbolism. In *Les Fleurs du mal*, he uses a complex set of symbols to evoke the struggle between good and evil in his anguished existence. Poets Paul Verlaine (1844–96), Arthur Rimbaud (1854–91), and Stéphane Mallarmé (1842–98) experimented with symbols and language to discover new forms of reality in visions of mysterious beauty in unknown worlds.

The 19th century also produced outstanding novelists. Henri Bayle (1783–1842), who wrote under the pseudonym of Stendhal, was a Romantic novelist who excelled in analyzing the passions and moral codes of his characters in his best-known work, *The Red and the Black*. Honoré de Balzac (1799–1850) wrote more than a hundred novels and stories, grouped under the title *La Comédie humaine*. His ability to create memorable characters and to describe their world in precise detail made him a leader of the realist movement. *Madame Bovary*, the novel by Gustave Flaubert (1821–80), is a good example of realistic observation. The bourgeoisie was shocked by the description of Emma Bovary's monotonous life in a country town and her desperate search for happiness in a liaison that ends in her suicide. Naturalism, an extension of realism, described the life of the working classes in the newly industrialized society. Emile Zola (1840–1902) kept detailed journals of his observations, which he then transformed into novels such as *L'Assommoir* and *Germinal*.

The last 30 years of the 19th century saw an explosion of genres, from the sentimental novel to adventure and science fiction, and the beginnings of the modern detective novel. Popular novels by Alexander Dumas (1802–70), such as the *Count of Monte Cristo*, and Jules Verne (1828–1905) *Around the World in Eighty Days* are considered "classics" in their own right.

Related Web links: classiclit.about.com for Balzac, Baudelaire, Flaubert, Hugo, Maupassant, Zola (E); http://abu.cnam.fr/BIB/index.html, see *Auteurs* (F); members.aol.com/balssa /balzac/balzac.html (E)

Literature in the 20th Century

The two world wars in the 20th century introduced into literature the theme of the individual's role in a society torn by war, violence, and political conflict, which led to the search for new values. However, the century began with the quest for self-knowledge in the novels of André Gide (1869–1957) and the functioning of memory in the novels by Marcel Proust (1871–1922). Eventually consisting of seven books, the first of which was published in 1913, Proust's *Remembrance of Things Past* explores the influence of subconscious thoughts on our character.

Poet Guillaume Apollinaire (1880–1918) is considered the pioneer of the surrealist movement. André Breton (1896–1966), also a poet, became the movement's leader after the horrors of World War I had shattered a young generation's belief in the civilizing values of rationalism. The surrealists analyzed the subconscious workings of the mind in order to examine wider social problems. Paul Eluard (1895–1952), Louis Aragon (1897–1982), Robert Desnos (1900–45), and Jacques Prévert (1900–77) were among the young poets influenced by surrealism.

The French consider literature an essential art form, and the novelist has always been held in high regard in French society. Novelists André Malraux (1901–76), Jean-Paul Sartre (1905–80), Simone de Beauvoir (1908–86), and Albert Camus (1913–60) developed the notion of the committed writer engaged with the political and ethical problems of society. Sartre's *Nausea* (1938) and Camus's *The Outsider* (1942) emphasize the "absurdity" and meaningless of life in an irrational world. Malraux's *The Human Condition* (1933) and Camus's *The Plague* (1947) propose an ethical code based on human brotherhood arising from shared suffering. De Beauvoir's book-length essay *The Second Sex* (1945) is at the origin of woman's liberation. In the 1950s the traditional form of the novel came under attack by the "new novelists," including Nathalie Sarraute (1902–99), Claude Simon (1913–), Alain Robbe-Grillet (1922–), and Michel Butor (1926–). They rejected the traditional plot and concentrated on atmospheric details and coincidences in the setting. Popular women writers included Marguerite Duras (1914–2000) and Marguerite Yourcenar (1903–87), who moved to Maine in 1940.

The government recently instituted an annual Fête de la lecture (Reading Festival), held in Paris in October, to encourage the French public to keep reading. The literary tradition in France is revived each year with a number of awards, the most prestigious of which are the Prix Goncourt, the Prix Femina, the Prix Medicis, and the Prix de la Critique Littéraire. Internationally, French Nobel Prize winners for Literature since World War II include André Gide (1947), François Mauriac (1952) Albert Camus (1957), the poet St-John Perse (1960), Jean-Paul Sartre (1964), who refused to accept it, and Claude Simon (1985).

Related Web links: classiclit.about.com for Camus, Sartre, Yourcenar, Prix Goncourt (E)

Economic Policy

After World War II, France's chief economic concern was reconstruction and the modernization of its industry. The state played an essential role in this process: it nationalized the major banks, the coal industry, gas and electricity distribution, and some of the country's larger industrial interests.

As a major colonial power, France remained relatively isolated from world trade circuits because of trade with its colonies until their independence in the late 1950s. Decolonization, entry into the European Coal and Steel Community (ECSC) in 1951, and then the advent of the European Economic Community (EEC) in 1957 with the signing of the Treaty of Rome, revolutionized France's economic structures and ended its commercial isolation. By 1973 only 3.5 percent of French imports and 5.1 percent of its exports involved the Franc Zone countries, which mainly consisted of France's former African colonies.

The principle of free circulation of people, goods, services, and capital within the EEC opened a trade arena of 348 million consumers to French companies. The European Common Agricultural Policy (CAP) contributed significantly to modernizing France, and the resultant growth in agricultural production was spectacular. In industry, free circulation of goods and capital was also a stimulus to French companies and increased their number abroad. EEC integration facilitated the restructuring of French industry, freed capital to fund research and development, and led to the development of an extensive service sector. Meanwhile, the government subsidized ambitious industrial programs in aeronautical construction and nuclear development. As a result, 76 percent of the country's foreign trade was directed toward industrialized countries in 1973, with 55 percent of France's exports within the European Community.

The *trente glorieuses* (30 glorious years) of continuous French economic growth that began in 1945 came to an end in 1975. In addition to monetary instability, France was faced with competition from the United States and Japan in the technologically advanced sectors, and from developing countries for labor-intensive industries. In order to become more competitive, companies increased productivity and laid off workers. As in other European countries at the time, unemployment soared. The volume of France's trade grew, in particular with the EEC nations. Exports represented an average of 27 percent of the GDP, which is a lower proportion than Germany but is higher than that of the United States or Japan.

In the monetary area, introduction of the European Monetary System (EMS) in 1979 and the Treaty on European Union, which went into effect in 1993, committed France, along with its partners, to work toward Economic and Monetary Union (EMU). As a prerequisite of monetary union, inflation and interest rates had to be kept in check and exchange rates stabilized. The European Monetary Institute was established in 1994 and a central European bank in 1999. The euro became the single European currency in 2002.

Traditional and Service Industries

As in other prosperous industrial countries the traditional industries in France have been declining. Production of iron and steel has decreased by a third and the labor force by 70 percent. Pechiney dominates aluminum production.

The textile and clothing industry has introduced new technologies and exports a third of what it manufactures, though the industry is in deficit and the number of employees is contracting. The major textile companies are Chargeurs-Textiles (wool) and DMC (cotton), at Mulhouse.

Construction and public works companies are fairly large employers. Bouygues, SGE (Société générale d'entreprise), Dumez-GTM, Eiffage, Spie-Batignolles, and Sogea are the major companies completing public works projects in France and in other countries.

In manufacturing, the automobile industry is fourth in world production, producing 3.5 million cars and more than 500,000 utility vehicles and exporting over 60 percent of its production. Renault and PSA (Peugeot and Citroën) have invested in robotization, advanced technology, and development of external markets.

Naval construction, specializing in large cruise ships and tankers, is located at Saint-Nazaire, at the mouth of the Loire River, and at Le Havre, at the mouth of the Seine. France ranks among the top constructors of leisure craft (Bénéteau and Jeanneau).

The chemical industry ranks fourth in world production, transforming domestic raw materials (potassium, sulfur, salt) or treating imported materials. The petro-chemical industry is dominated by the Compagnie française des pétroles.

In high-technology industries (*industries de pointe*), electronics is dominated by two major companies: Alcatel-Alsthom specializes in equipping electric power stations, and Thomson produces equipment for defense and domestic consumer markets. The aerospace industry exports about half its production: Airbus makes civil aircraft, and Dassault-Industrie makes military aircraft. The Arianespace program, an active space industry, includes telecommunications and observation satellites (SPOT, Hélios).

France currently ranks fifth in the world for arms exports. And, this high-technology, state-dependent, strategic industry is quite profitable for the large companies involved: GIAT-Industries, Dassault, l'Aérospatiale, Thomson-CSF, and Matra.

Both state and private groups are involved in bioindustry research. Water treatment and the treatment of air and waste products are the main eco-industry activities.

The tertiary sector provides 70 percent of the GDP and 65 percent of the nation's employment, in public services (transportation telecommunications, postal service, electricity, water) and commercial services.

The French banking sector contributes 4 percent of GDP. The Paris financial market ranks fifth in the world in stock market capitalization, and the French insurance industry ranks fourth.

BUSINESS
Changing Work Patterns

Until well into the 20th century, France was largely a rural nation. At the end of World War II, however, the mechanization of agriculture forced most of the rural population off the land and into urban centers, an event known as the *exode rural* (rural exodus). In the ensuing 30 years of continuous economic growth (the *trente glorieuses*), France adapted to this change. The workforce became more skilled and enterprising, with a huge increase in the number of white-collar professional and managerial workers (*les cadres*). Today, traditional industries have declined massively and been replaced by high-technology industries, especially in the realms of aerospace, defense, and telecommunications. The services sector has also boomed and employs almost three-quarters of the working population.

This economic revolution has had a particular impact on two traditional work sectors: the peasantry (*la paysannerie*) and the working class (*la classe ouvrière*). The peasantry, who lived on the produce from their small plots of land, have disappeared and been replaced by farmers (*agriculteurs*), who lead lives similar to the rest of the population. The working class has eroded because of the automation of industry and the rapid growth of computer technologies. Traditional working-class jobs requiring no qualifications have virtually disappeared, and class consciousness has declined with the expansion of the sprawling middle class. Thus, France has lost two of its national symbols: its rural majority (although 86 percent of French people still believe that agriculture has an important role in national values) and its revolutionary proletariat, which was the power base of the Communist party.

Globalization (*la mondialisation*), which has forced company mergers and worker layoffs, and the computerization of industry (*l'informatisation*) have changed traditional work patterns. Opportunities for stable, full-time employment are decreasing, and flexibility has become the new imperative among employers and employees. Twenty percent of French workers are now engaged in more fluid, unconventional forms of employment involving fixed-length duration, job sharing, telecommunication, and outsourcing. In the year 2000 alone, flexible work contracts increased by 15 percent.

Traditionally, the French have viewed work as a moral observance, capable of redeeming all. While this attitude still exists among more conservative members of society, other perceptions now prevail. More and more people value work as a source of security, revenue, emotional support, and liberty, rather than as a duty. Career aspirations have also changed, as people become frustrated with the often unrewarded Metro, *boulot*, *dodo* (train, job, sleep) existence and look for personal fulfillment in their professional lives. Today, the career paths most favored by French youth (researcher, doctor, journalist, teacher) are not necessarily those with the highest incomes.

Agriculture

France is the leading agricultural country in the European Union, with 22 percent of the total EEC production and a third of the agricultural land (55 percent of French territory).

Restructuring more than 40 percent of the agricultural land in France has resulted in the disappearance of small, economically unviable farms and an increase in highly productive large farms suitable for exploitation with modern equipment. Today, large farms are located primarily in the Paris Basin (Beauce, Brie, and Picardie). Smaller farms are mainly found in the Southwest and in the coastal regions of the Mediterranean. Prior to World War II, farming families and agricultural workers made up 55 percent of the population. Today they constitute only 5 percent.

The two main cereal crops in France are wheat and corn, and France is the world's largest producer of sugar beets, a major world producer of wine and spirits, and third in the EU in fruit and vegetable production. The French beef herd is the largest in the EU, and in pork production, France ranks second behind Germany. Pork consumption has been growing rapidly (75.2 pounds per person), whereas beef consumption (57.2 pounds per person) has declined as a result of the "mad cow" epidemic at the end of the 1990s. The sheep herd remains average. Chicken breeding has expanded, with large batteries in the West and Southwest.

Fertilizer consumption multiplied sixfold in the last 50 years. Though widespread use of chemical products has eliminated most pests and diseases, making French agricultural yields among the highest in the world, ecologists and food safety organizations have pointed out the threats to public health. Genetic research has led to the breeding of better plant varieties. In the realm of animal breeding, vaccinations, control of dairy production, and stock selection by artificial insemination have contributed to increased milk and meat productivity, as well as higher quality.

The food-processing industry's contribution to French exports is notable and increasing, and it is now the third largest employer in France. Wine and spirit sales head the list, followed by cereals and milk products, such as cheese.

French agriculture has greatly benefited from the European community agricultural policy, or PAC (*Politique Agricole Commune*), which supports production and modernization by providing financial aid for development of infrastructure and ecologically sustainable farming. Eighty percent of the EU's budget is allocated to PAC. Sizable funding has been channeled toward developing rural areas, modernizing farms, and improving the land. However, this policy has created an oversupply of agricultural produce, resulting in lower prices and lower returns to producers. There are frequent demonstrations by French producers though they willingly accept the huge subsidies they receive from the EU.

Related Web links: cemagref.fr for research on agriculture, water, forest, rural life (E, F)

BUSINESS
Ecology and Energy

Professions linked to the environment are expanding, and ecology is an important aspect in all sectors of industry, especially in the fields of chemistry, biology, agronomy, geology, hydrology, law, and computer science. Problems of water and waste treatment and the disposal of airborne toxins need to be solved before techniques of nonpolluting production become more widely used.

Industrialization of the food supply, genetically modified food (OGM, for *organismes génétiquement modifiés*), and animal cloning are new concerns. There is fear that under pressure of the global economy, the pursuit of short-term goals will not be compatible with principles of scientific accountability and precaution. Biological food and biologically produced food (*aliments biologiques*) are perceived as less dangerous.

Bio Farming in Europe
(Amount of agricultural land devoted to bio farming)

Austria	11%
Sweden/Denmark	4%
Finland/Germany	2%
France	0.4%

France now provides 51 percent of its energy needs, but it still depends on hydrocarbons. For example, 2.1 million tons of oil are produced annually from local deposits in France (Landes and Brie), and imports account for 83 million tons.

Electricity production, managed by Electricité de France (EDF), has increased tenfold in the last 40 years. Nuclear energy contributes 75 percent of total electricity production in 57 reactors in the Loire and Rhône valleys; thermal power stations provide 11 percent; and hydraulic power stations, in the Alps, Pyrénées, and Massif Central, provide 13 percent. Natural gas produced at Lacq, in the Southwest, is decreasing, and France now buys foreign natural gas from Algeria (22 percent), Norway (30 percent), and the Netherlands (15 percent). Most of the coal mines in the Nord-Pas-de-Calais region have closed.

Consumption of Primary Energy

Oil	41.5%
Electricity	36.5%
Gas	13.6%
Coal	6.6%
New energy sources	1.8%

Related Web links: finances.gouv.fr/ogm for questions, links, and glossary for OGM (F); agriculture.gouv.fr/alim/ogm/welcome.html, see *Cartes* for maps of bio experiments (F); edf.fr is a French electricity site (E, F); cea.fr is a government atomic energy site (E, F)

Banks and Credit

The large French banks are among the most powerful in Europe. The merger of La Banque nationale de Paris (BNP) with Paribas in 1999 made the merged bank the leading one in France and the third largest in the world. The Société générale is also an important bank. Branches of large French banks are located throughout the country. As in the United States, they allow customers to rent a safe to store money, jewels, and other valuables. Students and visitors can open an account free of charge. Foreigners can change money at some banks, and there are also numerous foreign exchange offices (*le bureau de change*).

The French frequently use personal checks to pay for purchases in supermarkets and shops. Checks are accepted with confidence because, under French law, to give a worthless check is punishable by a large fine or imprisonment. Credit cards from French banks allow customers to pay for their purchases in shops and to withdraw cash from ATMs located in banks, post offices, train stations, airports, commercial centers, and some department stores. The most common credit card is the Carte Bleue, which the French also use abroad.

In fact, credit cards were slow to be accepted. Buying consumer items on credit went against the French tradition of keeping as much money as possible in savings (*l'épargne*), which would be spent only on essential items. At the same time, the French nurtured a mistrust of the banking system, and it was not uncommon for wealthy peasants and prudent bourgeois to convert savings into gold coin and hide it at home in a woolen sock, popularly known as *le bas de laine*. These habits gave the French a reputation for being stingy and reluctant to spend money without compelling reasons. Even today, the French demand value for their money and expect their purchases to last. They may have joined the consumer society, but not the throwaway society.

Related Web links: bnpparibas.com for bank site and ad gallery (E, F); **bnp.fr** for bank branches, services (F); **socgen.com** for bank site that includes euro information and a link to its **voonoo.net** portal (E, F); **carte-bleue.com** for credit card site (E, F); **mastercard.com** for ATM locator in France (E); **banque-france.fr** for history of banknotes, the euro, and la Zone Franc (E, F)

Aeronautics and Space Industries

In October 1999 a new company was formed in Europe that changed the face of the French aeronautics and space industries. The European Aeronautic, Defense, and Space Company (EADS) brought together the French company Aerospatiale Matra, Germany's DaimlerChrysler Aerospace, and the Spanish Company CASA, creating the largest aerospace company in Europe and the third-largest worldwide. With its headquarters in Amsterdam, in the Netherlands, EADS employs 88,879 people. Its aim is to encourage other partners to join to create a giant unified European company in this sector.

EADS is the major shareholder (75.8 percent) in Airbus, the French- and German-based company that produces passenger and freight aircraft used by major airlines throughout the world. Airbus is now neck and neck in aircraft production and orders with the American company, Boeing. The two companies share the world market. Toulouse and Hamburg are the manufacturing and assembly centers for the Airbus planes. In December 1970 a French-German agreement produced the Airbus Industrie consortium. In 1971, CASA, the Spanish manufacturer, joined the program. In 1972 the Airbus A300-B1, the world's first twin widebody, which can seat 300 people, took off from Toulouse. The company produced two more models, the B2 and the B4, but struggled until 1977 when the American carrier Eastern Airlines placed an order for 30 aircraft. Throughout the 1980s and 1990s, Airbus flourished, producing more sophisticated passenger aircraft. The model A340-600 is the longest in the world and can transport 380 passengers; the A380, to be put into service in 2006, will transport 550 passengers. Airbus is currently working on the A3XX, which will transport 656 passengers over 8,500 miles. The company also produces military, surveillance, and freight aircraft, as well as helicopters, for the EADS parent company.

France has a majority share in the European Space Agency (ESA), which launches communication satellites and the SPOT land-observation satellites from the space center in French Guiana. The first *Ariane* rocket was launched from there in 1979. In 1999 the 121st rocket was launched. In the summer of 2001 the biggest satellite ever built in Europe for the ESA, *Envisat* (Environment Satellite), weighing 3.3 tons and the size of a bus, was launched on an *Ariane 5* rocket from French Guiana. This satellite monitors the planet for environmental damage to oceanic, atmospheric, and terrestrial environments. EADS has a 23.8 percent share in the French company Arianespace, which is the European leader in launching satellites for countries around the world. Founded in 1980, Arianespace is one of the great successes of the French space industry.

Related Web links: cnes.fr for Ariane space program, photos, news of flights (E, F); eads.net for information on Airbus planes, fighters, helicopters, satellites (E, F)

Automobile Industry

Renault and Peugeot-Citroën are car names synonymous with France. For more than a century these two companies produced cars that were exported throughout Europe, but more than that, the majority of the French drove Renaults, Peugeots, and Citroëns.

In the last ten years the automobile industry in France has undergone a major restructuring, with new business alliances forming between French and Japanese car manufacturers. This is a major evolution from the time when Louis Renault (1877–1944) and his two brothers, Marcel and Fernand, founded the Renault car company in 1899. In 1946 the company was nationalized and grew into a major state-run industry until the 1970s, when the international oil crisis halted the economic boom. Renault is worldwide company now, with a major share in the Japanese car company, Nissan.

Renault and Peugeot-Citroën compete against each other in the European and world markets. Peugeot-Citroën claims to be Europe's second-largest carmaker, with 13.4 percent of the market in passenger cars and commercial vehicles. Renault claims the premier position for Western Europe with a 10.8 percent share. Peugeot-Citroën is intent on exporting its cars, especially to Central Europe and China, but Renault has embraced globalization as well. In addition to its accord with Nissan, it has acquired Samsung and Dacia. Renault has also taken a stake in AB Volvo Global Trucks and entered into an agreement with the Italian company Benelli to develop and market a range of Renault scooters, which were launched in 2001. Both French companies are eager to develop new technologies, and in 1999 they received funding for a joint research project aimed at developing a fuel-cell-powered car.

Renault and Peugeot-Citroën have established regional manufacturing plants. The most radical development in the French automobile industry was the construction of a new car plant in the North of France by Toyota, the Japanese manufacturer. The first car rolled off its production line in 2001. Prior to the output from the new plant, the government had been intent on protecting the French automobile companies. It had imposed a quota on the number of Japanese cars that could be sold in France. Now the Japanese, employing French workers, are able to produce cars that can be sold in France and the rest of Europe. Coming on the heels of the Renault-Nissan alliance, this modern plant, a model of cooperation between two of the world's car-producing giants, seems to symbolize the future of the French automobile industry.

Related Web links: renault.com (E, F); **psa.fr** for French automaker sites (E, F)

Working Life

The French population is made up of *les actifs*—those who work or are seeking employment—and *les inactifs*—students and retired people. The working population is 43 percent of the total population of France, and the upper echelon of the employed are still predominantly male and middle-aged. Longer periods of education mean that French people start work later in life, and given the state-imposed retirement age of 60, French working life is among the shortest in Europe. Since 1999, when the 35-hour week was introduced, the workweek in France has been one of the shortest in the world.

Everyone is entitled to five weeks of paid vacation per year. There are also ten public holidays. The workday typically begins earlier for wage earners than for nonwage earners, between 7:30 and 8:30 A.M. The duration of breaks depends mainly on the profession. The traditional several-hour lunch break is now generally one hour. Despite changing work patterns, the French engage in less part-time work than other Europeans, with only 16 percent of *les actifs* working part-time, unlike the United Kingdom and the Scandinavian countries, where this figure is 25 percent.

Employment in France is divided among three economic sectors. The primary sector (fishing and agriculture) employs only 3 percent of the working population, even though France is the second largest agricultural producer and exporter in the world after the United States. The secondary sector (industry) employs only 25 percent of French workers. The tertiary sector engages 72 percent of the working population, making France the second largest exporter of services in the world.

The French government has divided the working population into six socioprofessional categories:

1. *les agriculteurs exploitants* (farmers, 4.2%)
2. *les artisans, commerçants*, and *chefs d'entreprise* (self-employed craftsmen, tradesmen, and company directors, 7.5%)
3. *les cadres et professions intellectuelles supérieures* (management and the traditional and learned professions, 12.3%)
4. *les professions intermédiaires* (including middle management and technicians, 21%)
5. *les employés* (white-collar workers, 27.6%)
6. *les ouvriers* (blue-collar workers including farm workers, 26.4 %)

Social mobility between the categories is limited and depends largely on academic success.

Workers are employed either in the private or public sector, and in the latter case are called *fonctionnaires* (civil servants). The average wage in the private sector is lower than in the public, 130,790 francs compared with 148,120 francs in 2001. The state continues to be the biggest employer and employs more than 25 percent of the working population.

Related Web links: travail.gouv.fr/index.asp for the Ministry of Employment (E, F)

Women at Work

The revolution of the modern French economy has been one giant leap for women. Between 1968 and 1993 the number of female wage earners grew from 5.2 to 8.7 million, an increase of 65 percent. In contrast, the number of male wage earners increased from 10.1 to 10.7 million, or only 6 percent. Today, women account for 45 percent of the working population, compared to 42 percent in 1990, and they earn 40 percent of total household income. More than two-thirds of women with two children work.

The massive participation of women in the workforce is undoubtedly the result of the feminist movement of the 1970s, which challenged patriarchal oppression and conventional views on marriage, the family, and sexuality. Social change to achieve gender equality has been gradual in France and is still far from complete. Until 1965 a wife did not have full control of her personal property and earnings, and her husband could forbid her to join the workforce. The prestigious Ecole Polytechnique, where the nation's leading administrative and business elite studied, refused admission to women until 1972.

French women now enjoy a number of unique social provisions, which have facilitated their professional careers. Maternity leave in France is longer than most countries (16 weeks, with entitlements to 84 percent of salary), and children can attend free public nursery schools (*l'école maternelle*) all day from the age of two upward. In addition, two weeks of paternity leave for men was mandated in 2001.

Serious inequalities persist, however, between men and women in professional life. Even though 53 percent of *baccalauréat* graduates and 55 percent of students in the *classes préparatoires* (entrance courses for the *grandes écoles*) are women, they make up only 30 percent of management positions, and less than 10 percent are company directors. Male incomes are generally one-third higher than female incomes for equivalent employment, and women are concentrated in insecure, unqualified, part-time jobs. The unemployment rate is also higher among women than men (14 percent to 10 percent in 1996). French women remain underrepresented in politics. They account for 5 percent of the Parliament (which consists of the National Assembly and the Senate), as opposed to 43 percent in the Swedish parliament, 31 percent in the Netherlands, and 21 percent in Germany. The recent French law on *parité*, which requires an equal number of men and women to run as candidates for election, will undoubtedly result in more women in politics.

The persistence of such inequalities is largely due to traditionally sexist attitudes toward women, which are slow to change in France. A 1995 study revealed that only half the population believed that women should have the right to work if they want to. The French have also been reluctant to create feminine equivalents of conventionally masculine titles or trades. Among the few titles that have been adapted are *la députée* for a female member of the Parliament and *la ministre* for a female government minister.

Trade Unions

Trade Unions (*syndicats*) are significant players in protecting workers' rights and negotiating better working conditions. Initially, the unions were allied strongly with communism and parties of the left and played a political role. There are three main trade union blocs in France that the government consults on issues affecting work and salaries: the Confédération générale du travail (CGT), Confédération française démocratique du travail (CFDT), and Force Ouvrière (FO). The CGT is the oldest union, founded in 1895, and affiliated with the Communist party. In 1992, Nicole Notat became the first woman to lead a union when she was elected leader of the CFDT. A number of other unions, which represent particular professions such as farmers and teachers, have emerged over the years. The Confédération générale des cadres (CGC), for example, is specifically for managers (*les cadres*). The main employers' organization is the Médef (Mouvement des entreprises de France), which is often an opponent of the unions.

Since 1970 trade unions in France have undergone a rapid decline. By 1996 only 8 percent of workers belonged to a union. This is the lowest rate of union membership in Europe and even among Western nations in general. Membership is higher in the public sector (20 percent) than in the private sector (6 percent). In a 1999 survey, only 42 percent of wage earners said they had faith in the unions, down from 47 percent in 1998.

A range of explanations has been offered for the decline. The erosion of the working class (*la classe ouvrière*) has undermined a traditional source of union support, as have the fading of class consciousness and the development of an individualist culture. The French are increasingly critical of trade unions; more than two-thirds believe that unions act out of political motivations rather than concern for the interests of workers. The French are also weary of the aggressive approach taken by unions, which has often led to an impasse in negotiations; instead, many would prefer constructive cooperation between workers and employers. French youth are the most critical, with three-quarters having never participated in collective action. Furthermore, all companies have a *comité d'entreprise* that brings together management and employees (some of whom are union representatives) for direct discussions that can resolve conflicts.

Related Web links: cgt.fr, cfdt.fr, force-ouvriere.fr for trade union websites (F)

Unemployment

Automation and computerization have placed a heavy strain on French employment markets in the postwar decades, but the oil crisis of 1973 sparked an economic catastrophe, causing unemployment (*le chômage*) to soar in the 1980s and peak in 1997, when 12.6 percent of the population was out of work. Unemployment has affected all socioprofessional categories and remains a major concern in France, even though it fell to 8.7 percent in 2001.

Young people have primarily been affected by the employment crisis in France. In 1997 the unemployment rate among those younger than 25 was 28.1 percent, more than double the overall rate. In 2001 it had fallen to 16.4 percent. The problem is particularly acute among those who possess no qualifications, particularly youth of North African background. Unemployment is four to five times worse for them than for those who have achieved academic success.

The government has responded to the crisis with a number of measures. In 1988 a monthly allowance, the *revenu minimum d'insertion* (RMI), was awarded to job seekers older than 25. Recipients of the benefit, called RMIstes, numbered more than a million in 1995 but have since declined, in concert with falling unemployment rates. Despite this support, most RMIstes cannot find employment. The government has also introduced a range of financial incentives to encourage companies to maintain or increase the number of employees. Other measures to combat unemployment include lowering the retirement age, shortening the workweek, developing integra-tion programs for the unemployed, and, to combat unemployment among young people, the government-sponsored program *emploi-jeunes*.

In order to find work, job seekers register with the Agence nationale pour l'emploi (ANPE), which was established by the government in 1967. But many new jobs are at the SMIC (basic wage) rate and offer employment on a part-time, interim, or contractual basis. The specter of joining the unemployment lines at the ANPE has affected French attitudes toward education, with parents demanding that their children learn employable skills as well as the traditional intellectual skills. And unemployment has also brought political disillusion. The extreme right has had success recruiting supporters by claiming that fewer foreign-born workers would translate to more jobs for the French. And the government has restricted immigration from Africa and criticized European Union policies that it believes threaten French workers.

France is the fourth largest economic and commercial power in the world, but high rates of unemployment and job insecurity combined with rising levels of poverty and the marginalization of jobless youth pose a serious threat to social cohesion, which is one of the basic values of the French Republic.

Related Web links: anpe.fr offers guidance for job seekers (F); **tripalium.com** has information on employment legislation (F)

Business Culture

Every country has a distinctive business culture. When you arrive in an American office for a business appointment, you're offered coffee. In France you are not usually offered anything to drink. The American business office will often have a comfortable atmosphere, with paintings or prints on the wall, plants, reference books, and a family photograph and a discreet nameplate on the desk facing the visitor. It is an extension of home. In France, offices are often cramped and have few of these friendly features.

American male executives wear suits but will receive visitors with their jackets off. The French are more formal. They don't take their jackets off, although middle managers often wear sport coats. The dress code is formal: a tie and suit or jacket for men; a classic, discreet outfit for women. In France, women executives prefer casual elegance (*chic décontracté*) to "power dressing." In summer, women do not hide their sun-tanned legs under panty hose.

Introductions to a man or a woman in the business world involve shaking hands and using the appropriate titles and greetings; for example, *"Bonjour, Monsieur le Directeur/Madame la Directrice."* And when introductions are made, it is the man who is introduced to a woman, a younger person to an older one. When introduced, you give your name and your function in your firm. The word *vous*, the polite form of "you," not the more personal *tu*, is used.

When you enter a meeting room, you do not choose your own seat. The organizers will show you the appropriate seat; otherwise, you sit with the people with whom you work. The person who holds the higher position (*le supérieur hiérarchique*) will sit at the end of the table or in the center, next to his or her colleagues. And unlike Americans, the French usually don't arrive punctually for a meeting. They are often up to ten minutes late, during which time those who are present chat and exchange information.

A strict hierarchical organization within a company is still prevalent in France. The tendency is not to act until a decision is made and passed down by a more powerful executive. This stifles personal initiative among salaried employees, who see their role as implementing their superior's decision and sticking to the rules, though beneath this formal structure personal relationships often create a parallel network of indirect channels of information. Little direct communication takes place between the different sections of a company, which reduces opportunities for staff to cooperate in sharing ideas and information that might improve the company's efficiency. However, the influence of multinational companies is changing these traditional French business practices. Large French firms with foreign clients, or those competing for international contracts, are changing the fastest.

Business Conversation

A French business meeting begins with a general discussion before getting down to the topic at hand. The discussion allows the participants to get to know each other and their opinions. In the high context culture of France, establishing trusting relationships between people is a necessary prelude to doing business. During the discussion, the general business climate, economic trends, market conditions, and competing companies will be touched on before details of the subject are considered. This indirect approach and the theoretical analysis that precedes looking at financial details frustrate Americans, who like to get to "bottom-line" financial commitments and profits to be made. What's more, Americans, accustomed to making sharp points, find the French long-winded. And if the meeting begins late, as is often the case in France, the lengthy introductory discussion will likely strike an American, to whom punctuality is a virtue and time is money, as more time wasted.

Americans also tend to proceed more rapidly to wrap up a deal, and they give more importance to the practical details of the final written agreement, setting out strict conditions if things go wrong. The French are people-oriented. They place more value on the unwritten agreement and on the goodwill of both parties. If they have not developed a good feeling about the people and company with whom they are negotiating, they will be unwilling to enter into the agreement. This approach may appear circuitous and disorganized to Americans, whose thrust is to arrive at a conclusion. To the French, it makes sense: they are simply deciding whether they can trust the other party, despite the projected financial benefits from the deal.

The same pattern of behavior is evident at business lunches or dinners, which usually begin at one in the afternoon or eight at night. There will be a general conversation until the dessert, when the business topic is finally discussed. For the host company, the meal is an opportunity to know the people involved in the proposal better. Another appointment will be necessary before any firm agreement is reached.

The French interpret American directness as brusqueness. For their part, the French are more diplomatic. They don't like confrontation. During a conversation, when a speaker is interrupted before he or she has finished, the French don't consider this offensive, but proof of intellectual brilliance. And they don't like to lose face. Instead of giving a direct "no," for example, they will suggest a need for more information. Body language will usually reveal more about what they are actually thinking than what is said. For the French, it is necessary to save appearances and for things to look good up front.

Related Web links: goeurope.about.com/cs /etiquette, see *France* for etiquette (E)

Business Cards

A business card is an indispensable part of professional life. Americans hand over their business cards immediately, because it gives personal information quickly. Time for Americans is a succession of sequenced separate events, and efficiency means dealing with each event as quickly as possible while giving it your full attention.

For the French, the impressions made during a face-to-face meeting, and the information gained indirectly during the conversation, are more important. They prefer to give out business cards at the end of a meeting. Their elastic concept of time and the high value given to interaction with people enables them to deal with several people and events simultaneously, while gathering the information they need from the person who will eventually present his or her business card. The different function of the business card in France can be frustrating for Americans. Sometimes the French even forget to hand over their cards at the end of an appointment!

Some features of French business cards are:

- **Format:** The narrow card (2 by 4 inches) is commonly used in the professional world. It is easy to fit in your wallet and to give to someone who is introduced to you. The largest card (3 by 5 inches) for use with envelopes (3.5 by 5.5 inches) is ideal for congratulations or brief correspondence. There is also a card of intermediate size that is used less often.
- **Choice of paper:** This is crucial. It is important to avoid fanciful styles. The classic white card suits French formality best. To them, fancy colors convey a lack of seriousness.
- **Printing:** Embossed cards are considered more refined than standard printing.
- **Lettering:** Nowadays, roman characters are preferred to calligraphic letters. Some people mix both styles, with their names in roman characters and their title in calligraphy. Generally, name and title carry different fonts. Telephone numbers are written on the left and the address on the right, but world communication through new means of information exchange has modified this conventional layout.
- **Wording:** For men, the first name comes before the family name. French people don't use initials. For women, the same procedure applies. Traditionally, married women use *Madame* and their husband's name. The last name can be centered in the middle or placed on the left-hand side.

Greetings and Correct Forms of Address

The formal etiquette of shaking hands or kissing on both cheeks (*la bise*) when meeting or saying "good-bye" remains a strong tradition for all French people. Good friends who greet or bid each other farewell with the informal "*Salut!*" will also shake hands or offer *la bise*.

People meeting for the first time, or of unequal social or professional status, shake hands and say "*Bonjour*, madame" (or "monsieur" or "mademoiselle") without adding the person's name. The formal farewell is "Au revoir, madame" (or "monsieur" or "mademoiselle"). The informal farewell to a friend is "*Salut*," or "*Salut tout le monde*" (Good-bye, everybody) to a group of friends. The Italian good-bye, ciao, is also used among friends.

When saying "good-bye" to a group of men and women in a casual situation, the formal term of address — "Au revoir, mesdames" or "Au revoir, messieurs" — is shortened to "Au revoir, messieurs-dames."

If you meet an acquaintance on the street or in a building and stop, you say "*Bonjour*" and shake hands. If the person is older, or holds a higher position, you say "*Bonjour*, madame" (or "monsieur" or "mademoiselle"). If you don't stop, you simply nod and smile, or say "*Bonjour.*" People in villages and small towns where there is a friendly atmosphere stop and greet each other in the street. You only add a person's family name when greeting them if you know the person well ("*Bonjour*, Madame Dumont"), and it is friendly to do the same to the concierge of your apartment building. To respect good clients, a shopkeeper may include the family name to show that he or she knows them. When customers enter a shop in country towns they may say "*Bonjour*, messieurs-dames" if there are people of both sexes in the shop.

After five or six in the evening "*Bonjour*" is replaced by "*Bonsoir*" (Good evening) as a greeting and farewell. "*Bonne nuit*" (Good night) is only used before going to bed.

When you stop and shake hands, the oldest, the person with the highest prestige, whether a man or a woman, should offer his or her hand first. When wearing gloves, you take off your glove before shaking hands. You don't shake hands too firmly; it is more a touching of hands than a grasp. Shaking hands is expected, and if you have a dirty, wet, or injured hand, you would immediately excuse yourself or offer your wrist or your forearm instead. Clients do not shake hands with the taxi driver, shopkeeper, waiter, retail clerk, or office employee unless they know the individual personally.

When you greet someone you know, the initial greeting is followed by a de rigueur question about the person's morale or health. Informally, the question is usually, "*Comment ça va?*" or "*Ça va?*" (How are you?), and the response is usually "*ça va*" (I'm fine). In more formal situations you say "*Vous allez bien?*" and the usual response is "*Très bien, merci.*"

Kissing and Embracing

Foreigners comment that the French spend a lot of time kissing each other on the cheeks. Family members and close friends, both male and female, kiss each other on both cheeks the first and the last time they meet during the day. This kiss is called *la bise*, and it varies from region to region: one kiss on each cheek; one kiss on each cheek and a third on the first cheek; twice on both cheeks. Even casual friends kiss each other once on both cheeks, or twice or three or four times, according to local tradition.

This ritual is repeated when you greet or leave a group of friends; everyone gets kissed. If someone you don't know well kisses you on both cheeks, this is a spontaneous gesture that you don't have to reciprocate, but you show by your attitude that you appreciate the gesture.

Men, if they are friends, can kiss, but it is more common to shake hands with a little tap on the shoulder or on the back. At family gatherings, French men kiss and hug each other when they meet and say good-bye.

The custom of the *baisemain* (a kiss on the hand) comes from the Middle Ages: the vassal paid homage to his lord by kissing his hand; it was regarded as a sign of respect. Over the centuries, knights escorting ladies used the *baisemain* as a gracious gesture to greet them. While bowing, they took the lady's hand delicately and touched it lightly with their lips. However, a man who kisses a lady's hand is regarded as old-fashioned today, or as a seducer. On formal occasions men of the upper bourgeoisie and aristocracy may still kiss the hand of a married woman instead of shaking her hand when they greet or say farewell to her. They do not kiss a gloved hand or a young girl's hand. This formally polite custom is disappearing along with other rules of rigid etiquette.

La bise is more a cheek-to-cheek than a kiss. The French consider kissing on the lips an erotic gesture and only for lovers. In fact, lovers openly give each other long kisses in the street, in cafés, and in public places, and this doesn't attract stares of general disapproval. When spring comes, people can be seen everywhere walking hand in hand or kissing, and radio stations play the new love songs that will become top hits during the summer vacation.

Some language notes are in order. The verb "to kiss" is *embrasser* or *s'embrasser*, "to kiss each other." The noun is *un baiser*. There is a verb *baiser* that often confuses foreigners because the French never use it to mean "to kiss"; rather, it means "to screw."

Friendship

The French make a clear distinction between friends (*amis, amies*) and acquaintances (*connaissances*). Foreigners have often observed that when among the French it is not easy to be accepted as a friend rather than an acquaintance. A casual relationship develops into friendship only after a considerable amount of time.

In France, professional relationships are clearly separate from personal ones. For instance, work colleagues don't go out and relax together on a Friday night. And, in contrast to American society, where your lifestyle is defined by your work, in France a clear distinction is made between work and family life.

The French usually have a small number of friends—*grand(e)s ami(e)s*—in addition to their immediate family. Friends who expect loyalty and sincerity from each other tend to belong to the same social background, and remain true friends throughout their lives.

Making friends in the South of France (le Midi) seems to be easier than in the North. Southern people (les Méridionaux) are thought of as more joyful, chatty, and demonstrative with their feelings and emotions. People from the North are considered more reserved and tend to take more time to make friends. It is not uncommon for northerners to criticize the smiling, open attitude of southerners as superficial. Northerners claim that friendship for them is something deeper and longer lasting.

Patterns of friendship are changing as the younger generation is influenced by the European Union. They travel more, have become more outward looking, and have adopted a more relaxed approach to life. Students automatically use the more personal *tu* (you) with students from other countries instead of *vous*, which is traditionally used when people meet for the first time. In addition, shared interests and intellectual affinities are increasingly the reason for becoming friends across frontiers and within France. Such friendships cut across social barriers, which previously limited the possibilities of making close friends outside one's social group.

A changing aspect of French social life is the increasing number of community-based "associations" (*la vie associative*) in sports, the arts, and music. These are often promoted by local councils and reflect a growing awareness of the need to communicate and establish links within neighborhoods. Indeed, urbanization has produced more lonely people living alone. These are often older widowed or divorced people without a family, but there is also a growing number of single people who have never married. The growth of neighborhood cultural associations and leisure clubs is a response. They help foster contacts between people. An official response is S.O.S amitié (S.O.S. friendship), a free counseling service offering help to depressed and lonely people.

Love and Romance

France has a worldwide reputation for love and romance, and Paris is often called the City of Love. The French do not hide their emotions from the public gaze. Amorous encounters take place in cafés, and park benches attract necking couples. Many famous French artists have captured moments of passion, such as *Le Baiser* (*The Kiss*), a sculpture by Auguste Rodin. The progress of the women's movement in France has not changed young women's expectations. French women expect to be courted, and they expect men to compliment them on their looks and clothes; when men and women meet, they enter into a coded game of seduction. A popular saying in France is that *l'amour* (love) rhymes with *toujours* (always).

A surprising 72 percent of young French 15- to 25-year-olds believe they will experience *L'Amour* with capital A, ideal love that lasts forever.

France has given English the expression *amour fou* (madly in love). Je *t'aime* (I love you) and *je t'adore* (I adore you) are frequently spoken by lovers to express their affection for each other. There are numerous French expressions of endearment. For instance, women can be divine (*mon ange*), edible (*mon chou*), simply cherished (*ma chérie, chérie, mon amour*), or sophisticatedly called "darling."

Having a romance with a French person is an exotic fantasy for many foreigners, whose imagination is titillated by stereotypes of the French spending their time making love, of French men as the best lovers and French women as the sexiest. The accordion strains of many Parisian love songs have graced romantic Hollywood movies set in France, and a large proportion of the French films exported to other countries have a love plot. The Folies Bergère and the cabarets in Pigalle as well as the Lido on the Champs-Elysées have also made their contributions to tourists' impressions of erotic Paris.

French history has helped build this exaggerated image. The 12th-century theologian Abélard and his lover Héloïse, who became a nun, lived out the quintessential story of the star-crossed lovers. United in death, their tomb is a popular attraction in Père Lachaise Cemetery in Paris. Most French kings had celebrated mistresses who had an influential role in public life. The myth of the good-hearted mistress willing to sacrifice her personal happiness for the benefit of her lover's public family image was popularized by Alexandre Dumas's 19th-century novel *La Dame aux camélias*, which inspired the libretto of Verdi's popular opera, *La Traviata*. The well-known 20th-century existentialists Jean-Paul Sartre and Simone de Beauvoir carried on a lifelong open relationship before the eyes of the world. François Mitterrand, President of France (1981–95), revealed just before his death that since the 1970s he had a mistress with whom he'd had a daughter, a revelation that did not cause moral outrage in France.

> **Related Web links: musee-rodin.fr**, see *Collections* then *Sculpture* for *The Kiss* (E, F); **folies bergere.com**, see *Archives* for photos on cancan; **lido.fr** (E, F); **moulinrouge.fr**, see *History* (E, F)

Dinner Invitations

An invitation to dinner at home is often given by phone, but if it is a very formal occasion, a written invitation card (*un carton*) is sent.

You dress appropriately for the style of the dinner. Men usually wear a suit and tie. If it's a casual dinner, they may wear a shirt without a tie, but casual dress does not mean sneakers and jeans. Women dress elegantly because they want men to appreciate their company.

It is usual to arrive 10 to 20 minutes after the set time for either a dinner or a party because you don't want to stress your hosts while they are still making last-minute preparations for the evening.

Guests bring a small present: a box of chocolates and maybe a box of candy for your hostess's children. A *bouquet composé* (a bunch of mixed flowers) is always welcome. It is not a French custom to bring a bottle of wine. Your French host will have already chosen different wines to go with each dish. Usually when the hostess accepts the gift she says, "*Oh, il ne fallait pas*" or "*Vous n'auriez pas dû!*" ("You shouldn't have gone to the trouble" or "You didn't have to"), but this does not mean you actually shouldn't have or that she does not like the offering. Her surprise is a conventional attitude to let you know that even if you'd come without any present, you would have been welcome.

In France, guests are not usually given a tour of the house or apartment. They are led from the front door, where their host takes their coat from them in winter, to the lounge for an aperitif, and then to the dining room.

You are offered the choice between nonalcoholic and alcoholic beverages as an aperitif; it is not usual to drink beer.

The hostess announces when dinner is ready to be served. Guests wait until they are told where to sit at the dinner table. Male guests will draw back the chairs of female guests and then wait until the hostess is seated or until they are told to be seated before sitting down themselves. If the guests of honor are a couple, the woman sits on the right-hand side of the host and the man on the right-hand side of the hostess. Other guests are seated alternating women and men, grouped according to their mutual interests.

At the end of the meal the guests are invited back to the lounge room, where the conversation continues and coffee and liqueurs are served. The hostess will open the chocolates she has been brought and offer them to the guests, and later she will serve a refreshing nonalcoholic drink before the guests depart.

Table Manners

When guests are invited, the table is set with the cutlery and glasses for each person arranged in a set pattern.

The same plate is used for the lettuce salad after the main course, but a new plate is usually used for cheese if it is not sepa-

1. Water glass 2. Red wine glass 3. White wine glass 4. Soup spoon 5. Hors d'oeuvre or fish cutlery
6. Main course cutlery 7. Dessert cutlery

There are no bread and butter plates. The crusty French bread is placed on the table beside your plate. It is not eaten with butter or margarine.

Table manners are generally more formal than in America. You place your napkin in your lap and rest your wrists on the edge of the table and sit straight in your chair. After the guests have been seated by the host according to a seating plan and the first course is served, wait until the hostess says *"Bon appétit!"* and starts eating. When the main course is served, you may be told to start while your meal is hot, rather than waiting until all are served. If dishes are passed around for you to serve yourself from, men present the dish to women before helping themselves. When passing a dish in front of someone, you say *"Pardon."*

rated from the main course by a lettuce salad. You don't cut the lettuce leaves into tiny pieces but may use a piece of bread to push the lettuce, which in fact is served in small pieces, onto your fork. You don't wipe up the dresing on your plate with bread. Cheese is eaten with a cheese knife and bread. A knife and a fork are always used in a restaurant, and often at home, to peel and eat fruit.

You don't help yourself to wine. The host makes sure that your glass doesn't remain empty, but glasses are normally only half filled. Guests are expected to be impressed by the food served by the hostess and the accompanying wines chosen by the host.

Conversation

The French attach special importance to conversation. It is a skill that can be learned and developed into an art. The literary salons of the 17th and 18th centuries established the rules. Women of intellect and sophistication presided over the salons, the Marquise de Pompadour (1721–64), for example, King Louis XV's official mistress. Philosophers and artists gathered in her salon to discuss the new theories and ideas of the Age of Enlightenment.

Conversation with dinner guests is expected to be pleasant and witty, on topics that will interest everybody. The weather, money, or events at work are rarely talked about. Talk about money is avoided because people's salaries, incomes, or the cost of their houses or apartments and its furniture could potentially cause embarrassment. The host and hostess don't try to impress guests by mentioning how much expensive items cost. Guests simply comment on their beauty and quality. The reason for not discussing money may be found in the long French tradition of an aristocracy more inclined to leisure than work. People's age or physical appearance is not discussed but their intellectual brilliance is. Topics of social and cultural interest, food, politics, and vacations take place frequently and give everyone the opportunity to exchange ideas and voice an opinion.

At family meals parents encourage children to join in the conversation and express their opinions. From an early age, schoolchildren are taught to reason and to analyze a topic from different points of view. Oral examinations are an important part of their education and excellent training for discussing ideas.

Conversations around the table can be controversial. An Anglo-Saxon observing the French in conversation might well be struck by the fact that they speak out, interrupt each other, and argue intensely, to the point where it seems they will be enemies forever. And then the discussion subsides and everyone is smiling and at ease with each other. Why? Because all the participants are expected to express their opinions frankly and to defend them when someone disagrees. Intelligent disagreement can be one of the main pleasures of conversation, even between close friends.

Some foreigners say that the French prefer discussion to action. One anonymous Anglo-Saxon businessman, impatient with the delays in acting on a decision because of the French need to discuss its principles, parodied the French attitude as "It sounds all right in practice, but does it work in theory?" The French themselves would probably not take umbrage at this characterization. The time devoted to discussing abstract principles is characteristic of a people whose ideals are intellectual rather than pragmatic.

However, surveys indicate that the French are conversing with each other less and less, especially in the big cities. Casual conversations with local shopkeepers are down by 26 percent from a few years ago, and conversations with colleagues and neighbors are down by 12 percent. The pace of life, stress, and the rise of individualism all factor in this decline.

CUSTOMS
Gestures

Italians are often parodied for their dramatic gestures when they speak. The French, especially southerners, also gesture a lot. Even naturally undemonstrative French people draw on a large stock of facial expressions and bodily gestures to add force or nuance to the spoken word.

Americans are socially trained to smile a lot; the French are not. In fact, when asked for an opinion, their first reaction is to pout. Foreigners not used to this reaction may incorrectly interpret it as a sign of rudeness or contempt for people from other countries.

Almost no gesture is universal, but some gestures are at least multinational. The American gesture for "crazy"—circling the index finger near the temple—closely resembles the French gesture with the same meaning: pointing the index finger at the temple and twisting the hand back and forth. The English expression "my foot" translates into French as "*mon oeil*" (my eye), and the French expression has a convenient gesture that can accompany or replace it: pulling the lower eyelid down slightly with the index finger. This gesture is also a convenient and quick way to indicate to the other listeners that you don't believe the speaker's version of events. To say "I don't know" or "Beats me" (*Je n' sais pas*), a French person can pout, raise eyebrows, push his or her head forward slightly, raise shoulders, and raise the hands to shoulder level with palms out and upward.

The French start counting from the thumb, not the index finger. An American ordering two beers in France with the index and middle finger might well receive three, however energetically the American's thumb was curled out of sight.

While conversing, the French tend to stand or lean closer to each other than Americans do. Two French speakers standing close, leaning toward each other, and employing the standard set of gestures might convey to an American observer that the two are speaking intensely and reacting emotionally. This is a conversational style and habit, not an illustration of uncontrollable emotions.

However, when the French get behind the wheel of a car, their emotions are uncontrollable. Insulting other drivers with rude gestures and bad language is a national sport. Anyone else on the road becomes the enemy, keeping the driver from getting to his or her destination as quickly as possible. As French drivers weave in and out of traffic lanes, they hurl insults at the drivers who have forced them to do this, by driving too slowly or by respecting the safety rules. If you intend to drive in France, be prepared!

Related Web links: french.about.com for an article on French gestures (E)

Dress Code

The French pay a lot of attention to what they wear and generally dress more formally than Americans. They take particular care with matching their clothes and accessories. The expression "BCBG" (*bon chic bon genre*) is often used to describe elegantly dressed people. The French have adopted the English word "look" to describe someone's appearance: *Tu as vu son look?* (Have you noticed how he/she is dressed?). Criticizing how someone is dressed, and especially the casual attire of foreign tourists, is a common topic of conversation between friends in a café.

France is internationally famous for its high fashion industry. The *haute couture* parades in Paris of the new winter and summer fashions by the top designers attract fashion writers from all over the world. The high fashion creations of the *grands couturiers* are very expensive and seldom bought, but what French people wear is strongly influenced by the new season's fashion trends. Designers produce less expensive ready-to-wear collections. The top fashion houses also produce extensive ranges of accessories, perfumes, and cosmetics. Yves Saint-Laurent, Chanel, and Hermès are famous fashion houses. Several others, including Dior, Givenchy, and Louis Vuitton, are controlled by the biggest French luxury goods conglomerate, LVMH, which is chaired by one of France's richest men, Bernard Arnault. The French spend 5 percent of their disposable income on clothes. They save money by buying well-known brands, including Gap, during the end of season sales in June and January.

Women doing the daily shopping tend to dress elegantly rather than casually. Their favorite accessory is a scarf, even when they don't wear a coat. Men are now spending more time and money on their appearance and on cosmetic products. On formal occasions, men wear a suit and tie more frequently than a tuxedo (*un smoking*). Students dress more formally than their American counterparts. Streetwise young people, with urban attitude, adopt American fashions. You rarely see people wearing shorts in the streets in big cities even in summer. At work, executives wear recognizable brands more frequently than employees. Working women do not wear panty hose in summer.

People dress more casually on weekends for outdoor activities, but if they're going to church or a family luncheon, they dress formally. Tourists visiting churches are expected to avoid sexually provocative clothing such as brief shorts and low-cut tops. When dressing elegantly, the French prefer neutral tones and avoid bright, flamboyant colors. In summer, on vacation, they will wear bright but not clashing colors. Their secret is to match colors and clothes with a flair and chic that characterizes *le look français*.

Related Web links: ysl-hautecouture.com, chanel.com, dior.com, givenchy.com, vuitoton.com, lvmh.com for French fashion houses (E, F); **frenchfashion.com** for online shopping of French collections (E)

Time and Punctuality

The French have their own concept of punctuality. It is accepted behavior to arrive a little late for a personal appointment, and guests may arrive up to half an hour late for a dinner at a home without upsetting their hosts. For a business appointment, people may arrive up to ten minutes late without being expected to apologize. When catching a train, the French have to be punctual because the national railway system (SNCF) has an enviable reputation for its trains leaving and arriving on time.

The French tend to separate their lives into periods of work and periods of pleasure. The latter have a certain sanctity, especially mealtimes. The day begins early for French families with schoolchildren. Even kindergarten classes (*école maternelle*) for children age three to five begins at 8:30 A.M. and doesn't finish until 4:30 P.M. However, there is a two-hour break for lunch from 11:30 to 1:30. Many mothers take their children home for lunch. The other children are served a hot meal in the school cafeteria. The traditional two-hour lunch break for workers has become one hour in large urban areas because many workers now travel greater distances to work and don't have enough time to go home for lunch. In many country towns, most shops will close for a lunch period, usually 12:00 to 2:00 P.M. The evening mealtime frequently takes place during or after the nightly television news broadcast at 8:00.

The annual month-long summer vacation breaks the year into two parts for workers. These are further broken by one- or two-week vacations in winter, which are often spent skiing, and the long weekends of Toussaint (November 1) and Pâques (Easter). All French salaried workers are officially entitled to five weeks of annual paid vacation.

The length of the French workweek is set by the national legislature. In the year 2000, a 35-hour workweek for salaried workers was introduced. Additional working hours will be paid overtime. Managers and executives in large companies tend to work until 7:00 P.M. Large stores are not allowed to open on Sundays.

The French calendar week begins on Monday rather than Sunday. The expressions *huit jours* (8 days) and *quinze jours* (15 days) mean "a week" and " a fortnight." The word *prochain* (next) used with a weekday does not mean "in the next week," as it does in English. For example, *vendredi prochain*, when spoken on a Wednesday, means the Friday two days away, and not *vendredi en huit* (Friday in 8 days). Wednesday is commonly a day off for kindergarten and primary schoolchildren and a half day for high school students. On the other hand, both are in class for half a day on Saturday. Trials are being conducted in some parts of France to have no classes on Saturday and give pupils a full weekend.

Politeness and Directness

Foreigners sometimes find the French rude and dismissive. One reason is the directness and frankness with which the French express their feelings and opinions. They are accustomed to speaking their minds with each other without fear of offending the listener, and they expect their listeners to respond with equal candor. Foreigners may also interpret the way the French look at them as challenging and patronizing. It is, rather, a reflection of their interest in other people. People watching is a frequent French pastime.

With each other, the French are sociable. They constantly greet one another, shake hands, and exchange tokens of politeness. Customers entering small shops greet shopkeepers with "*Bonjour, messieurs-dames*" (roughly equivalent to "Good day, ladies and gentlemen") and depart with "Au revoir, messieurs-dames." One person's "*Merci*" ("Thank you") is always acknowledged with "*Je vous en prie*" or "*Je t'en prie*" ("You're welcome") or the less formal "*De rien*" ("Don't mention it"). People eating together offer "*Bon appétit*" to each other. "*Pardon*" ("Excuse me") or "*s'il vous plaît*" begin a request to an acquaintance for information or to a stranger for street directions. Passing ahead of another person, as when squeezing through a crowd, is also excused with a "*Pardon*." Personal criticism is always preceded with an apology, which the French see as transforming the criticism into a polite observation rather than a personal attack.

People use professional titles in conversation, when they are applicable, to signify polite respect: *Monsieur le Directeur/ Madame la Directrice*; *Monsieur/Madame le docteur*; *Maître* (for an attorney or famous artist); *Monsieur le Cure/Mon Père/Ma Sœur*; *Monsieur le Pasteur*; *Monsieur/Madame le Professeur*; *Monsieur/ Madame le maire*.

In the 1970s the government was concerned that the French reputation for rudeness was discouraging the influx of tourists, who make a significant contribution to the national economy. It launched a campaign asking the French to be polite and welcoming toward tourists. The response was an attempt to communicate with tourists in their native languages, rather than insisting on speaking French, as had been the custom. Today, French children begin learning English in primary school. People in the tourist industries speak English, as do the younger generations of graduates from business schools. French willingness to communicate in English has accompanied expanding international perspectives and economic globalization.

Standing in Line

Americans may set the world standard for the orderliness of their lines at bus stops, taxi stands, and ticket windows, which they take as a manifestation of their civic responsibility and polite respect for each other. French behavior suggests that they do not accept the American standard in this matter, as in so many others.

Despite recent attempts in public agencies to make people form a single line (*une file d'attente unique*), French lines are disorderly affairs, and everyone seems to have a logical personal reason to break into the line (*resquiller*).

Lines quickly become large rather than long because newly arriving people try to stand side by side with those already in line. If for any reason people try to go to the front, the others in line will shout: "*La queue!*" (The line!). Often, an angry discussion takes place, with the person who is trying to get in at the front justifying why he or she should be allowed to do so, before retreating indignantly to the end of the line. From there the newcomer is likely to keep a vigilant watch to prevent anyone else from breaking into the line. If someone makes a valid mistake about the direction of the line, the traditional apology—"*Pardon!*"—is barely sufficient to calm the suspicions of the people in line, who will no doubt be exasperated by the slow pace that lines move in France.

Banks have recently instituted a red line or a sign to mark the distance between the line and the other customer at the counter. However, don't be surprised if someone stands right next to you while you're dealing with the teller.

Lines at the post office are famous for being long and time consuming. This is because the post office not only takes care of the mail, but is also a people's bank, with associated banking transactions. In the public offices of state facilities and big companies, customers must take a number and wait their turn instead of waiting in line. This doesn't stop people from trying to get served at the counter ahead of people waiting with a number.

Lines publicly demonstrate the lack of discipline, the single-minded devotion to individualism, and the reluctance of the French to acquiesce to any group organization. This national pastime to find a way around a government regulation or administrative decision is called *système D*, an expression that says a lot about the French temperament. The D stands for *débrouillard*, which means "resourceful" in literal translation but implies a great deal more. *Débrouiller* is "to untangle," and so, from the French point of view, the chaos of a French line is a logical consequence of a mass of individuals untangling the knotty problem of getting to the head of the line. The French practice *la débrouillardise* in all aspects of life, whether getting a broken electrical appliance to work, cutting into lines, or finding a way to pay less tax. The French compliment *Il/Elle sait se débrouiller* (He/She knows how to get things done) is always sincere and expresses admiration for a person's resourcefulness.

Astrologers and Superstitions

A defining characteristic of the French is their belief in the power of logic and reason. Schoolchildren are taught from an early age to develop the analytical skills to solve all problems. This intellectual training sets the pattern of their decision making at home and at work in their adult life. In view of this, it is paradoxical that there are 50,000 professional astrologers and fortune-tellers in France (twice as many as priests), and that 16 percent of the population have consulted them. The horoscopes published in many daily newspapers and in popular magazines have been read at one time or another by 75 percent of the population.

This strong interest in the irrational and the supernatural extends to the ancient traditions of Druid priests, sun worshipers, and witchcraft. In the popular *Asterix* comic book, one of the main characters, Panoramix, is a Druid who mixes a magic potion that makes people strong, and thus able to defeat invaders.

Some of the bad luck omens in France, in decreasing order of popularity, are

- *Mettre le pain à l'envers:* Putting the bread upside down. Bread is an essential item in the French diet.
- *Ouvrir un parapluie à l'intérieur d'une maison:* Opening an umbrella in a house.
- *Casser un miroir:* Breaking a mirror means seven years of unhappiness.
- *Passer sous une échelle:* Walking under a ladder.
- *Etre 13 à table:* Thirteen people sitting at the table.
- *Un vendredi 13:* Friday the 13th.

- *Offrir des couteaux ou des aiguilles:* Offering knives or needles. You can avoid the bad effect by offering a coin in return. Note that a very popular folding knife called the Laguiole is often given as a present in France.
- *Croiser un chat noir la nuit:* Crossing a black cat at night.
- *Renverser du sel sur la table:* Spilling salt on the table. To ward off ill fortune, take a pinch of salt and throw it over your left shoulder.

Good luck omens in France, in decreasing order of popularity, are

- *Trouver un trèfle à quatre feuilles:* Finding a four-leaf clover.
- *Marcher sur une crotte du pied gauche:* Walking on a animal's dropping with the left foot.
- *Mettre un fer à cheval au-dessus de sa porte:* Putting a horseshoe above your door.
- *Voir une coccinelle s'envoler:* Seeing a ladybug flying. This announces good weather.
- *Toucher le pompon rouge du béret d'un marin:* Touching the red pompom on a marine's beret.
- *Voir un arc-en-ciel:* Seeing a rainbow.

Students, colleagues, and friends wish each other good luck before an exam or a difficult undertaking by saying "Merde!" ("Shit!").

Related Web links: **horoscope.fr** for horoscopes, astrology, tarot, etc. (F)

Family

Family is generally thought to be more significant in France than in Anglo-Saxon countries. It is the nucleus of daily, social, and cultural life, and for a majority of the French, the family is the only place where they feel comfortable. The legal concept of the ideal family dates from the Napoleonic era. Napoléon's Family Code entrenched in law the absolute power of the father to make all decisions concerning other members of the family. The shape of the family underwent significant changes in the 1960s and 1970s, when the father's power and marriage itself was altered by legal reforms regarding contraception, abortion, divorce, and women's rights. Blended families, single parent families, and families of unmarried parents with children are now an accepted part of French life.

Families with a large number of children have become the exception, and they are usually families in which at least one parent is a foreigner. Between 1990 and 1999, the number of families with two or more children decreased. Families with three children decreased by 9 percent, while those with only one child increased by 3.5 percent and those with no children increased by 3.3 percent. During the same period, single parent families increased by 22 percent, and in 88 percent of such families a women was the single parent. Thirteen percent of children younger than 15 were in these families. Unmarried parents account for 40 percent of France's babies.

Also between 1990 and 1999, the number of people living alone increased by 25 percent. Today, one out of eight people lives alone and single people make up 12.6 percent of the population. Families with no children and people living alone are now more numerous than families with children.

French parents and their children generally spend a lot of time together and participate in many activities. Mealtimes, when parents and children sit, eat, and talk together, play an essential role in maintaining the family unit. Vacations are usually spent together and often include a stay at the country home of members of the extended family. The extended family also gets together for major events and holidays.

During the economic difficulties of the 1990s, moral and financial family support for children unable to find employment assumed even more importance. The *baccalauréat*, which is the end of high school public examination, is a significant milestone for young people. Compulsory military or civil service, abolished in 2000, was also a milestone. Young people in France are increasingly influenced by American popular culture. It influences how they dress and their choice of entertainment. According to a recent survey, young people are most concerned about relationships (36%), followed by health issues (29%) and emotional problems (28%).

> **Related Web links: droitdesjeunes.gouv.fr** for a guide to youth health, family, employment, sexuality, drink, national service, with quiz (F); **lebaccalaureat.com** for guidance for students (F)

Family Functions

French families often get together every weekend, as well as for major events such as baptisms, first communion, weddings, and funerals. They also get together on holidays: Christmas, Mother's Day, the low-key Father's Day, as well as the recently enacted Grandmother's Day.

A few months after a baby is born, a Catholic French family will gather to celebrate the child's baptism. A godmother and godfather will be chosen, often from members of the child's extended family, and they will offer gifts (*dragées*, which are sugarcoated almonds) to the baby and to its family. A baptism is also the chance for the family to get together and share a long and sumptuous meal.

The next major celebratory rite of passage involving the whole family is the child's first communion. In France, a child has two communions, the first and the second, referred to as the *communion solonelle*. On this occasion, the children, boys as well as girls, wear a long white robe. Relatives and friends gather after the religious ceremony at the home of the child's parents, offering gifts to the child. It is also customary to offer *dragées* to the guests.

The family also gets together to celebrate Christmas, which in France is celebrated on December 24. The family meal begins in the afternoon and lasts all day. The family will then go together to midnight mass, after which some families exchange presents. In other families, gifts are placed in stockings around the fireplace of the family home, or at the foot of the children's beds, and are not opened until the next morning.

New Year's festivities are usually not celebrated with the family, but with friends. Nonetheless, children will often receive a New Year's gift from their grandparents, known as an *étrenne*—an envelope filled with money.

At Easter the family will traditionally gather at the home of the grandparents, to share chocolate eggs, chocolate chickens, or chocolate rabbits. These are often hidden in the garden for the children to find.

To mark Mother's Day, the children will present their mother with a gift, often a potted plant, a photo, flowers, and chocolates. Father's Day is a more subdued celebration, an occasion for children to exercise their artistic creativity and make presents for their fathers. Weddings are large affairs, bringing together the whole family from all corners. Even family members who live on the other side of the country will attend a family wedding. French couples must publish *les bans* (the official marriage notice) at least two weeks before the wedding and then marry at the town hall to satisfy the requirements of a civil marriage. Two people are required as witnesses. Usually only very close relatives and friends will attend this ceremony.

It is the optional religious wedding ceremony that involves the whole family and many friends. Afterward, the guests will toast the newly married couple and extend to them their best wishes.

Related Web links: http://fr.dir.yahoo.com/societe /fetes_et_jours_feries for links for Christmas, Easter, Halloween, Religion, Holidays (F)

Meals

The daily routine of meals has changed in France. The traditional three-course lunch was the main and most important meal of the day. Today, the main meal is more likely to be dinner. This reflects changes in the French lifestyle, especially in the cities, where people travel longer distances to work. With the traditional two-hour lunch break being replaced by a one-hour lunch, the workday ends sooner. However, 50 percent of French workers will return home for lunch if they live less than three miles from their place of work. And the two-hour lunch break still prevails in smaller towns in rural areas. School cafeterias provide a state subsidized full meal for those children who cannot return home for lunch.

Meals for a typical workday consist of a light breakfast (*le petit déjeuner*) of coffee, chocolate, or perhaps tea, and buttered pieces of bread or baguette, sometimes with jam. Cereals are now more acceptable as a breakfast food. Lunch (*le déjeuner*) is likely to be a three-course meal if eaten at home or in a work cafeteria, or else just a main course or take-out food. Dinner (*le dîner*) would begin with an entrée of soup or salad; followed by a main course of chicken, meat, or fish, with vegetables or pasta; then cheese and dessert or fruit. Bread, mineral water, and wine are also part of dinner. Only young children tend to have snacks between meals, usually the *goûter* after school. It is likely to consist of a fruit juice or hot chocolate, with biscuits, cake, fruit, or a little yogurt.

The main meal is traditionally a family affair at which parents and children discuss the day's events at school and work. The French spend an average of 33 minutes at the dinner table during the week, and 43 minutes on the weekends. Some French families follow the modern trend of leaving the television on during meals, to the detriment of the conversation. Sunday lunch, either at home or in a restaurant, remains a long meal at which family and friends often gather. The aim is good food and drink and good conversation. It is often followed by an activity together such as a *promenade*.

Related Web links: **rh.nestle.fr**, see *Enfant* and *Etudiants* for information and games on nutrition and eating habits (F)

Comfort

The French today spend more money on housing than on food. The choice of the home itself as the center for family and personal life, and the desire for more creature comforts, such as electrical and other household appliances, accounts for this increased spending in recent years. In addition, utility and maintenance costs are greater.

Higher unemployment, the possibility of working from home, more years in school, and longer life expectancy have meant that the French spend more time at home. They find within the family the security, tranquillity, and conviviality they need to feel protected from the seemingly threatening world they see, hear, and read about on television, radio, newspapers, and magazines. The family remains the core value in French society, and the home is the favored place for family celebrations, leisure, and rest.

In more than eight households out of ten there is an inside toilet, shower, or bath and central heating; 10 percent of French homes have at least two bathrooms, and 17 percent have two toilets. Homes in rural areas that have traditionally had only basic comforts are gradually catching up with urban homes. Still, lack of minimum sanitary requirements is more common in rural areas (10 percent) than in cities and towns (5 percent). The dwellings of homeowners are more comfortable than those of tenants. Life in the HLM low-rent, high-rise, state-subsidized condominiums lacks the usual comforts.

Income level has a greater impact on the comfort of those who live in houses than in apartments. Forty-six percent of the poorest households lack central heating. The oldest houses are the least comfortable: 16 percent of those built before 1949, in contrast with 2 percent built 20 years after the war, and 0.3 percent built in the last 30 years.

The size of an average residential house today is 1,042 square feet, compared to 856 square feet 20 years ago. The size of a typical apartment has remained the same (689 square feet), but the number of rooms per apartment has increased to 3.0. The number of rooms per residence has also increased in houses, to 4.8. But it should also be noted that at the same time, the number of people living in a household has diminished, and today averages 2.5. One residence in ten is overpopulated; two out of three are underpopulated. Overpopulation is rare in individual houses but more prevalent in apartments, which house lower income tenants in large cities and their suburbs.

A survey of reasons given by apartment dwellers for being unhappy with their accommodation yielded the following results:

	PEOPLE UNDER 30	PEOPLE OVER 65
Noisy neighbors	23%	7%
Dust and pollution	21%	14%
Uninteresting view	20%	10%
Lack of light	19%	5%
Unpleasant smells	9%	5%

Household Appliances

Almost all French households are equipped with large electric appliances. Ninety percent or more have a refrigerator, stove, washing machine, and vacuum cleaner. And the typical household has a dozen smaller items of domestic equipment (iron, hair dryer, coffeemaker).

Ownership Rates of Other Electrical Household Appliances:

Iron	98%
Hair dryer	83%
Coffeemaker	79%
Hand mixer	78%
Frying pan	67%
Microwave oven	52%
Standing mixer	46%
Deep fryer	35%

Those who lack these items are most often single people who have not yet set up their own apartment, poorer households, or older people who do not have use for them. A separate clothes dryer is still not common (20 percent), because of the extra consumption of electricity it requires.

Only 42 percent of French households have a dishwasher, and sales have progressed relatively slowly over the last 30 years. There is a big difference between social groups in its use. More prosperous households, or those that include children, are more likely to own a dishwasher.

Households that have several of the same appliances vary according to level of income. Approximately 15 percent of households have more than one refrigerator. The average age for a refrigerator is nine years. It's eight years for a freezer, seven for a dryer, and six for a dishwasher.

The cost of household appliances has remained low, and in the last 20 years has fallen by 2.2 percent, while the consumer price index for goods and services has risen by 32 percent.

There is an increasing demand for household items and services that make life easier and save time, effort, and money. These include: automatic opening/shutting doors and windows; garden and indoor plant-watering systems; distance control of heating, lighting, audiovisual, and electrical appliances; optimization of energy use; burglar alarms; gas/water/fire alarms; and connection to municipal services (police, doctors, firemen). As for the future:

- 81 percent would like solar panels installed on the roof to provide the energy for heating and lighting.
- 57 percent would like a domestic robot to do the vacuuming and clean the house.
- 43 percent want a miniature greenhouse, which would enable them to grow vegetables, fruit, and herbs for personal consumption.
- 38 percent would like a kitchen robot capable of cooking and making meals.

Furniture

Reduced spending on furniture in French households (2.9 percent) can perhaps be explained by the fact that people move less and thus need to buy major items of furniture less often. Today, furniture is less an indicator of social status than it was in the past. Young people give greater importance to leisure items such as audiovisual equipment. For example, a large television screen may take the place of a sideboard, and a stereo system unit may replace a small cupboard. Purchases of bedroom furniture have not fallen as much because it responds to concerns for comfort and health, which are a priority: 44 percent of women and 27 of men say they suffer from sleep problems.

Lack of innovation in furniture design may also explain the reduction in furniture purchases. Modern demand is for functional, light, modular furniture, especially for larger items such as tables, wardrobes, sideboards, divans, armchairs, and kitchen furniture. Smaller items are less affected by this trend. Modern mid-range products and ready-to-assemble furniture have become popular. The tendency is toward modular furniture, because modular units allow different arrangements of the component parts to suit the various members of the household.

Today, households want furniture that is multifunctional, movable, light, modular, pliable, stackable, and foldaway, so that space can be saved. Young people are attracted by exotic styles. High-income households are attracted to ultramodern designer furniture.

Beautiful antique pieces of furniture can be seen in many French homes. In fact, France has a long tradition of distinguished furniture makers, and antique furniture is highly prized and passed down from one family generation to the next. A popular address for buying antique furniture is the *marché aux puces* (flea markets) at Saint-Ouen, Paris. It's open on Friday mornings, and on Saturday, Sunday, and Monday. In a 17-acre area there are 2,500 dealers, 700 clothing stalls, and 20 restaurants. Eleven million people visit each year, and spend $600 million.

Three well-known markets in the *puces*, all in the rue des Rosiers, are:
- **Serpette:** International film stars shop here. There's a wide selection of antiques, from 18th century to art deco, as well as paintings, jewelry, and luxury luggage. 110 rue des Rosiers.
- **Dauphine:** This is on two levels underneath a glass roof, and includes 150 antique dealers. 140 rue des Rosiers.
- **Vernaison:** This market, a labyrinth of 300 stands, dates back to the 1920s and offers silverware, curios, porcelain, and fabrics. 99 rue des Rosiers.

Related Web links: antikita.com is the official site of Saint-Ouen des puces market, with links to 1,400 different antique dealers, decorators, restorers, insurers, and transporters (E, F)

DAILY LIFE
Domestic Gardens

Fifty-three percent of the French people say that they garden, at least occasionally. This proportion is similar to the number of households that have a garden (56%). Almost all of them (94%) have a garden that averages 10,900 square feet. Those who live in apartments create an interior garden: 4 million households have a balcony, terrace, or veranda. Owners of a second residence (12 percent of the population) also enjoy gardening.

However, when it comes to gardening, on a terrace or in a garden, France ranks at the bottom of European countries:

Netherlands	96%
Greece	94%
United Kingdom	94%
Italy	86%
Belgium	86%
Denmark	85%
Germany	83%
Luxembourg	79%
Portugal	70%
Spain	70%
France	58%

In France, around 40 billion francs (about $5.6 billion), or 2,000 francs per household ($280), is spent per year on gardening. The purchase of maintenance products and equipment account for half of this sum. Main gardening suppliers are no longer large supermarkets but garden centers and markets, which offer a greater variety of products and competitive prices. French women are more likely to tend an ornamental garden than men, but the majority of vegetable gardens are maintained by men. The proportion of gardens devoted to strictly utilitarian use (vegetable gardens) has decreased: 1 percent today, compared to 7 percent 20 years ago. Gardening is a frequent activity among people between the ages of 50 and 64 (68 percent). Gardeners spend an average of six hours gardening per week in spring and summer. Increasingly concerned about protecting themselves, they wear suitable shoes and gloves, and are purchasing new products that appear on the market.

Less time spent at work, and an increasing desire to live in harmony with nature without giving up the comforts of home, seems to explain the increase in gardening in France. Considered a pleasant pastime (47 percent of liberal professions and managers, 32 percent of workers), 44 percent say that the gardening activity itself is more important than eating what the garden produces. Gardening as a means of beautifying one's immediate environment is the second most common reason given for pursuing this pastime. Indeed, paying attention to the beauty of the garden has become more important, especially if the garden is small. Four out of five gardens have a lawn, and over 50 percent of French households have a lawn mower.

Gardening as a Leisure Activity

	M & F		MALE		FEMALE	
	GARDEN	OFTEN	GARDEN	OFTEN	GARDEN	OFTEN
Ornamental	40	27	38	28	42	26
Vegetable	21	15	25	19	17	11

Pets

The French are a nation of animal lovers. The English have a reputation for being great pet lovers too, but France is the European country with the most pets. Great Britain is second and Italy third.

Fifty-two percent of French homes have a pet. Cats are slightly more popular than dogs, and 45 percent of homes have both a cat and a dog. You'll find a fish in 10 percent, a bird in 6 percent, and a pet rodent in 5 percent.

Paris has more dogs than children, and dog owners often enter restaurants with their dogs. The German shepherd is the most popular breed in France, followed by the poodle and the Breton spaniel.

The large dog population in Paris explains why, when walking in the streets, you have to watch where you step. Dog owners don't carry poop scoopers and don't often guide their dogs to the curb gutter to relieve themselves. The gutters are flooded with water at specified times by council employees to keep them clean. Other council employees, dressed in green, ride scooters along the sidewalk and clean up the dog poop through a long hose of a machine that's like a vacuum cleaner. Despite this, there always seems to be plenty of dog poop waiting in the streets for unsuspecting tourists.

The French spend 16 million francs a day ($2.2 million) on pets. In addition, nine out of ten cats and half the dogs are given to their eventual owners as presents and so cost nothing. A lot of the money is spent on the 3,000 tons of pet food bought each day. Seventy-six percent of the cats are fed with canned food. Three million francs ($420,000) are spent each day on the health and grooming of pets. Eighty thousand dog owners and 3,000 cat owners buy health insurance policies for their pets. And when cherished pets die, some grieving owners have them buried in the famous pet cemetery in Asnières, a suburb of Paris.

Just before the summer vacation period is dangerous time for pets. Some owners will abandon them because they don't want to take care of the pets while they're on vacation. Some of these abandoned pets find their way to the Sociétéé protectrice des animaux (Animal Protection Agency) where the lucky ones will be adopted by new owners.

Though the French love animals as pets, hunting is also a popular pastime in France, involving 1.6 million (only 1 percent of whom are women). France has the greatest number of hunters in Europe, followed by Spain, Italy, and Great Britain. The increased political power of the Greens has led to demonstrations against hunters when the official hunting season opens in the fall.

Related Web links: spa.asso.fr for advice and legislation from the Society for Protection of Animals (F)

FOOD AND DRINK
The Eighth Art

Gastronomy, the pleasures of the table, has always played a great part in French life. Referred to as the Eighth Art, French cuisine is famous around the world.

It's said that the Italian chef Marie de' Medici (1573–1642) brought with her to France, as a safeguard against the uncertain quality of food preparation in her adopted country, which began the French tradition of fine cooking. The Renaissance was also the time when vegetables (beans, potatoes, maize) from the Americas made their appearance in Europe, along with turkey, which replaced the peacock among chefs at the end of the 16th century. There was also a revolution in table manners, with the introduction of the fork and the dining room, though it was confined to the royal and aristocratic classes.

However, it was under the absolute monarchy of Louis XIV (1638–1715) that French cooking reached new heights. Sumptuous feasts, staged in a theatrical manner, became an element of glorification of the king. Under Louis XIV the importance of etiquette, *le service à la française* (all the main courses were served at the same time), and the art of table conversation became a national institution. At the same time, La Varenne published *Le Cuisinier français*, which sold 100,000 copies, and French playwright Molière (1622–73) wrote, "*Il faut manger pour vivre et ne pas vivre pour manger*" (You must eat to live and not live to eat), perhaps in reaction to the gastronomic excesses of the royal court. The supremacy of service *à la française* was to be challenged in the 1880s by service *à la russe* (serving courses in succession and not all at the same time).

The great gastronomic revolution of the 18th century was due to the French cook Beauvilliers, who in 1765 opened a *bouillon*, the first restaurant in Paris. During the French Revolution the former chefs of the aristocratic houses, deprived of their employment, opened restaurants in Paris, and thus great cuisine came to the streets, to become the domain of the growing bourgeoisie. French chefs such as Marie-Antoine Carême (1784–1833) and Auguste Escoffier (1846–1935) popularized French culinary traditions internationally. It was accompanied by intellectual reflection on gastronomy by Alexandre Grimod (1758–1838), who wrote *Almanach des gourmands* (1803); Alexandre Dumas (1802–70), of *Three Musketeers* fame, who wrote the *Grand Dictionnaire de cuisine*, published two years after he died; and Brillat-Savarin (1775–1826), the first influential food writer. In his 1825 *La Physiologie du goût* (*The Physiology of Taste*), Brillat-Savarin discussed the physiology of various foods and their effects, such as the sexually stimulating effects of truffles. His aphorism, "*Un bon repas favorise la conversation; un bon vin lui donne l'esprit*" (A good meal encourages conversation; a good wine makes it spirited), still holds true for the French today.

Related Web links: frenchfood.about.com for recipes, articles, links (E); france.diplomatie.fr /label_France/france/dossier/gastro/terre.html for a history of French gastronomy (F)

Regional Cooking

Although French cuisine is seen as a uniform way of national cooking, it is actually a composite of different regional and local cuisines that take their identity from the area and its produce. Regional products have become very popular in France, and are synonymous with ideas of quality, trustworthiness, origin, and the concept of *terroir*. Literally translated as "soil," *terroir* has also come to mean a "locality" that is part of an area (*pays*). Products of the soil—whether vegetables, cereals, fruits, wine, cheese, or meats—have their local flavor, related to the character of their *terroir*. It is this uniqueness of the foods of different regions that the French prize.

The main gastronomic regions of France include Brittany (crustaceans, crêpes called *galettes*, biscuits, ciders, and cider liqueurs); the Pyrenées (cured hams, lamb, and chorizo sausage); Alsace and the Northeast (*choucroute*, brioche, pork, cheeses, Riesling wines, beer, mirabelle plum liqueur, and champagne); Provence and Languedoc-Roussillon and the Mediterranean coast (olive oil, *salade niçoise*, ratatouille, bouillabaisse, and *pastis*); Rhône-Alpes (*boeuf bourguignon*, snails, Bresse chicken, *andouillettes*, *clafoutis cake*, cheeses, and Beaujolais and Burgundy wines); and the Southwest (foie gras, cassoulet, truffles, *confit de canard*, wild mushrooms, goat cheese, and Bordeaux wines). The Ile-de-France around Paris now grows a narrower variety of produce, so the best of regional produce is welcome in the kitchens of the Paris region. In many domains, Paris influences the provinces, but in the food domain it's the other way around, with numerous restaurants in Paris specializing in regional cuisine, creating a mosaic of gastronomic France.

The myth of French culinary savoir faire comes from the determination to do just about anything in order to achieve a sublime taste. Foie gras symbolizes this unique French characteristic. This pâté made from the enlarged livers of force-fed geese has become a luxury revered by the French and an integral item on the festive menu, like champagne. Special orders are placed in advance for fine foie gras, which is exported all over the world. It is often eaten with another French regional specialty, truffles. Pigs and dogs are trained to find black truffles, a fungus that grows symbiotically on hazelnut roots and is considered a delicacy. French food eccentricities such frogs legs are less common on French menus these days but persist as national clichés. In the past this particularity gave rise to the popular, and derisive, British moniker for the French, whom they called "Frogs." Until World War II the French generally ate within their regions, however these days "gastrotourism" is a favorite pastime for the French, and for international tourists as well, who enjoy the experience of sampling regional cuisine and produce in Paris and around France.

Related Web links: frenchfood.about.com, see subject *French chefs* for links; **alain-ducasse** **.com** for restaurants and a biography of Alain Ducasse (E, F)

Food and Restaurant Guides

France has two famous restaurant guides, the *Michelin Red Guide to France* and the *GaultMillau Guide France*. Both cover Paris and the provinces, and they are taken extremely seriously by the French and the rest of the culinary world. Inclusion or exclusion in these guides can make or break a restaurant's reputation. Each guide is linked to different traditions of French cooking.

The Michelin guide first appeared in 1900 as a motoring guide. It introduced its star system (*l'étoile de bonne table*) in 1926, when it was awarded to 46 establishments. The practice of awarding two and three stars began in 1931. Three stars denotes an establishment that has "exceptional cuisine worth a special journey, with fine wines, faultless service, and elegant surroundings." Two stars represent "excellent cooking worth a detour, with specialties and wines of first-class quality." One star signifies "a very good restaurant in its category." In the 2000 edition there were 22 three-star, 70 two-star, and 407 one-star restaurants in France. One million copies of the Michelin guide are sold each year. Some French chefs have been in the elite group for many years, such as Paul Bocuse, whose restaurant near Lyon has had three stars for 35 years; and Pierre Troisgros, whose restaurant at Roanne has had three stars for 32 years. Thanks to the *Michelin*, the French chefs who form part of the elite group are treated as kings, and their restaurants as places of food worship.

The bright yellow cover of the *Gault-Millau Guide France 2000* is not the only feature that distinguishes it from the red-covered *Michelin*. Launched in 1969 by two food critics, Henri Gault (1929–2000) and Christian Millau (1929–), as an alternative to the Michelin, its own rating system is based on scores (1 to 20) and three different toques (chef's hats) to denote quality. The toque prestige denotes luxury restaurants, the toque classique represents comfortable or elegant restaurants, and the toque bistro denotes neobistro, brasserie, and auberge establishments. Under this system, nine elite chefs scored 19 out of 20. In the 2000 edition there were 137 toques prestige, 2,572 toques classiques, and 1,232 toques bistros. In an article in the 1973 guide, Gault and Millau brought about the revolution in French cooking known as nouvelle cuisine. Until then French cooking was characterized by the use of butter and rich sauces. The two critics challenged French chefs to innovate by using fresh produce, reducing the cooking time of food to preserve the flavors of the ingredients, and to simplify sauces. They also challenged traditional rules, such as the sacrosanct pairing of red wine with meat and white wine with fish. The *Gault-Millau* has strongly influenced modern French ideas about food and eating habits not only in restaurants, but also in the home. It has provided a philosophy that corresponds to changes in people's lifestyles.

Related Web links: frenchfood.about.com see 2000 feature article on "Ordering in a French Restaurant" (E)

Great Chefs and Famous Restaurants

Like fashions, food in France is subject to trends. Nevertheless, certain restaurants and certain chefs have become synonymous with fine French cuisine, and when they have strong loyalties to particular regions, they have helped create reputations for regional dishes. Until the 1970s two restaurants consistently received three stars in the Michelin guide: La Tour d'Argent in Paris, for its signature dish, *caneton Tour d'Argent* (duck); and the 234-year-old restaurant Lapérouse on the left bank in Paris, for its dishes *gratin de langoustines Georgette* (shellfish), and *poulet poêlée du docteur* (chicken). With the advent of nouvelle cuisine in 1973, a new generation of chefs became famous. Bernard L'Oiseau, Joël Robuchon, Alain Senderens, and Michel Guérard, founder of *la cuisine minceur* (lean cuisine) movement. They were joined by a new group, described as innovators of *le nouveau régime*, which includes the use of authentic produce and flavors, and acceptance of ingredients and ideas from other national food traditions, such as Asian cuisines. Two major names in this group are Pierre Gagnaire and Alain Passard.

Paul Bocuse (1926–), who along with Alain Ducasse (1956–) has attained celebrity status, made his native Lyon region famous because of his restaurant at Collonges-au-Mont-d'Or, which belonged to his father and grandfather. In 1959 he took over the restaurant, and by 1965 he had won three Michelin stars. In 1975 he was made a member of the Légion d'Honneur by President Valéry Giscard d'Estaing. Bocuse has taught all over the world,

has published many books of his new cuisine, and has a business that is listed on the French stock exchange. Similarly, Alain Ducasse has an empire estimated to be worth 100 million francs ($14 million). He has restaurants in France, London, and New York (where there is a fixed-price menu of $160 plus wine and coffee) and the corporate giant Vivendi as a major shareholder in his company. In 1987, Ducasse took over as executive chef of Le Louis XV restaurant at the Hotel de Paris in Monaco. In 1990 that restaurant won three stars and made Ducasse, at 33, France's youngest three-star chef. In 1998 his restaurant at the Hotel Le Parc in Paris was also awarded three stars, and Ducasse became the only chef to hold six Michelin stars at the same time. He is renowned for coaxing the essential flavors from his ingredients, of revealing rather than concealing flavors, and for the fusion of French with other cuisines.

Related Web links: frenchfood.about.com, see *French chefs* for links; **alain-ducasse.com** for restaurants and a biography of Alain Ducasse (E, F)

Wines and Spirits

French wines and liqueurs are famous throughout the world. France is the second largest wine producer. Italy produces more wine, but the French drink more of it, about 55 liters a year, considerably less than the average of 100 liters a year in the 1960s. The French consume about double the quantity consumed by other Europeans. Wine consumption is decreasing, particularly among young people. Most French houses and apartment buildings have a *cave* (cellar) where wine is stored. Wine for daily meals can be bought in supermarkets or a wine shop (*marchand du vin*). One of the most famous restaurants in Paris, La Tour d'Argent, has 500,000 bottles of wine stored in its cellar, with 9,300 different types of wine to choose from.

A distinctive feature of the industry and its wines is the classification system guaranteeing quality and authenticity. Wines labeled *Appellation d'origine contrôlée* (AOC) or with a controlled origin label have a guaranteed origin. Wines labeled *Vins délimités de qualité supérieure* (VDQS), or labeled Superior Quality have a guarantee of quality. VDQS wines are less prestigious than those classified AOC, which are controlled according to the type of vine, the area of production, alcohol content, and viticulture practices. Produced from "less noble" types of wine but still controlled are the *vins de pays* (local wines), one of the most famous of which is *Beaujolais*, a light red wine produced in southern Burgundy. The third Thursday in November is a ritual in France—the day the first of the year's new Beaujolais wine is tasted. All over France, and all over the world in 150 locations including New York, Tokyo, and Moscow (where the wine is flown), there's a race to be the first to taste the new Beaujolais ("*Le Beaujolais nouveau est arrivé!*").

The most famous French wine-growing regions are Alsace (for white wines) and Bordeaux and Burgundy (for both red and white wines). Tradition still governs a special meal, which is preceded by an aperitif of champagne (brut or rosé), *kir* (white wine and black currant liqueur, cassis), a *kir royal* (champagne and black currant liqueur), or a *pastis* (an aniseed-flavored spirit mixed with water, a popular summer drink in the South). At the commencement of the meal a light wine (white or red *sancerre*, a pinot noir, or white wine from Alsace) is served. With the main course of meat or game, the wine is usually a quality red; with dessert a mellow wine such as a sauterne or champagne is served. With coffee, a fruit liqueur or a *digestif* such as cognac is usual. The vineyards around the city of Cognac in the Charente region near the Atlantic coast produce the prized after-dinner spirit.

Ancient associations of wine growers and their friends promote the wines of the region. Among the most illustrious is the *Confrérie des chevaliers du Tastevin* at the castle of Clos de Vougeot near Beaune, which celebrates the great vintages in Burgundy.

Related Web links: frenchfood.about.com, see *French wine* (E)

Water, Juices, and Beer

The French drink a large quantity of mineral water (*eau minérale*) and choose their water with as much thought as they choose their wine. The Ministry of Health must recognize genuine therapeutic qualities before it will allow a water to be labeled *eau minérale*. Mineral waters are marketed according to their therapeutic qualities. The natural springs from where the water derives were once famous as therapeutic spas where people went to "take the waters." Mineral water can be either *gazeuse* (sparkling) or *plate* (flat). Perrier and Badoit (sparkling) are well-known brands, as are Vitel, Contrex, and Evian (flat). The French lead the world in consumption of mineral water, drinking 112 liters a year, followed by the Italians (101 liters), the Germans (80 liters), the Spanish (55 liters), and the Americans (45 liters). Both water and wine appear on tables at mealtimes. However, 59 percent of the French drink tap water every day. Tap water is served in restaurants only upon request.

Cider, produced from the apple orchards in Normandy and Brittany, is also a popular drink. For breakfast, the French will most likely choose coffee (45 percent), followed by hot chocolate, fruit juice, or tea (10 percent), and then either water, milk, or chicory drinks. France has the lowest consumption of fruit juices in Europe, with only 15 liters consumed on average by each person in a year, in contrast to 35 liters in Germany and 45 liters in the United States. French children enjoy drinking water mixed with cordials (*syrops*), often made from real fruits, such as strawberry, raspberry, lemon, and mint. Grenadine syrup (a mixture of different fruit syrups) is very popular, as is Orangina, an orange-tasting soft drink. For a long time Coca-Cola was unpopular in France because it reminded French children of medicine. However, today it is popular among French teenagers, who also enjoy most of the major American soft drinks. Perrier is now also marketing their mineral water flavored with popular fruit flavors such as lemon, orange, and mandarin.

The north and east of France, which border beer-drinking Germany, Belgium, and the Netherlands, have a beer-drinking tradition and produce two popular brands of French beer: Kronenbourg and Kanterbrau. France, however, is only the seventh-largest beer-drinking country in Europe. It was a Frenchman, Louis Pasteur (1822–95), who successfully devised a method to kill disease-producing organisms in beer in 1873 by raising the temperature in the brewing process. Cafés serve both alcoholic and nonalcoholic drinks. If you order *une bière*, you'll be served bottled beer, which is more expensive than *un demi*, or beer on tap.

Related Web links: perrier.com (E, F); danone.com/bottled_water.html for Evian and Volvic (E), brasseries-kronenbourg.com (F); http://guy.massart.free.fr for cider-making process (F)

Cheese and Chocolate

Charles de Gaulle once commented on the difficulty of governing a country that made as many varieties of cheeses as there are days in the year. This great variety has made France famous as a cheese-loving and -producing country. Only the Greeks eat more cheese (2.2 ounces per day, compared to 2.0 ounces for the French). Every French main meal includes at least one kind of cheese, and often a selection of cheeses is served with or without a salad after the main course and before dessert. French cheeses are intimately associated with the regions and the *terroir* where they are produced. Normandy is famous for its creamy Camembert and Brie as well as its strong-smelling Pont-l'éveque; Poitou for its goat cheese; Auvergne for Cantal; and the Midi-Pyrénées region for the blue cheese made from sheep's milk, Roquefort. The most popular cheeses found in France in 1998 were Selles-sur-Cher (goat cheese), Livarot (from Normandy), Pouligny (shaped like the base of the Eiffel Tower), and Reblochon (from Savoy in the Alps). French cheese is exported throughout the world, but particularly to other members of the European Union, but a serious challenge to French cheese exports is the threat to French cheese-making practices from the European Union, since many cheeses are made from nonpasteurized milk, which is an essential element of their flavor. Enforcing the use of pasteurized milk would end a long tradition of distinctive French cheeses.

As for chocolate, the French regard it with great reverence; they consider it a "noble" food that is continually being refined in the search for new and purer tastes. According to surveys done by the National Chamber of Chocolate Makers, 70 percent of the French believe that chocolate should be part of the daily diet, and to this end each person in France eats 7.6 pounds a year. Nearly every French home buys chocolate (93 percent), and on special occasions chocolate is considered an essential part of the celebration. For example, in 1998, 38,500 tons of chocolate were consumed during holiday periods such as Easter and Christmas. On these occasions the patisseries and chocolate specialty shops throughout France devote whole windows to chocolate displays, and delight children with chocolate eggs, rabbits, and other animals. Paris is home to some of the *grandes maisons* of chocolate makers, like Dalloyau and La Maison du chocolat. There, you can buy pure chocolate (100 percent cocoa) or chocolate containing different percentages of cocoa and milk, with hazelnuts, preserved fruit . . . the list is endless. Since 1995, in Paris each December, at the Salon des saveurs (Salon of Tastes), new types of chocolate like chocolate with spices, or with algae, are displayed, testifying to the endless ways of experiencing the pleasure of eating chocolate.

Related Web links: franceway.com, see *Food & Drink* for cheese (E); fromages.com (E); chronicus.com, see *Temps moderne* for dossier on chocolate (F); confiserie.org for candy and confectionery (F); choco-club.com is an amateur chocolate-lover site (F)

Bread and Pastries

Although bread is now sold in supermarkets, the *boulangerie* (bakery) remains indispensable to the French way of life. *Boulangeries* produce 75 percent of the bread sold in France. Bread produced in factories (*pain industriel*) accounts for the rest of the market. In *boulangeries*, bread is baked fresh several times a day. Nearly half the French (46 percent) purchase their bread in the morning. In fact, though bread is an essential part of the French diet, the French eat five times less bread today than they did at the beginning of the 20th century, down from 722 pounds to 128 pounds per person per year. Meanwhile, the variety of breads available has increased, with over 80 regional and specialty types, but the French still love their baguette, which accounts for 80 percent of all bread sold.

The name of the long crusty French loaf indicates its thickness and weight: *la ficelle* is the thinnest; then comes *la baguette* (the commonest), then *la flûte* and *le pain*, of which there are different types, such as *pain de compagne* (country style bread). At meals, the French usually break bread with their hands and eat it without butter. Lunch in a café often consists of a baguette cut in half and sliced lengthwise to make *un sandwich* filled with ham, cheese, or pâté. Besides bread, a *boulangerie* will also sell croissants (eaten for breakfast or special occasions), *pain au chocolat* (a croissant filled with chocolate), and simple pastries like *un chausson aux pommes* (apple-filled pastry) or an *escargot* (pastry filled with sultanas and raisins and rolled to make a snail shape).

Since Marie-Antoinette's alleged callous reply to being told that the people had no bread during the French Revolution, "Well, then, let them eat cake!" bread has had enormous political significance in France. From 1789 to the present, no French government would dare allow the price of bread to climb out of reach of the poorest family. As a result, bread is heavily subsidized by the government and its price remains low.

The French cake shop, the *pâtisserie*, may sell bread in addition to its mouthwatering range of cakes, tarts, and elaborate pastries. Many of these pastries have religious or historical associations, for example *une religieuse* is a chocolate éclair shaped to resemble a nun; or *la tarte Tartin* is a caramelized apple tart named after a restaurant owner, Madame Tartin. On Sunday mornings the *pâtisseries* do a brisk trade in cakes and fruit tarts, which are bought for the Sunday lunch. For weddings and christenings, a *pièce montée*—a tall cone-shaped arrangement of caramelized profiteroles—is traditional. At Christmas the traditional cake is the *bûche-de-Noël*, a Christmas log.

Related Web links: boulangerie.net, see *Produits* for bread, pastries, regional specialties, manufacturers (F)

FOOD AND DRINK
Modern Eating

There is general agreement among food critics and chefs that French cuisine, despite the increased range of choices available to the French from foreign cuisines or from American fast food outlets, is maintaining its popularity and its identity. French food is still an important part of Gallic culture. Food education begins at school, in the cafeterias where most French children eat lunch provided by the government. This meal is strictly structured, consisting of an entrée, a main course, cheese or milk products, and dessert. The lessons learned about what constitutes a balanced meal remain with French children throughout their lives. However, the number of obese children over the age of ten in the Paris region has doubled between 1978 and 1995, from 6 percent to 14 percent. Some suggest that Parisian children have taken to "snacking," although the French eat only about 8 pounds of snack foods per year, compared to about 29 pounds for the British. For adults, the preferred snack foods in France are chocolate, cakes, bread, cheese, pizza, and croissants. Candy is not nearly as popular in France as it is in the United States, with 440,000 tons sold a year, compared to 1.1 million tons in America. For dinner, some of the traditions seem to be breaking down: only 24 percent of the French have an entrée, a main course, and dessert, while 53 percent choose to have just a main course and dessert.

A recurring discussion in France is the need to protect French cooking traditions against "progress." The French chef Joël Robuchon, who writes a regular column in Le Figaro, speaks for the traditionalists, demanding that French chefs take their inspiration from the regions and not adapt foreign cuisines. In 1997 in a survey conducted by the magazine Cuisine et vin de France, the classic regional dishes remained the best loved. These dishes included quiche lorraine, blanquette de veau (veal), steak-frites (steak with fries), confit de canard (duck), and choucroute garnie (sauerkraut). Among the younger generations the situation was different. They preferred foreign dishes like paella, chili con carne, and nem (spring rolls).

There is an enormous choice of food to eat in Paris; regional cuisine and foreign foods are available in many restaurants. Parisians go to North African restaurants to eat couscous, which is often listed by the French as one of their favorite dishes. They can eat at Chinese, Vietnamese, Laotian, and Indian restaurants. Thai food is seen as more exotic, and eating at a Japanese restaurant is viewed as a total cultural experience. Often, foreign food is adapted to French tastes. The food in Chinese restaurants in France, for instance, is blander than in other countries. Other adaptations are more unusual, such as pizza topped with goat cheese or merguez sausages. It's not uncommon to find French dishes, such as a green or tomato salad for an entrée or crème caramel for dessert, included on the menu in foreign food restaurants.

Related Web links: lefigaro.fr, see Art de vivre for gastronomy section (F); cuisineetvinsde france.com is a food and drink magazine site (F)

Hamburgers vs Baguettes

In July 1999 the European Union decided to ban imports of American beef from hormone-fed cattle. The Americans responded by taxing at 100 percent French products such as Roquefort and Camembert cheese. In Aveyron, sheep farmer José Bové and 300 fellow farmers whose livelihood depended on the sale of Roquefort cheese to America decided to protest outside the local McDonald's. This inspired a movement in France against what the French call *malbouffe* (bad nutrition) as represented by American fast food chains. It has grown into a protest against the industrialization of food-growing practices and a renewed demand for healthy, simple, and authentic produce, which in France means a return to homegrown regional foods. It is also a protest against the infiltration of the French food industry by American chains and against globalization.

Despite the visibility of fast food restaurants (*la restauration rapide*) in French cities and towns, the French spend only 19 percent of their eating-out budget in this type of restaurant when they eat out. Perhaps even more surprising, hamburgers represent only 1 percent of food consumed by young people, 15 to 24 years old. The French have also responded to American fast food restaurants by developing their own versions of fast food, such as the Quick chain. The fastest growing McDonald's alternative are the *sandwicheries*, which serve sandwiches *à la française*, like sliced baguettes with a range of different fillings. One of the most successful French fast food chains is La Brioche Dorée, which tells its customers to *mange vite, mais bien*

(eat fast, but well) and has combined a sandwich shop, *boulangerie*, and *salon de thé* into one convenient location. Other popular French chains are Aubépain, Pomme de pain, and Station Sandwich.

The other change in French attitudes concerning food results from the increasing distrust of industrial food-growing practices, intensified by the crisis in the British beef industry and the discovery of dangerous levels of toxins in Belgian poultry and pork products. The spread of mad cow disease (*la vache folle*) to France, Germany, and Italy heightened interest in organic (*bio*) produce. Although only 0.4 percent of the total food market, one in six French people claim to eat some products with the label *bio*, which must contain 90 percent organic ingredients. Such food, whose sources of production can be traced, is given an Agriculture Biologique (AB) label by the Ministry of Agriculture. Thus, "natural" does not necessarily mean "organic" in France. The trend, *manger bio* (eat organic), means a lot more than just replacing nonorganic foods with organic ones. It is an approach to eating that is balanced: less meat, more whole foods and cereals, and more fresh fruit and vegetables. With increasing government support, this way of eating and appreciating food may become more accessible to the French, who will no doubt adapt it to French culinary ways.

Related Web links: mcdonalds.fr, quick.fr, le -duff.com, for La Brioche Dorée fast food chains (E, F)

FOOD AND DRINK
Cafés

The café is one of the best-known symbols of French lifestyle. Cafés, sometimes called "bistros," are open from early till late, before and after restaurants have closed. They serve alcoholic and nonalcoholic drinks and food, but the café is far more than a place to eat or drink. It is a meeting place for friends, acquaintances, and students. The casual *On prend un verre?* (Let's have a drink?) or *On prend un café?* (Let's have a coffee—usually a short black espresso) can be an invitation to continue an interesting conversation with a new acquaintance, to take a break from grueling work or a boring routine, or to explore the romantic possibilities of a chance encounter. Some cafés are well-known as meeting places for artists or intellectuals.

The social importance of the *café* is reflected in its ubiquity in every French town or village. In neighborhood cafés, pinball machines (*les flippers*) are played by young and old. The pinball machine in France is more a prized feature than it tends to be in the United States; it is *not* acceptable to set a drink on the glass, for example. If you stand at the counter in the morning, you can take a croissant from the baskets placed there and pay for it along with your coffee later. The hard-boiled eggs on the counter are eaten for quick snacks. It costs less, by the way, to stand and drink at the counter (*le comptoir* or *le zinc*) than to be served at a table. A price list is displayed on the wall near the counter. Don't be surprised if prices vary greatly according to the location of the café. A simple cup of coffee in a smart area costs much more than in a neighborhood *café*.

There are conventional ways of greeting the waiters and the owners, who serve from behind the counter. Customers use the *vous* form, add "monsieur" or "madame" after *Bonjour*, and say "Au revoir" on leaving. You don't call the waiter with a snap of your fingers. You get his attention either by eye contact or calling to him, "Monsieur, *s'il vous plaît*." Avoid the old-fashioned term *garçon* for waiter, which is now considered condescending.

You have no obligation to pay immediately when you are served. If you're seated, the waiter leaves a ticket with the price on the table. You pay when you leave. The traditional tip (*le pourboire*) for the waiter has been officially replaced by a 15 percent service charge included in the bill. If you have the exact amount of the bill in cash, leave it on the table, without calling the waiter. If you want to leave a tip as well, leave it on the table; don't give it to the waiter in person.

Salons de thé, Pubs, and Bars

In the lively and densely populated environment of urban France, where people don't readily invite friends home, a café is a place where people meet and talk. It can also be a place to read a book or a newspaper (sometimes the café makes newspapers available to customers), to write, or to sit on your own over a drink. The café terrace opens onto the street (with a glass frontage in winter and chairs and tables outside in summer). It is a popular space for socializing or simply watching the passing crowd.

Salons de thé (tearooms) have recently become more numerous and fashionable. Originally, there were not many of them and they had the reputation of being elegant meeting places for upper-class women who had adopted the British custom of drinking tea and eating cake in the middle of the afternoon. In those French tearooms, ice cream was served and there was a much wider selection of delicate French pastries than in their British counterparts.

Their popularity in France reflects a desire to meet for a light meal in a place less crowded than a café and less expensive and formal than a restaurant. You don't go to a *salon de thé* just to drink; you go to a café for that. A wide range of customers from diverse social backgrounds, both men and women, now eat, drink, and enjoy conversation in the relaxed and chic atmosphere of a *salon de thé* at lunchtime and during the afternoon. These establishments can serve wine with lunch but continue to offer many different types of tea as well as coffee and nonalcoholic drinks, in addition to cakes and pastries. They rarely remain open for dinner, and unlike cafés, the staff of a *salon de thé* is generally feminine. Another traditionally British meeting place that is challenging the universal appeal of the French café for beer drinkers is the pub. British-style pubs serving many types of beer are now common throughout France. On average, the French drink 37 liters of beer per person per year and 66 liters of wine.

Bars in France grew out of the American bar tradition and tend to be more specialized nighttime meeting places than cafés. Harry's Bar at "Cinq Roo Donoo" (5, rue Daunou) near the Opera House in Paris is well-known and was a haunt of Ernest Hemingway, among others. Bars are more expensive than cafés and they don't serve coffee. Often they are part of discothèques and nightclubs. The Bastille area in Paris has become the fashionable location for bars frequented by young people.

Related Web links: france-boissons.com is the largest distributor of wines, beers, and sodas in France (F); parispubs.com, nycbeer.org/paris for reviews of Paris pubs (E); cafeguerbois.com for Parisian cafés in the 19th century (E)

Landscape and Climate

France enjoys a privileged geographical position in Europe, and, with a fairly temperate climate, is endowed with a diverse and spectacular range of landscapes. It is the only European country that is part of both the Mediterranean region and of northern Europe. It is called *l'hexagone* due to its roughly hexagonal shape, which consists of three seaward coasts (the Channel, the Atlantic, and the Mediterranean) and three land-bound sides (Belgium/Luxembourg, Germany/Switzerland/Italy, Spain).

A large part of France consists of fertile plains, including the three coastal plains of Flanders, the Landes, and Languedoc. The mountain ranges are all below a line running from Bayonne, in the Southwest, to Strasbourg, which borders Germany in the east. Mount Blanc, in the Alps, at 15,515 feet, is the highest mountain, while the Pyrénées, between Spain and France, rise to over 9,700 feet. France has five important rivers. In order of their size within France, they are: the Loire (660 miles), the Seine (465 miles), the Garonne (315 miles), the Rhône (314 miles), and the Rhine (117 miles). The variations of climate in France can be grouped in three categories: Atlantic, Continental, and Mediterranean. The Atlantic climate is influenced by the ocean. In the north and in Brittany it can be misty and wet, while in Aquitaine it is more likely to be hot and sunny. The Continental climate affects central and eastern France. Winters are dry and cold, summers hot and dry, with rainy periods in spring and fall. The Mediterranean climate is characterized by hot,

dry, sunny summers, with generally mild winters. However, it can also be subject to violent storms and the mistral and tramontane winds. The French spend a lot of time talking about the weather. They listen to the forecast on radio and, at night, on television. In fact, weather forecasters are regarded as celebrities.

Brittany, on the Atlantic coast, is mainly a forest region, with pine, oak, beech, and birch trees, to which the heath and ferns add a unique color. The Mediterranean influence is seen in the landscape of the Rhône Valley, with its chestnut trees in the north and olive groves to the south. Vineyards and orchards, and lavender and rosemary bushes testify to a favorable climate. The mountainous regions of France offer spectacular scenery, from the rocky gorges of the massifs to the snow-encrusted peaks of the Alps or the Pyrénées. Man has helped shape the beauty and harmony of the French landscape through agriculture and architecture, from the vineyards to the villages clinging to the hills of the Mediterranean.

> **Related Web links: meteo.fr** for weather by region, wind, temperature, satellite picture (F); **cnrs.fr** is the national center for scientific research (F); **jadot.net/carto** has relief and 3-D maps of France (F); **rando.net/cartes/france /2frame.htm** for a zoom-in map (F)

Flowers, Gardens, and National Parks

In France, as in many countries, red roses are a symbol of love and beauty. They also became the symbol of the French socialists when François Mitterrand was elected President. Chrysanthemums, however, are not given to your loved ones unless they are dead. The French traditionally place chrysanthemums on family graves in visits on Toussaint (All Saint's Day) on November 1. A flower is also associated with Labor Day (*fête du Travail*), when lily-of-the-valley (*muguet*) is given to friends and family in order to bring them happiness (*un porte-bonheur*).

The French style of garden (*jardin à la française*) is geometrical, and includes ponds, fountains, and statues; the landscape architect André le Nôtre (1613–1700), who designed the gardens of the Palace of Versailles, originated it. In Paris, the Tuileries Gardens near the Louvre and the Luxembourg Gardens near the Sorbonne are examples of the style. The impressionist painter Claude Monet's (1840–1926) garden at Giverny, north of Paris in the valley of the Seine, has been maintained with the help of American philanthropists and attracts crowds of admiring visitors. It was in Giverny that Monet painted his radiant *Nymphéas* (*Water Lilies*) series from 1899 to his death.

France protects the flora, fauna, and ecological environment in seven large national parks covering nearly 3.2 million acres, and in 36 regional nature parks covering 13 million acres. The national parks in the Alps and the dates they were established are Vanoise (1963), with 107 mountain peaks above 9,750 feet, and Ecrins (1973). Pyrénées Park was opened in 1967, and Cévennes, in the Massif Central in the center of France, in 1970, and classified a world reserve of the biosphere by UNESCO in 1985. The other three national parks are Mercantour (1979), inland from Nice; Port-Cros (1963), on the Mediterranean coast, and including small islands and a marine reserve; and, outside mainland France, Guadeloupe (1989), which is also part of UNESCO's world reserve of the biosphere and contains the active volcano La Soufrière. The regional nature parks are scattered across France and include the Camargue, the famous wildlife area in the estuary of the Rhône river, and Corsica in the Mediterranean. There are 23 major aquariums, mainly on the French coast from Antibes (Mediterranean) to Arcachon (Atlantic) and Saint-Malo (English Channel).

The internationally famous French underwater explorer Jacques Cousteau (1910–97) contributed greatly to raising the awareness of the French to the beauty and richness of marine life and the necessity of protecting the environment.

Related Web links: parcsnationaux-fr.com for seven national parks (F); parcs-naturels-region aux.tm.fr for 40 regional parks (E, F); chateau versailles.fr is the official Versailles site, with 360-degree panoramas (E, F); cousteau society.org is the society founded by Jacques Cousteau (F)

The North and East

The North (Nord Pas-de-Calais, Picardy, Champagne-Ardenne)

Nord Pas-de-Calais in the 19th century was France's major industrial region because of its coal, steel, and textile industries. With the decline of those industries, the region has undergone many changes. Maintaining and developing its agricultural interests, largely in the Picardy region, it is the world's top producer of chicory. The vineyards of Champagne and its world-renowned producers (Veuve Cliquot, Roederer, Tattinger, Heidsieck, Laurent-Perrier, Moët et Chandon) have also helped create the gastronomic reputation of the region. New industries are also developing: domestic glassware at Arques, wool at Tourcoing, mail-order businesses at Roubaix. And with the construction of the Channel Tunnel, Lille has become the center of a European transportation network.

The East (Lorraine, Alsace, Franche-Comté, Burgundy)

In recent years, Lorraine has been suffering from the decline of its coal mining and iron and steel industries. Lorraine's rich history attracts many tourists. The principal city, Metz , has retained much of its medieval architecture, while Nancy, the capital of the Dukes of Lorraine, has the magnificent Place Stanislaus, reflecting the city's past, when it was a center of the art nouveau movement. Although the Alsace region's geographical location on the left bank of the Rhine River made it subject to territorial disputes between France and Germany, it is today experiencing economic and cultural expansion. It has a rich agricultural and industrial base. The principal town, Strasbourg, is home to the European Parliament and the Council of Europe, making it an influential city in European politics. The picturesque mountainous region of the Vosges is covered in pine and oak forests and is known for its thermal baths, and its lakes and cheeses.

The principal city of Franche-Comté, Besançon, is the capital of France's watch and clock-making industry and of high-precision engineering. The Peugeot car firm has its headquarters at Montbéliard-Sochaux, and Alsthom is a leader in the engineering and rail industries.

Burgundy is famous the world over for its vineyards. It's also known for its beef cattle and cuisine. Along the Route du vin (wine route) you will find the vineyards of the *grands crus* with the wonderful vintages such as Gevrey-Chambertin, Clos-Vougeot, Vosne-Romanée, Pommard, Meursault, and Puligny-Montrachet. Tourists visit Burgundy for its Romanesque and Gothic architecture, many examples of which still survive in Autun, Auxerre, Beaune, Dijon, Fontenay, and Tournus.

Related Web links: champagne-multimedia.com (E, F); champagne-ardennes.com (E, F); pays-du-nord.fr (F); alsace.fr (E, F); vinsalsace.com for *Route du vin* (E, F); en-lorraine.com (F); citesortie.com for Franche-Comté (F); burgundy.net (E, F)

Ile-de-France

The region surrounding Paris is called the Ile-de-France. It consists of the inner suburbs of Paris, *la banlieue*, with la Seine-Saint-Denis, les Hauts-de-Seine, and le Val-de-Marne; and the four departments of the outer suburbs, which are le Val-d'Oise, les Yvelines, la Seine-et-Marne, and l'Essonne. Paris and these departments make up the largest urban area in Europe, with a total population of 10.9 million, 2.2 million of whom live in Paris itself. Nearly 20 percent of the total population of France lives in this region.

Although the description of France as "Paris and the French desert" has lost much of its truth, Ile-de-France remains the headquarters of most political, economic, and financial decision making, despite 30 years of a government policy aimed at decentralization. Ile-de-France is the "economic brain" of the nation, and most French and international corporations are based here, as well as all government departments and the national headquarters of public agencies. Construction and heavy industry also have a strong presence in the region, most notably in the metal processing, chemical, pharmaceutical, aeronautic, and automobile industries.

The Ile-de-France is also the principal intellectual, cultural, and scientific center of the country. The *grandes écoles*, universities, research laboratories, cultural institutions, public and private radio and television networks are all concentrated here. Paris is a major press, publishing, and arts center, as well as home for a number of international organizations, including UNESCO and the OECD. The region is a transport hub for the national train network (the TGV high-speed train, and the RER regional train network) and for air traffic, with Roissy and Orly airports.

The Ile-de-France is rich in history and in natural beauty, which make it the major tourist center of France. In addition to the charms of Paris, tourists flock to see the spectacular castles (Versailles, Fontainebleau, Chantilly, Compiègne, Saint-Denis, Saint-Germain Vaux-le-Vicomte), the theme parks (Disneyland and Asterix), and the huge forests (686,660 acres of green space, which attract 100 million local and international tourists a year). The magical combination of history, natural beauty, and economic and cultural dynamism make this region of France the world's most popular tourist destination.

Related Web links: proloc.com for maps of Paris and suburbs (E); http://perso.wanadoo.fr /ornicom/ for a listing of Ile-de-France parks and zoos (F)

The West

Brittany, Normandy, and the Loire Region

Brittany, whose capital is Rennes, was the land of the Celts in the 5th century. It is still the land of legends and myths, enjoying a revival of Celtic culture, and of landscapes of strange and sometimes mysterious rock formations. Brittany used to be relatively isolated because of its geographical location in the northwest of France, but improved road and rail links have changed it from a land of emigration to a major agricultural (vegetables) and meat-producing (pork) region. The automobile and telecommunications industries are well-established in Brittany, and the ports of Lorient, Douarnenez, and Roscoff are maritime centers for the fishing industry. Brittany is also a center for oceanographic research and tourism (Saint-Malo and le Mont-Saint-Michel). Once considered one of the poorest regions of France, Brittany today is prosperous as well as culturally dynamic.

Normandy, with its famous and beautiful hedge-separated fields, while still a region of agriculture and milk production, has diversified into industry and tourism. Lower Normandy has a number of light industries (light engineering, motor vehicles, and electronics) and a significant tourist industry, with a dynamic capital, Caen, on the Channel. Upper Normandy has France's second and fifth largest ports, Le Havre and Rouen, on the Seine, and is a center for the oil refining, chemical, and motor vehicle industries. Many Parisians have country houses in Normandy, whose beaches were chosen for the invasion during World War II that eventually led to the Liberation of France.

The Loire region (Pays de la Loire) holds second place in France in terms of agricultural production and livestock breeding. The port complex of Nantes–Saint Nazaire (fourth largest in France) is the industrial hub of the region and a center of naval construction and oil importation. The TGV (high-speed train) that links Nantes, the principal city, to Paris in two hours has helped make Nantes a major administrative and insurance center. The famous chateaux of the Loire are a major French tourist attraction, as well as its vineyards and the fine hunting and fishing in the Sologne and Berry areas.

Related Web links: rennet.org for Rennes (F); ville-saint-malo.fr (E, F); saint-malo.com (E, F); monum.fr for Mont Saint-Michel (F); ville-le havre.fr (E, F); http://perso.wanadoo.fr/mvgs /lehavre.htm (F); asteria.fr for a virtual tour of Brittany; rouen.fr (E, F); multimania.com/nantes (F); loirevalley.org/tourisme (F)

The Center and Southwest

The Center (Auvergne, Limousin, Centre, and Poitou-Charentes)

The Center is primarily an agricultural and livestock-raising region. The Beauce plain produces cereal crops (wheat, sugar beet), and Touraine produces flowers, mushrooms, fruit and vegetables, and wine. Cognac and butter are the specialties found in the Charente area. Poitou-Charentes is the main oyster-producing region of France. Industry is concentrated in the Auvergne, a mountainous and isolated region of France. For instance, the Michelin tire company has its main factory here, at Clermont-Ferrand. There is a strong artisan tradition in textiles (tapestry at Aubusson), leather, and porcelain (Limoges) which survives today. A new industry of building pleasure boats is at La Rochelle on the coast, also a popular tourist destination. The theme park Futuroscope, built at Poitiers and dedicated to the image, has contributed to the growth of tourism in the region. Other attractions for tourists are the beaches, walking and hiking, and the thermal spas of Vichy and La Bourboule. Limousin and Poitou-Charentes are also known for their many Romanesque churches (Saint-Savin, Talmont, Poitiers, Aulnay, Saint-Junien).

The Southwest (Aquitaine and the Midi-Pyrénées)

The Center and Southwest share the Atlantic side of the *hexagone*, and the Midi-Pyrénées shares the land border between France and Spain. Two cities form the focus of these regions: Bordeaux, for Aquitaine, and Toulouse, for the Midi-Pyrénées. For many years, Aquitaine's prosperity has been linked to the vineyards of the Bordeaux region (like Médoc, Saint-Emilion, Graves), another of France's famous wine-producing areas. This region is known for its good climate, fertile lands, and easy lifestyle. The Atlantic coast (the Landes) is a popular tourist destination. Inland from Biarritz is the Basque country. Described as an "ancient and mysterious race," the Basques still maintain their traditions, language, and culture. Toulouse is known as the *ville rose* (rose-colored city) because its buildings were constructed from rose-colored bricks. It is the principal city of the Midi-Pyrénées, the largest of France's regions, extending from the Atlantic coast to the Massif Central. The Airbus and the Ariane rocket are assembled at Toulouse, which is the center of France's aerospace industry. After Paris, it is the second most important city for technological research. This region offers spectacular scenery, like the valleys of the Dordogne and the Garonne. It is also the location of some famous French specialties: foie gras, cassoulet, and the truffle omelet.

Related Web links: rando.net and rando-massif central.com have details on walks (F); causses-cevennes.com (E, F); ville-vichy.fr (E, F); crt-auvergne.fr (E, F); larochelle.fr (E, F); irochelle.com has 360-degree panoramas and history (F); futuroscope.fr (E, F); voyager-en-france.com/bordeaux (E, F); arttoulouse.com for history, monuments, photos (F); mairie-toulouse.fr (E, F); best-of-perigord.tm.fr for Dordogne (E, F); infobasque.com (E, F); bascoweb.com (F)

The South

Rhône-Alpes, Languedoc-Roussillon, and Provence-Alpes–Côte d'Azur

This area is the second economic center of the country, after Paris and the Ile-de-France. Located on the route between southern and northern Europe, it has always been an area of commercial and political significance. Lyon, where the Rhône and Saône rivers meet, was the capital of Roman and Christian Gaul. Today it has the second largest urban agglomeration in France and is an important manufacturing and services center (electrical and mechanical engineering, chemicals, clothing, financial services). It is also a large university center, along with Montpellier in Languedoc-Roussillon and Aix-Marseille in Provence. Lyon, Marseille, Montpellier, Grenoble, and Nice are dynamic commercial and cultural cities, and the latter two are centers of scientific research.

Provence-Alpes–Côte d'Azur owes its prosperity largely to the Mediterranean coastline, its excellent climate, and its natural beauty. Nice and St. Tropez are famous resort towns, as is Cannes, the location of France's most famous film festival. The sunny climate has given the landscape strong colors and smells, as around Grasse, a city of perfume and flowers, and is home to several famous perfume manufacturers. There are the beautiful historic cities of Arles, Aix, Les Baux, and Avignon, which in 2000 was designated cultural capital of Europe. Marseille, France's largest port and Europe's second (after Rotterdam), dominates much of the region's economic life, with its oil refineries, iron and steel production, chemicals, and foodstuffs. To the west of Marseille, in the delta of the Rhône River, the Camargue is a marshy plain that is home to wild horses and bulls and bird life. The people of the Camargue have a unique culture very much linked to their environment and have developed a reputation as being great horsemen. The Alps, of course, is known to skiers from around the world, and boasts numerous ski resorts.

The plains of Languedoc-Roussillon are covered with vineyards, thanks to the gentle climate of the area. The long coast of beautiful beaches is crowded with tourists in the summer. Montpellier is an important university town, and a cultural and commercial center. The most celebrated Roman bridge still standing in France, the Pont du Gard, is close to Avignon and Nîmes, which is also the center for bull-fighting in the South. Carcassonne is a beautiful walled medieval city and today a thriving artistic haven for local artists, potters, and sculptors. The painter Toulouse-Lautrec was born at Albi, where a museum displays his famous posters and drawings.

Related Web links: bsi.fr for Cévennes; **alyon.asso.fr** for a Lyon guide and old postcards (F); **mairie-lyon.fr** (E, F); **avignon-et-provence.com**; **cogito.fr/marseill/marseill.htm** for history, culture, cuisine, tourism (F); **mairie-marseille.fr** (E, F); **mtblanc.net** for panoramas, walking, skiing (F); **camargue.com** (E, F); **cannesinfo.com** for 360-degree panoramas (E, F); **nova.fr/Saint-Tropez** (E, F)

French *Départements*

01 Ain
02 Aisne
03 Allier
04 Alpes-de-Haute-Provence
05 Hautes-Alpes
06 Alpes-Maritimes
07 Ardèche
08 Ardennes
09 Ariège
10 Aube
11 Aude
12 Aveyron
13 Bouches-du-Rhône
14 Calvados
15 Cantal
16 Charente
17 Charente-Maritime
18 Cher
19 Corrèze
20A Corse-du-Sud
20B Haute-Corse
21 Côte-d'Or
22 Côtes-d'Armor
23 Creuse

24 Dordogne
25 Doubs
26 Drôme
27 Eure
28 Eure-et-Loir
29 Finistère
30 Gard
31 Haute-Garonne
32 Gers
33 Gironde
34 Hérault
35 Ille-et-Vilaine
36 Indre
37 Indre-et-Loire
38 Isère
39 Jura
40 Landes
41 Loir-et-Cher
42 Loire
43 Haute-Loire
44 Loire-Atlantique
45 Loiret
46 Lot
47 Lot-et-Garonne

48 Lozère
49 Maine-et-Loire
50 Manche
51 Marne
52 Haute-Marne
53 Mayenne
54 Meurthe-et-Moselle
55 Meuse
56 Morbihan
57 Moselle
58 Nièvre
59 Nord
60 Oise
61 Orne
62 Pas-de-Calais
63 Puy-de-Dôme
64 Pyrénées-Atlantiques
65 Hautes-Pyrénées
66 Pyrénées-Orientales
67 Bas-Rhin
68 Haut-Rhin
69 Rhône
70 Haute-Saône
71 Saône-et-Loire

72 Sarthe
73 Savoie
74 Haute-Savoie
75 Paris
76 Seine-Maritime
77 Seine-et-Marne
78 Yvelines
79 Deux-Sèvres
80 Somme
81 Tarn
82 Tarn-et-Garonne
83 Var
84 Vaucluse
85 Vendée
86 Vienne
87 Haute-Vienne
88 Vosges
89 Yonne
90 Territoire de Belfort
91 Essonne
92 Hauts-de-Seine
93 Seine-Saint-Denis
94 Val-de-Marne
95 Val-d'Oise

GEOGRAPHY
Overseas Departments and Territories

Charles de Gaulle granted independence to France's last colonies when he returned to power in 1958. The French influence nevertheless still remains in the former African colonies of Cameroun, Congo, Côte d'Ivoire, Gabon, Guinée, Niger, Mali, Sénégal, Chad, and Togo. The French, for their part, maintain policies of cooperation, and have an emotional attachment to these countries.

Certain lands overseas still belong to France. Overseas France is administratively divided into *départements d'outre-mer* (DOM) and *territoires d'outre-mer* (TOM). The DOM are Guadeloupe, Martinique, French Guiana, and Réunion; the TOM are New Caledonia, French Polynesia, Wallis and Fortuna, Saint-Pierre-et-Miquelon, Mayotte, and the French Southern and Antarctic Territories.

The DOM and TOM are subject to different administrative systems. The four nations in the DOM became French *départements* in 1946 and for the most part are subject to the same legislation as metropolitan France. The *territoires d'outre-mer* (TOM), in contrast, are only subject to metropolitan France in the areas of defense, foreign relations, justice, and currency. Local affairs in the TOM are managed by an assembly elected by universal suffrage. In all Overseas Departments and Territories, the French government is represented by a High Commissioner or an administrator holding the rank of Prefect, while the people are represented in the Parliament by one or more deputies and also by a senator.

Although the inhabitants of the TOM have full French citizenship and elected local governments, they are also able to leave the French Union if they wish. Some have chosen independence—Afars and Issas (Djibouti), and three islands in the Comoros—while for others the decision is a complex one. An independence movement in New Caledonia, led by the indigenous Kanak people, has been striving for complete independence from France for most of the 20th century. This has occasionally led to violent clashes between the Kanaks and the French government. Among the DOM, a disorganized nationalist movement is running a guerrilla campaign against government by the French, in the hope of gaining independence.

The DOM and TOM are extensions of French language and French-influenced culture around the world. The international network of French language and culture is further promoted by organizations of the Francophonie, the community of countries where French is the official language or where a significant part of the population speak French. Forty-nine such countries from Europe (France, Belgium, and Luxembourg), Canada (Quebec), Africa, the Middle East, and Asia meet every two years for a Francophone summit.

Related Web links: insee.fr, see *Votre Région* for data on Guadeloupe, Guyane, Martinique, Réunion (F); **guadeloupe-antilles.com** for Guadeloupe links and photos (F)

Health and Fitness

The state of health of the French has greatly improved over the last decades. The mortality rate has declined considerably. Today, French women have a life expectancy of 82.1 years, which is 7.9 years longer than for men.

The French are renowned for their enjoyment of drinking and smoking, and excessive alcohol and tobacco consumption together account for one in five deaths a year. In the national psyche, drinking is associated with celebration, pleasure, and conviviality. The French consume the largest amount of alcohol in the European Union, with an average of more than 14 liters of pure alcohol consumed per year. Today, alcohol consumption is decreasing under the influence of changing lifestyles and government campaigns to reduce the high number of road accidents caused by intoxicated drivers. Today, young French people, men in particular, are less inclined to drink an aperitif before and a liqueur (*digestif*) after their meals.

Tobacco consumption is also decreasing. France now ranks seventh in the European Union, with Greece, Ireland, and Spain heading the list. Today, 29.8 percent of those between the age of 18 and 64 smoke, compared to 33.6 percent ten years ago, with 65 percent more of the smokers men than women. Since 1992 the government has been promoting antismoking campaigns.

In contrast, the use of sedatives in France has increased. The French take over three times more tranquilizers and sleeping pills (230 tablets per day for every 1,000 people) than other Europeans. In the past 20 years, spending on prescribed medicines has tripled while individual purchases have doubled. French consumption of medicines in general is higher than in other developed countries, and France has become the largest European producer of pharmaceutical products. However, for all the attention that the French demand of their doctors, they often prefer home remedies, consume herbal teas for stress or insomnia, and employ homeopathic treatment for various ailments. Many also believe in "taking the waters" at a spa such as Vichy, and mineral water named after a spa is popular at home as a remedy for various minor ills.

Possibly from a growing awareness of sedentary habits such as watching television, of increased stress in modern life, and work fatigue, the international fashion of jogging and aerobics has become popular since the 1980s. When the French say *faire de la gym*, they don't usually mean "to do gymnastics," but to do aerobics in a fitness center. At the same time, the French still enjoy less glamorous, more rural exercises as means of keeping fit (*garder la forme*), such as country walking and cycling.

Related Web links: sante.gouv.fr dossiers on health issues (F); sante.gouv.fr/htm/pointsur /tabac for the campaign against tobacco (F)

Health Care

The French set great store by their health (*santé*). It was in France, after all, that Louis Pasteur (1822–95), made his discoveries in microbiology. More recently, the research team at the Institut Pasteur, under Luc Montagnier (1932–), were the first to discover the AIDS virus, and the international humanitarian group of doctors Médicins Sans Frontières (Doctors without Borders) monitors and tries to alleviate world health catastrophes. France spends 9 percent of the national budget on health, double the amount 40 years ago and more than any of its European partners. Sixty-seven percent of the French say they are worried about their health. This is no doubt why the French visit their doctors frequently and expect a high level of service involving prescriptions and medical examinations.

The national health system in France has been part of the social security system (*la sécurité sociale*) since 1945. One of the first in Europe, this system reimburses every citizen's medical and hospital expenses. An overwhelming majority of 72 percent think that reimbursement of health costs should be the same for everyone despite his or her income.

France has the lowest rate of cardiovascular disease in the European Union, with 61 cases for 100,000 inhabitants, in contrast to the United Kingdom (200 cases) and the United States (176). However, the cancer rate in men (311 for 1,000 inhabitants) is the highest in the European Union. Cancer is the main cause of death in men (lung cancer) and the second cause of death in women (breast and cervical cancer). The number of appendicitis operations carried out each year in France is among the highest in the world (355 operations for 100,000 inhabitants); 2.5 times more than in the United States (141) and 3.6 times more than in the United Kingdom (97).

In any one year, more than 10 percent of the French are the victims of approximately 8 million domestic accidents that occur during the course of daily life—at home, at school, or during leisure activities. This is the highest proportion of such accidents in Europe.

As can be seen in the chart below, which refers to the year 1997, more than 500,000 people die each year in France. A quarter of these deaths is caused by illness or an accident before the age of 65 and involves men more than women.

Causes of Death

	MEN	WOMEN	TOTAL
Circulatory system	79,585	93,592	173,177
Coronary	26,121	21,155	47,276
Cerebral vascular	18,037	25,431	43,468
Tumors	89,194	58,527	147,721
Accident/violent death	26,279	17,402	43,681
Respiratory system	22,131	20,391	42,522
Digestive system	13,924	12,509	26,433
Other causes	45,532	56,425	101,957
Total deaths	276,645	258,846	535,491

Related Web links: **paris.msf.org**, for Médicins Sans Frontières, highlight of world health catastrophes (F); **pasteur.fr** news, for museum, information on infectious diseases (F); **sante.gouv.fr /index.htm** for practical information on health (F)

Height and Weight

The average Frenchman is 5 feet 8.5 inches tall, and the average French-woman is almost 5 feet 4 inches tall, according to the latest survey available. The tallest are young men from 20 to 22, who are 5 feet 9.7 inches tall, and 18-year-old women, who average 5 feet 5 inches tall. Over the last 100 years, men have grown 3.1 inches, and women 2.7 inches. Young men are, on average, 1.8 inches taller than their fathers and 2.9 inches taller than their grandfathers.

The height hierarchy reflects the social hierarchy, in that executives and professional people tend to be taller. Senior managers are on average 1.6 inches taller than employees, while the difference is .8 inches for women. Male students are 1.6 inches taller than young farm workers, and 28 percent of male executives are taller than 5 feet 10.9 inches, compared with 14 percent of farm workers and 17 percent of employees. The average height differences between the socioprofessional categories are less marked for women.

The average Frenchman weighs 163 pounds, and the average woman 134 pounds. Since 1970, the average weight for men has increased by 4.2 pounds, while the average weight for women has not increased. Between the ages of 20 and 50, men gain 11 pounds and women gain about 16.5 pounds.

Seven percent of French people are obese (defined as 30 percent higher than their ideal height-weight value)—9 percent of the women and 5 percent of the men. This compares favorably with other European countries. In the United Kingdom, 16 percent of women and 13 percent of men are obese, and in Germany, 12 percent of women and 11 percent of men. Recent research reveals a disturbing increase in child obesity in France. Up to 10 percent of children are obese. The recent increase in child obesity is linked to an unbalanced diet, to the habit of eating between meals, which is a fairly recent occurrence in France, and to lack of physical exercise. Only 30 percent are attributable to heredity.

Among men, farm workers and those in the professions weigh more, on average, than salaried employees of the same age and height. Senior managers weigh 6.6 pounds less than farm workers. Among women, senior managers or those in the intellectual professions are the tallest, and also the slimmest (in relation to their height). Perhaps women who are trying to obtain high positions in the professional hierarchy watch their figures more than others. Women middle managers or technicians seem to be less concerned with weight, since they weigh over 13.2 pounds more than the average, even though they're not as tall. Women workers present the highest height/weight ratio.

Hygiene and Appearance

Hygiene has not always been a high priority for the French. Traditionally, they have neglected hygiene in favor of enriching the mind and, if they were religious, the soul. The body was only looked after when it was sick.

The magazines *Elle* and *Marie-Claire* can take credit for the improvement in women's hygiene after World War II. Sales of soap, deodorants, and toothpaste rose rapidly. And the provision of bathrooms in new apartments made it easier to wash. Today, 94 percent of homes have a bath and/or a shower, compared to 29 percent in 1962, 48 percent in 1968, and 70 percent in 1975.

The rediscovery of the body gained momentum in the late 1960s with the rise of individualism and the possibility for women to control their fertility. More people took up sports to keep fit, and later took up aerobics and bodybuilding. Advertising and the mass media promoted new models of cleanliness and personal image.

Fifty-five percent of the French have brown or black eyes, 31 percent have blue eyes, and 14 percent have gray eyes. The number of blondes is declining, and redheads are disappearing.

Fifty-two percent say they wash their hair two or three times a week, compared to 30 percent in 1984 and 40 percent in 1987. They go to the hairdresser on average seven times a year. In the mid-1970s one French person in two never went to the hairdresser. The ratio is now one in three. Women go more frequently than men; half go at least once a month, 21 percent every two months, 19 percent every three months, 6 percent every six months, and 5 percent once a year.

The French (men and women) spend more on perfume than their European neighbors. The average French person spends about $26 a year, compared with $17.50 in Spain, $15 in the United Kingdom, $14 in Germany, and $10.80 in Italy. The average bra size for French women is 90 B, and the average hip measurement is 37 inches. The shoe size for women averages 38.

Thirty-seven percent of French women over 15 think they are too fat. The part of the body they'd like to improve is their stomach (25 percent), legs (14 percent), thighs (12 percent), buttocks (9 percent) and bosoms (7 percent). Twenty-five percent would like to improve their whole figure, not just one part of it.

French women think that the best way of improving their figure is by watching what they eat (83 percent), getting physical exercise (72 percent), looking after their blood flow (8 percent), and having cosmetic surgery (3 percent). However, asked about the attributes necessary to seduce the opposite sex, a good figure ranks only fourth (23 percent), behind a pleasant, friendly personality (60 percent), a good sense of humor (50 percent), and intelligence (33 percent).

Related Web links: elle.fr, marie-claire.com for beauty, health, fashion, society, cuisine (F)

Prehistoric and Early France

The first artifacts of Stone Age civilization, dating from the Paleolithic period, were found in France. The science of the study of prehistory, paleontology, was itself founded in France in the 19th century. The Jesuit priest Pierre Teilhard de Chardin (1881–1955) achieved international fame combining paleontology and philosophy.

In 1868 three skeletons found in a cave near Les Eyzies in Dordogne came to be known as Cro-Magnon man — the first representatives of Homo sapiens. In the same vicinity in southwest France in 1940, the Abbot André Glory discovered the Lascaux caves, an underground treasure of prehistoric art. The walls depicted the life of the hunter 17,000 years ago, with pictures of bulls, cows, deer, and bison. In 1994 the Combe-d'Arc Cave near Avignon, dating from 28,000 years before Christ, was found, its walls covered with 300 prehistoric paintings, including sketches of rhinoceroses and mammoths.

In the Bronze Age, the area of France now known as Brittany was home to the civilization of the megaliths, the ancestors of Cro-Magnon man. The formations of huge raised stones there are similar to Stonehenge in England. About 1,000 years before Christ, the Celts invaded France. Better known as the Gauls, they are regarded by the French as their true ancestors. Brave but undisciplined warriors, this intelligent and practical people, inspired by their Druid priests, cultivated the land and built roads and ports. The Gauls ruled until the Romans, led by Julius Caesar, overcoming the fierce Gaul resistance, became the new rulers of France in about 52 B.C.

For the next five centuries, France, and in particular the southern region of Provence, became a flowering example of Latin culture. The Romans established an urban civilization, with Lyon the capital, and new cities such as Arles, Nimes, and Narbonne connected by a magnificent network of roads. The Romans left a legacy of architectural monuments that have survived to this day, as well as the Pont du Gard aqueduct, which is an engineering masterpiece.

In the 5th century a Germanic tribe, the Francs, became the new masters of Gaul and gave France her name. They made Paris their capital, founded a monarchy, and assured the triumph of Christianity. Clovis was baptized king of the Francs in 496. Three hundred years later Emperor Charlemagne restored order to a divided and disorganized land. The dream of Charlemagne was to reconstitute the Holy Roman Empire. With all political and religious power in his hands, and surrounded by thinkers and writers in his court at Aix-la-Chappelle, Charlemagne created an enlightened culture.

Related Web links: grandroc.com for the cliffs of Laugerie-Basse and Grand Roc in Dordogne (E, F); culture.gouv.fr/culture/arcnat for archeological sites (E, F); mnhn.fr/teilhard for Pierre Teilhard de Chardin (E, F); netnimes.com (F); http://pages.prodigy.com/charlemagne for Charlemagne history and links (E)

France in the Middle Ages

The Norman invasion in 885 weakened the power of the king in France and led to the creation of a feudal system dominated by lords who ruled over their lands the same way the kings had ruled. These lords had their courts and their own coats of arms and flags, and they administered justice and waged wars, often. They loved hunting and tournaments. A long-lasting reminder in France of the Normans is the Bayeux tapestry, which is not so much a tapestry as a simple embroidery which, in one continuous stream, presents 72 scenes that tell the story of the Norman conquest of England in 1066. Designed by an Anglo-Saxon artist and embroidered by English needlewomen for Bishop Odo of Bayeux, it now hangs in the Museum of Bayeux in Normandy. The chevalier, or knight who could wage war on horseback, became the romantic figure of the age. Toward the end of the 11th century, the Church enlisted the knights into its service and the first Crusades to recapture Palestine from the Muslims began. There were eight Crusades over two centuries. King Louis VII led the second crusade, and Louis IX led the final two. In 1212 thousands of children in France left for the Holy Land but never reached that destination, and were sold into slavery at Marseille or died of disease and hunger.

At the same time as the Crusades, court life in France was the scene of a new code of chivalry and courtly love between noble men and women. It was popularized by the poems and songs of the troubadours, and a frequent theme was the unconsummated love between a young bachelor knight and his lord's lady. French medieval life, heavily influenced by the Church, was characterized in architecture and sculpture by the Gothic style. A superb collection of medieval artistic activity can be seen in Paris in the National Museum of the Middle Ages.

The Hundred Years War (1337–1453) was the intensification of a long-standing rivalry between England and France. The English were already occupying Gascony in southwest France when they won the Battle of Crécy (1346) in northern France and then took Calais (1347). At their weakest moment, the French kings were forced to retreat south of the Loire River. It took them nearly a century to retake Paris. In one of the most famous moments in French history, Joan of Arc (1412–31) inspired the continuation of the successful French counteroffensive against the English and the strengthening of the monarchy. In 1429, she raised the siege of Orléans and had King Charles VII crowned in Reims. Two years later, in Rouen, she was burned at the stake as a heretic.

Related Web links: chronicus.com, see *Moyen Age* then *Documents* for royal family tree (F); cablenet.net/pages/book for secrets of the Norman invasion, including the Bayeaux tapestry (E); jeanne-darc.com for the museum in Rennes on her travels and life (F); musee-moyenage.fr for collections, tapestries, Gothic sculpture, stained windows, daily life from the Cluny Museum (F); georgetown.edu/faculty/schneidz /web.html#Medieval for medieval French links (E)

A National Hero and Heroine

History is very important to the French, and certain men and women have become legendary for their actions in defending France in a time of war. The earliest hero dates from the time of the Roman conquest of Gaul. In his account of the war, Julius Caesar mentions Vercingétorix, chief of the Avernes tribe, more than 40 times. Not only did Vercingétorix have to contend with the superior power of the Roman army, he had to ensure the unity of the various wayward tribes of Gaul. At the siege of Alésia in 52 B.C., Vercingétorix resisted valiantly for two months before capitulating to Caesar. It was not until the 19th century that he became the first great hero of the French, incarnating the spirit of resistance in defending French territory against a foreign force. What makes Vercingétorix a true hero in French eyes was not only his valiant struggle, but his dignity and pride in defeat. It is said that after capitulating, he proudly threw down his weapons at Cesar's feet and negotiated a merciful settlement for his soldiers. Vercingétorix was taken as a prisoner to Rome, where he died in 40 B.C.

Joan of Arc also symbolizes French patriotism. Faithful to the voice of Arcangel Saint Michael, which inspired her mission to drive the English from France during the Hundred Year's War, she has become a national icon. Born the daughter of landed gentry in Domrémy in the Vosges region of France in 1412, she convinced King Charles VII that she had been sent by God to save France from the English. Joan cut her hair and put on the armor of a soldier. At the head of the king's army, she lifted the English siege of the city of Orléans on the Loire River in 1429. Injured and captured in 1430, she was handed over to the English by their French allies, the Burgundians, to be tried by a religious court. Her English jailers refused to give her female clothing, and obliged her to choose between appearing nude or wearing male clothes, so she chose the latter. In the eyes of the court, which had earlier ordered her to give up her weapons and her male dress, this was a relapse, and she was burned at the stake in Rouen in 1431. How Joan of Arc has been remembered in French history has varied from century to century, but the power of her sacrifice in the defense of France has made her—in politics, the arts, literature, and the cinema—the supreme model of a national heroine.

Related Web links: alesia.asso.fr for the Institut Vitruve on the siege of Alésia and Vercingétorix's war with the Romans (F); spe.sony.com/movies /joanofarc for *The Messenger* movie background and games (E)

From the Renaissance to the Revolution

The Renaissance in France began with King François I, who reigned from 1515 to 1547. From his military campaign in Italy, he brought back artists and thinkers influenced by the Italian Renaissance. This led to an era of refinement and humanism is France, and encouraged a new interest in art, architecture, and decoration by the nobility. It can be seen today most prominently in the castles, or chateaux, that were built throughout the Loire Valley and elsewhere. The established Catholic religion was soon challenged by the birth of Protestantism. The religious wars that began in 1562, and climaxed with the violent Saint Bartholomew Day massacre of Protestants in 1572, were halted when Henri IV, the first Bourbon king, proclaimed acceptance of Protestantism with the Edict of Nantes in 1598.

The Bourbon monarchy reached its peak in the 17th century when Louis XIV (1643–1715), the Sun King (*le roi soleil*), reigned. His palace and surrounding gardens were built by 50,000 workers over 50 years at Versailles, near Paris. This imposing monument to the power and extravagance of the monarchy was imitated by other European royal families. Under Louis XIV, France expanded her maritime activities with the founding of the Compagnie des Indes orientales (East Indies Company) in 1664. In 1673, Joliet and Marquette explored the territories of the Mississippi, and in 1682, Cavalier de la Salle chose the name of Louisiana in honor of Louis XIV. The 18th century, of Louis XV and Louis XVI, was marked by frivolity and glittering receptions and balls at the court of Versailles.

In contrast, Paris became the center of *le siècle des lumières* (Age of Enlightenment). In writing and in literary salons run by accomplished women such as Louis XV's official mistress, Madame de Pompadour, Voltaire, Diderot, and other philosophers challenged the intellectual authority of the Church and the political authority of the absolute monarchy.

Louis XV lost the French colonies of Canada and India to England. And in 1789, Louis XVI, faced with overwhelming national debt and the intransigence of the nobles to pay higher taxes, was forced to call a meeting of the Estates-General. Thus began the events of the French Revolution and the demise of the monarchy.

It was, however, under Louis XVI that France intervened in the American War of Independence, where the French nobleman, the Marquis de Lafayette, became a hero, fighting alongside George Washington to end British colonialism. The cities of Lafayette in Louisiana and Indiana are named after him.

Related Web links: fordham.edu/halsall/sbook-francais.html for Internet medieval sourcebook (F); **chronicus.com**, see *Temps Modernes* then *Documents* for Edict of Nantes (F); **louis-xiv.de** for art, court, castles, and the life of Louis XIV (E)

The French Revolution

The six tumultuous years of the French Revolution, 1789–94, swept away the institutions of the Ancien Régime: feudalism, the absolute monarchy, and its powerful ally, the Church. The Estates-General consisted of the First Estate (the Nobility), the Second Estate (the Church), and the Third Estate (all other social groups). The latter declared its autonomy on June 20, 1789, and formed a National Assembly. More repressive measures by Louis XVI led to the storming of the Bastille prison on July 14. On August 4, 1789, the Assembly voted for the abolition of privileges, thus ending the feudal system.

The French Revolution was more than a political revolution that adopted the red, white, and blue flag. It was preeminently a social revolution that took power from the aristocracy and gave it to the bourgeoisie and the people. As a reaction to the knee breaches worn by the nobility, for example, a popular revolutionary group, the *sans culottes*, wore full-length pants. It was also a legal revolution, introduced by the Declaration of the Rights of Man and the Citizen (August 26, 1789), which stated: "All men are born and remain free with equal rights." Further, the Revolution led to the separation of the legislative, executive, and judicial powers. Administratively, the provinces were replaced with *départements*.

In September 1792, the Assembly was replaced by the Convention, elected by male universal suffrage. The Convention immediately proclaimed the First French Republic, adopted a new calendar—with 1792 becoming Year I—the rallying cry "Liberty, Equality, Fraternity," the patriotic anthem *La Marseillaise*, and a new system of weights and measures—the metric system. The Convention confiscated Church property and created a new religion based on Reason and Virtue.

Power passed to the Committee of Public Safety and Robespierre, and the Reign of Terror and mass executions began. More than 60,000 people suspected of betraying the Revolution lost their lives. In April 1792 the guillotine became the favored instrument of execution. Originally used in the Middle Ages, the physician Joseph Ignace Guillotin (1738–1814) improved the design. The guillotine's most famous victims were King Louis XVI and Queen Marie Antoinette (1755–93), who were beheaded in Paris on the square now called the Place de la Concorde. The excesses of the Committee led to its overthrow in July 1794. For the next five years the Directory ruled, reestablishing public order and stability, until Napoléon seized power in the coup d'état known as 18 Brumaire (November 9, 1799).

Related Web links: chronicus.com, see *Revolution française* then *Documents* for Declaration of the Rights of Man and Constitution (F); fordham.edu/halsall/mod/modsbook13.html for the 1789 Revolution, documents, in translation (E)

Revolutionary Figures and Napoléon

Of the many involved in the French Revolution, some of the participants have a special resonance today. Jean-Paul Marat (1743–93), for one, is remembered as the *l'Ami du peuple* (Friend of the People), the title of his revolutionary newspaper, which was published in Paris until his murder in July 1793 by Charlotte Corday. Elected to the Convention, Marat denounced the intrigues of those who would sabotage the Revolution and came to symbolize the figure of the journalist who defends a just cause. Another important journalist, Camille Desmoulins (1760–94), is known for the Call to Parisians on July 11, 1789, which resulted in the storming of the Bastille. Elected to the Convention in 1792, Desmoulins became a fierce critic of the Terror, through his journal *Le Vieux Cordelier*. He was supported by the revolutionary leader Georges Danton (1759–94), with whom he was sent to the guillotine by Robespierre. Danton, although associated with the Terror, has come to symbolize the values of the French Revolution. Maximilien Robespierre (1758–94), a lawyer who was an implacable defender of democratic principles, is remembered for his political manipulation and ruthless elimination of opponents. He was guillotined in 1794, marking the end of the reign of Terror.

Born in Corsica, Napoléon Bonaparte (1769–1821) was given a scholarship to attend military school in France. As the brilliant commander of the French army in Italy, he achieved national prominence in 1797 and then led the Egyptian campaign. In 1799 Napoléon organized the coup d'état to replace the Directory with three Consuls, of which he was the most powerful. He imposed an authoritarian, centralized regime. He instituted a state secondary and tertiary education system (*lycées and grands écoles*), and a distinguished service award, the Legion of Honor; stimulated industrial and economic activity by establishing the Bank of France; and in 1804 he completed the Civil Code (*Code Napoléon*), which unified the law throughout France, enshrined the principle of the equality of all citizens before the law, guaranteed property, and gave the father overriding authority within a family. His reorganization of the administrative and legal systems remains in place.

The Consulate ended in 1804 when Napoléon was crowned Emperor of the French. During the next ten years his army dominated Europe, but England's navy controlled the seas, limiting Napoléon's power to the continent. The failure of his Russian campaign led to Napoléon's abdication in 1814. Escaping from his exile on the island of Elba, he regained power in 1815, but was defeated at Waterloo. He was exiled again, this time on Saint Helena in the South Atlantic, where he died. His ashes were brought back to France in 1840 and placed in his tomb, which remains a popular tourist destination at the Invalides in Paris.

Related Web links: napoleon.org for the life and times of Napoléon (E, F); **napoleonica.org** for Napoléonic documents (F)

Emperors, Kings, and Republics

The 19th century was a tumultuous time for the French. There were wars with Europe and successive changes in the type of government, which included two empires, the restoration of the monarchy, as well as two republics.

After Napoléon's defeat by the English, a constitutional monarchy was restored in France. Louis XV's grandson, Louis XVIII, ruled from 1814 to 1824, and he was followed by Charles X (1824–30). The Revolution of 1830 installed a new king, Louis-Philippe, who was backed by the bourgeoisie. But his regime could not balance social order and the new liberalism of the age. The Revolution of 1848 and the Second Republic (1848–52) abolished the institution of the monarchy forever, as well as slavery. Napoléon's nephew, Napoléon III, was elected president but organized a coup d'état to become Emperor in 1852. The Second Empire (1852–70) oversaw the Industrial Revolution and the building of the French railways as well as the urban redesign of Paris by Baron Haussmann. France became involved in a series of wars—in Crimea, in Mexico, and, most important, with Germany. In 1870, Napoleon III was defeated by an invading Prussian army. This established a unified Germany, its annexation of Alsace and Lorraine, and led to the Third French Republic. A working-class insurrection in Paris (la Commune de Paris) during the invasion tried to establish a more radical government, but President Thiers violently suppressed the uprising in 1871.

The Third Republic began with a long period of political instability, but was to last until 1940. During the Belle Epoque (Beautiful Age) at the turn of the century, life was transformed, by the automobile, the telephone, and the cinema, among other modern inventions and manifestations. The Dreyfus Affair consumed the French from 1894 to 1899, when Captain Alfred Dreyfus (1859–1935), a Jewish soldier, was pronounced guilty of selling secrets to the Prussians and then proven innocent. The fierce political and religious controversy around the case, including novelist Emile Zola's (1840–1902) famous broadside, J'Accuse, revealed the anti-Semitism in French society.

During the 19th and into the 20th century, France consolidated its colonial holdings, the foundations of which had been laid by the monarchy of 1830 and during the Second Empire. In North Africa there was Algeria (1836), Tunisia (1881), and Morocco (1912). In black Africa, France controlled the Sudan, the Congo, and Chad. In the Indian and Pacific Oceans there was Madagascar, Reunion, Tahiti, and New Caledonia. In Asia there was Vietnam, Laos, and Cambodia. By World War II, France was the second largest colonial power in the world.

Related Web links: chronicus.com, see *Le XIXe siècle* then *Documents* for Emile Zola's *J'accuse* (F); http://humanities.uchicago.edu/ARTFL /projects/CRL for pamphlets and periodicals of the 1848 revolution (F); napoleon.org, see *Napoléon III* (E, F); library.nwu.edu:80/spec/siege for Paris Commune photos (E)

World Wars

Germany declared war on France on August 3, 1914. World War I developed into a trench war (1915–17) between the combined French and Allied forces and the German army in the north of France. The French won the Battle of Verdun in 1916, but with severe losses of human life that could only be described as a carnage. An armistice was signed on November 11, 1918, after the Americans had joined the Allied forces. Nearly 1.5 million French soldiers died in all, one-fourth of all young French males, which had an effect on both France's economic recovery and its population growth for decades. Although France regained Alsace and Lorraine, the loss of human lives that touched so many cities, villages, and households in northern France has never been forgotten. The proliferation of monuments to the war dead and the solemnity with which the armistice is still celebrated today testifies to this.

Germany under Hitler was again at war with France in 1939. In 1940 the French army collapsed quickly before the German tank offensive and a huge exodus of the French left Paris for the south. On June 25, 1940, the 84-year-old head of state, Marshal Henri-Philippe Pétain (1856–1951), signed an armistice with Germany. This officially ended the Third Republic and began a period of collaboration between Pétain's government and the Nazis. The Nazi army occupied outright the entire North of France and the Atlantic coastline, while the South had nominal independence. Pétain declared a "National Revolution" establishing a government whose capital was in the spa town of Vichy in central France. It was an authoritarian regime with the motto *"Travail, famille, patrie"* (Work, Family, Homeland). Collaborating with the Nazis, the Vichy government organized the deportation of French Jews, compulsory work in German factories to aid the Nazi war effort, and the creation of the Milice to fight the French Resistance movement. A memorial to the French Jews during the Vichy regime, known as the Memorial to the Martyrs of the World War II Deportations, was inaugurated in Paris on April 12, 1962. In the year 2000, July 16 was declared a national day of remembrance of the deportation. That date was chosen because it was on July 16, 1942 that 12,350 Jews were herded in the Winter Velodrome in Paris and sent to the concentration camps in Germany.

Related Web links: richthofen.com/france_at_war for France in World War I photos from the *War Times Journal* (E); **paris.org/Expos/Liberation** for World War II photos from Paris papers (F); **http://gallica.bnf.fr/ArchivesParole**, see *Corpus Sonore* for recording of politicians during World War I; **invalides.org** for museum collections from both world wars (E, F)

Resistance Heroes

Among the many heroes of the French Resistance during World War II, two stand out: Charles de Gaulle (1890–1970) and Jean Moulin (1899–1943). After the crushing German victory over the French, de Gaulle became the first public figure to resist. Refusing to accept the armistice, he escaped to London in 1940 and, from the studios of the BBC, broadcast his famous pleas to the French not to support Vichy and to fight against the Germans. "France has lost a battle, not the war" became his rallying theme. Grouping "Free France" under his leadership, General de Gaulle organized military support from the French colonies of Equatorial Africa. In June 1943, based at Algiers, he became President of the *Comité français de libération nationale* (French Committee of National Liberation) and fought against Hitler in Africa. When Paris was liberated in 1944, de Gaulle led a march by the liberators from the Arc de Triomphe down the Champs-Elysées and to Notre Dame, accompanied by the patriotic shouting of the French crowds. It is a moment that has remained in the collective memory as a symbol of the spirit of resistance of the French people.

Jean Moulin, leader of the Resistance within France, united the various underground groups in Nazi-occupied and Vichy-governed France. Some groups consisted of young men fleeing compulsory work in Germany, who had taken refuge in the mountainous regions of France, where they formed the Maquis. Other groups were often led by the Communists, who played a large role in organizing the French Resistance. The Vichy government revoked Jean Moulin's public service commission as a prefect after he refused to sign government ordinances. At the end of 1941 he escaped to London, but parachuted secretly back to Provence in January 1942, delegated by de Gaulle as his representative in the southern zone. His mission: to coordinate and unify all the forces of the Resistance. In May 1943, Moulin succeeded in bringing all the disparate movements of the North and South together in the Conseil national de résistance (National Resistance Council). Less than one month later he was betrayed to the Germans. Severely tortured by Klaus Barbie, head of the Gestapo in Lyon, Moulin died a prisoner of the Nazis on July 8, 1943. At the Liberation, de Gaulle paid tribute to his Resistance leadership. After the war, the name Jean Moulin slid into relative obscurity until 1964, when de Gaulle, now President of the Fifth Republic, decreed the transfer of his ashes to the national shrine of French heroes, the Panthéon in Paris.

Related Web links: **charles-de-gaulle.org** for biography, documents, photos (F); **csonline.net /moulinte/moul-g.htm** for the capture of Jean Moulin (E)

Liberation and a New Republic

After the psychological and emotional shock of defeat by the Germans, most of the French support went to Marshal Pétain, who signed the armistice. However, as the Nazi occupation became increasingly oppressive, French resistance grew stronger, both within and outside France. On June 18, 1940, Charles de Gaulle broadcast his famous patriotic call from London, urging the French people not to collaborate with the Nazis and to fight for a free France: "No matter what happens, the flame of French resistance must never be extinguished, and will never go out." After the Japanese bombing of the American fleet in Pearl Harbor in December 1941, the United States entered the war. On June 6, 1944, the American and Allied forces landed on the beaches of Normandy, and in liaison with the Resistance network worked toward the defeat of Hitler's army. Paris was liberated on August 25, and the war ended in Europe on May 8, 1945. Marshal Pétain was imprisoned for treason, while other Vichy collaborators were summarily executed or imprisoned after court trials.

The Liberation of France in 1945 signaled a new era of democracy for France, but it had a difficult beginning. Acclaimed as the savior of France, de Gaulle proposed a constitution for the Fourth Republic that gave more power to the president than to the elected representatives. When this proposal was defeated, de Gaulle withdrew from political life. The constitution finally approved in 1946 gave supreme power to the Parliament, but the large number of political parties created instability. As a result, there were 23 governments during the 12 years of the Fourth Republic.

In 1946, France became embroiled in a war for independence in its colony in Indochina which was to last until the French were defeated at Dien Bien Phu in 1954. In the same year, the Algerian revolt against French rule began. While France had granted independence to its colonies of Morocco and Tunisia without a fight, Algeria was unique because it had been integrated into the administrative structure of mainland France and a significant part of its population was French. In 1958, President René Coty (1882–1962), fearing a civil war between supporters of a French and an independent Algeria, called General de Gaulle back from retirement to form a new government. De Gaulle was sworn in on June 1, and in September a referendum approved a new constitution giving supreme power to the president. It was the birth of the Fifth Republic. In 1962, Algeria finally gained its independence from France.

Related Web links: stella-galaxy-usa.com /jeanbaud for a memoir on the beginning of war in Indochina (F); http://latis.ex.ac.uk/french /cooke for notes on the Fourth Republic, Algeria, Indochina, De Gaulle (E); dienbienphu.org for the battle site (E, F); fnaca.org is an Algerian War veterans' site (F)

Republic

France is a republic. *"On est en république!"* is a popular French expression. The First Republic, founded in 1792, was the result of the French Revolution of 1789, in which the middle class, the peasants, and the working class rose against the absolute powers of the monarchy and the excessive privileges of France's aristocracy. These events signified the end of the Ancien Régime and the beginning of modern democratic France. In the two centuries since, France has lived through five republics, a constitutional monarchy, and two empires. Three of the five republics were heralded by the revolutionary cry *"Aux barricades!"* (To the barricades!), reflecting that significant political and social changes in France came about more from explosive ideological conflict than from smooth gradual change.

The Declaration of the Rights of Man and of the Citizen in 1789 expressed the guiding principles of the new republic. It embodied the ideals of the 18th-century Enlightenment: equality of all people; the obligation of government to guarantee equality, liberty, safety, and property; the separation of legislative, executive, and judicial powers.

The First Republic (1792–1804) lasted until Napoléon Bonaparte proclaimed the First Empire in 1804. Imperial though they were, victorious Napoléonic armies carried the ideals of the Revolution to the lands it conquered and thus sowed the seeds for democratic government in much of 20th-century Europe.

After Napoléon's defeat in 1815 a constitutional monarchy reigned until the Second Republic (1848–52) abolished it. Napoléon III, in turn, ended the Second Republic and established the Second Empire (1852–70).

Napoléon III was defeated by an invading Prussian army after a brief war that unified Germany for the first time in its history and led to the Third French Republic. A working-class insurrection in Paris (*la commune de Paris*) during the invasion was aimed at bringing about a more radical government, but the new, conservative Third Republic (1870–1940) repressed the movement violently, survived World War I, and saw its political institutions endure until Hitler's military invasion in 1940. The Fourth Republic was established after World War II, in 1946. It knew chronic instability and 23 governments before ending in 1958, when Charles de Gaulle established the Fifth Republic with a new constitution, giving France a stability that it still has today.

All five French Republics have paid homage to the democratic principles of the 1789 Revolution, and the Republican slogan — *"Liberté, Egalité, Fraternité"* — has become a constant in the rhetoric of all modern French political parties. The traditional conclusion of an official presidential address to the French people is *"Vive la République! Vive la France!"* (Long live the Republic! Long live France!). The French may nurse a popular fascination with the lives of the British royal family, but republican sentiment runs very deep in French society, and it determines both the national and international attitudes of the French.

IDENTITY
"French-ness"

What does it mean to be French? Despite a high international profile, the French are no longer sure. Several decades of heterogeneous immigration have raised questions in France about cultural identity.

The French nation, comprised of French-speaking citizens, is a relatively modern creation. During the last decades of the Third Republic (1910–40), a uniform national culture based on republican values was imposed, and the chief transmitters of this culture were the school, the army, the trade unions, and the Communist party. Immigrants and people of different regional cultures were forced to conform to the dominant national culture. Today, the assimilation of immigrants is more complicated. North Africans, for instance, are culturally and ethnically more distinct from the French population than were previous waves of European immigrants to France. These immigrants are generally Arabic speaking, Muslim, poor, and tend to form communities in the suburbs of large towns. Furthermore, the institutions that traditionally ensured the diffusion of French culture have declined: schools are in crisis, the Catholic Church competes with Islam, military service is no longer compulsory, and the extreme right National Front has challenged the Communist party for popularity.

Recent immigration has reawakened old fears of Muslim fundamentalism and bitter memories of the Algerian War, and the recessions of the 1980s and 1990s have exacerbated tensions between the French and immigrants. With the end of the economic boom of the *trente glorieuses*, and the reduced need for labor, many unemployed French workers feel that immigrants no longer have a place in France. In addition, anxieties about national identity lead many to seek refuge in nostalgia, for which reason some are attracted by the National Front's strident nationalism and attacks on immigrants. The National Front defines nationality by ethnic background, not by citizenship. This view of national identity motivated the French government in 1993 to adopt legislation that says citizenship is no longer given automatically at birth to the French-born children of immigrants, but granted upon application when they became adults at the age of 18.

Despite fears of immigrant ghettos, France's immigrants (7.8 percent of the population), including those from North Africa, are being integrated into society. The children of immigrants speak French and go to state secular schools, and in 1988 almost 80 percent of second-generation North Africans chose non-Arabic spouses.

The victory of the French soccer team at the 1998 World Cup has become a symbol of French integration, since the players were of different ethnicities and their victory depended on teamwork. The French were united in their praise for the heroes, among them Zinédine Zidane, the son of North African immigrants living in the suburbs of Marseille.

Related Web links: front-national.com for the National Front (F); **raslfront.org** is one of many anti-Front sites (F); **zidane.fr** for the official site of Zinédine Zidane (E, F)

Symbols and Decorations

The most popular international symbol of France would probably be the Eiffel Tower, built in 1889. For the French, however, the most important national symbol is the red, white, and blue flag—the *tricolore*—which dates from the Revolution. It was adopted on July 14, 1790, the first anniversary of the storming of the Bastille, and can today be seen flying above the entrance of all public buildings. Since the creation of the European Union by the Treaty of Maastricht in 1992, the blue flag of the Union with its circle of 12 yellow stars is displayed beside the French flag at all official national ceremonies.

Like the flag, the French national motto, "*Liberté, Egalité, Fraternité,*" and the national anthem, the "Marseillaise," date from the Revolution and symbolize the values of the French Republic. Foreigners are often surprised by the warlike words of the "Marseillaise." This is because it was written in 1792 by a military captain, Claude-Joseph Rouget de Lisle (1760–1836), as a war song to motivate his troops. An allegorical woman named Marianne, chosen in 1792 during the First Republic to represent France, is another national symbol. Her head is on French stamps and coins, and a sculpted head of Marianne and a photo of the French president are on display in the office of every French mayor.

The rooster (*le coq*) is not an official symbol of the French Republic but has become a popular emblem. Emperor Napoléon I replaced the Republican rooster with the eagle, but since World War I the eagle has represented Germany and

the rooster has been the emblem of French patriotism. The cartoon character Asterix, invented by Goscinny and Uderzo in their comic books, beginning with *Astérix le gaulois* (1959), has become emblematic of the French spirit of individualism and shrewd inventiveness, especially when foreign adversaries threaten France's independence. Asterix is the 20th-century counterpart of France's most popular heroine, Joan of Arc, who "kicked the English out of France."

The date of the storming of the Bastille, July 14, is France's national day. This is an affirmation of the Republican and democratic values that have inspired the French tradition of opposition to oppression in all its forms since the "declaration of the Rights of Man and of the Citizen" in 1789.

A small red ribbon or rosette worn on the left lapel of a man's or woman's coat denotes the highest state award, the Légion d'honneur, created by Napoléon Bonaparte in 1802. Each state honor has several grades: a ribbon for *chevalier*, the lowest grade; a rosette for *officier*, the next grade; a rosette on a silver bow, or *nœud* for *commandeur*, *mérite* (blue); Ordre des Palmes académiques (for service to education, mauve); Ordre des Arts et des Lettres (for contributions to arts and literature, green). These honors are awarded in the name of the President of the Republic.

Related Web links: abcparislive.com for Eiffel Tower webcam (E); **elysee.fr**, see *Institutions* for symbols: coq, Marianne, flag, Marseillaise, Liberté, seal (E, F); **asterix.tm.fr** (F)

IDENTITY
Cocorico and Grandeur

The rooster (*le coq gaulois*), the emblem of France, symbolizes vigilance. It arose in the mid-17th century when an official French medal depicted a rooster chasing the Spanish lion. France's enemies, in reaction, began to caricature France as a rooster. The French then adopted the rooster as its official emblem, using it on the flagstaff of its army regiments during the July monarchy (1830–48) and the Second Republic (1848–52). The seal of the French Republic since 1848 shows the allegorical Liberty seated at a rudder decorated with a rooster. French sports teams use the rooster as their emblem in international competitions.

The crow of the rooster in French is *cocorico*, not cock-a-doodle-doo as in English. French parodists and cartoonists use *le coq gaulois* and its *cocorico* to lampoon French nationalism and chauvinism. If one French person is seen as boasting too much about personal successes, another person in the group is liable to deride the behavior with a "*Cocorico!*"

The rooster on the bell towers of French churches has another history. It represents only the rooster that crows at daybreak. The militant secular government of the 1789 Revolution confiscated Church property and replaced the crosses on church bell towers with roosters.

Also central to French mythology is *grandeur*. This was the heart of the concept of France that General de Gaulle developed to restore the self-confidence and pride of a country that had surrendered to the German army and had to accept Nazi occupation from 1940 to 1944. The Vichy regime (officially l'état français, 1940–44) under Marshal Pétain collaborated with Hitler and carried out Hitler's policies in France, while General de Gaulle commanded the Free French Forces and the French Resistance from exile. Although de Gaulle's army played a relatively small role in the Allied Liberation of Europe, and Pétain's collaboration weakened France's moral position in the armistice, de Gaulle insisted that France occupy an equal footing with the Soviet Union, the United Kingdom, and the United States at the Yalta Conference at the end of the World War II.

During de Gaulle's presidency of the Fifth Republic from 1958 to 1969, his determination to make France an independent power on the world stage guided his foreign policy. While repeatedly affirming France's *grandeur* and democratic principles, he became the self-proclaimed voice of the developing countries that were struggling to gain independence, and he frequently criticized the hegemony and foreign policy of the two super powers: the United States and the Soviet Union.

De Gaulle's foreign policy added arrogance to the foreign image of the French themselves, and that image has resurfaced every time a French president, however pro-American the regime in question, has taken an independent view in world affairs.

The French Year

The calendar year begins on January 1, as does the fiscal year, but the lives of the French are programmed to begin a new year at the end of August, when workers have relaxed during their four-week summer vacations and the new school year starts (*la rentrée des classes*).

The rhythm of the year is linked with annual events in each season. In autumn, which, like the new working year, begins in September, the vineyards produce the year's new wine. The new autumn and winter fashions have been launched by leading fashion designers in August. The calendar of the school year has been influenced by another ancient agricultural tradition: farmers plow their fields in autumn and harvest the crops in summer.

Each year, major literary prizes are awarded in autumn, and the winning books become popular Christmas presents. The Festival of American Cinema is held in Deauville on the Normandy coast. The first rounds of the French soccer club championships are played, the International Motor Show draws huge crowds to Paris in October, and costumes are planned for Halloween parties.

The winter ski fields attract large crowds during the Christmas holiday, and many French workers will spend the fifth week of their annual vacation entitlement skiing in January or February. In January, the Six Nation Rugby Tournament is held and the shops put on their winter sales. The university break in February separates the first and second semesters.

In spring, nature reawakens, the countryside becomes a popular weekend destination, and plans are made for summer vacations. Students in their final year of high school begin studying for the all-important *baccalauréat* examinations in June. The Paris marathon is run in April, and the quarter- and semifinals of the European Soccer Cup match national teams.

The international Cannes Film Festival in May begins a series of cultural festivals that last until the end of summer, particularly in the South of France. Theater in Avignon, music in Aix-en-Provence, dance in Montpellier, and song in La Rochelle (les Francofolies) are some festival highlights. The Fête de la Musique throughout France on the night of June 21 marks the beginning of summer.

The final of the French Soccer Cup is in May. The French International Tennis Championships on the Rolland-Garros courts in Paris in June are followed by the Tour de France, the bicycle race that winds around the country for a month until the final sprint down the Champs-Elysées in late July. Bastille Day on July 14 and the end of the Tour de France signify the beginning of the summer vacation period.

The International Air Show takes place at Le Bourget Airport in June, French shops hold their summer sales in July, and summertime, which began in April, lasts until September, when clocks are turned back an hour and the yearly cycle begins again.

Related Web link: See page 193.

Legendary Places and Events

Certain monuments, institutions, and events have a special resonance in the French national psyche. For example, there are the national commemorations on the Ile de la Cité in the middle of the Seine, before the magnificent Gothic cathedral of Notre Dame, (1163–1245). This is where the Liberation of Paris from Nazi Occupation was celebrated in 1944 after General de Gaulle led a parade of Resistance fighters from the Arc de Triomphe down the Champs-Elysées. When French presidents die, a national commemorative mass is held in Notre Dame.

In 1806, to celebrate his greatest military victory, the Battle of Austerlitz in 1805, Napoléon laid the first stones of his triumphal arch, the Arc de Triomphe. Political upheavals interrupted, and the Arc, built in the Roman style, was not completed until 1836. Standing 164 feet high, the Arc has become a memorial to more than Napoléon's victory at Austerlitz. It contains the Tomb of the Unknown Soldier, dedicated to all the French soldiers who lost their lives in World War I. Other friezes show French soldiers defending their nation. There is also an eternal flame that burns under the Arc, the site of an annual wreath-laying ceremony during which the French President, on May 8 and November 11, officially marks the anniversaries of the end of the two world wars, in 1918 and in 1945. The Arc is now the customary starting point for victory celebrations and parades.

The Champs-Elysées from the Arc de Triomphe to the Place de la Concorde is the route taken by the military parade every July 14; by political parades such as the one organized by supporters of General de Gaulle, who restored order after the month-long student and worker strikes and demonstrations in May 1968; by celebrations such as the Bicentennial of the French Revolution in 1989 and the beginning of the new century with the year 2000; and by the enthusiastic celebration of France's victory over Brazil in the final of the World Soccer Cup on July 12, 1998.

On the left bank of the Seine, in the Latin Quarter, the Panthéon (1764–90) is devoted to the patron saint of Paris, Sainte Geneviève. The Revolution changed its function to a repository for the ashes of French heroes.

On May 21, 1981, his first official day as the new President of France and the first Socialist President since the Fifth Republic began, François Mitterrand (1916–96) chose the Panthéon for a ceremony to mark the start of an era of change. Watched by a joyous crowd and carrying a red rose, the symbol of the Socialist party, he walked into the Panthéon and bowed in front of the tombs of the Socialist pacifist hero Jean Jaurès (1859–1914), the Resistance hero Jean Moulin (1899–1943), and Victor Scholcher (1804–93), defender of the Rights of Man. In 1995, Mitterrand decreed that the ashes of Marie Curie be placed in the Panthéonm making her the first woman interred there.

> Related Web links: **paris.org**, see *Monuments* for Notre Dame, Arc de Triomphe, Panthéon (E, F); **elore.com/Gothic/contents.htm** Notre Dame (E)

Francophonie

The French are passionate about their language. And so too are millions of others, spread across five continents, who make French the second language of international communication. There are currently 120 million speakers of French as their first, second, or adopted language, and another 61 million occasional French speakers. French is spoken as an official or major language in more than 40 countries outside France.

Historically, French was the language of the elite in Europe. Continental sovereigns used the language to communicate among themselves, and in the 18th century it became the language of diplomacy. Treaties were written in French until the World War I, when Georges Clémenceau agreed that the Treaty of Versailles should be written in French *and* English. French remains an official language of a number of international organizations, such as the United Nations, UNESCO, and the International Olympic Committee, and the working language of bodies such as the European Commission.

In 1967, leaders of newly independent Francophone Africa formed the Association internationale des parlementaires de langue française (International Association of French-speaking Parliamentarians), which brought delegates from 22 countries to Brussels to defend and promote French language and culture in French-speaking countries. The French quickly mobilized to coordinate this venture, creating the Comité de la francophonie (Committee of Francophonie) in 1973, and the Haut conseil de la francophonie (High Council of Francophonie) in 1984. Francophone countries have attended "Summits of Francophonie" since 1986 to affirm their linguistic and cultural ties. After the summit in Hanoi (1997), Boutros Boutros Ghali, the former Egyptian Secretary General of the United Nations, became Secretary General of the Organisation internationale de la francophonie. The number of states and governments participating in the summits has doubled over 30 years; there were 55 in 1999 at the summit in Moncton, Canada.

The French are keenly sensitive to the perceived menace that English represents to the integrity of their language. There has been renewed concern over the evolution of franglais, the hybrid of French and English that has been a result of the dominance of English in new technologies, especially the Internet. The spread of English must not overshadow the dynamic work of writers, filmmakers, singers, and artists from the myriad Francophone countries who enrich the language and contribute to its widespread transmission each year.

Related Web links: diplomatie.gouv.fr /francophonie/hcf for Haut conseil de la francophonie (F); francophonie.org for Organisation internationale de la francophonie (F); aupelf-uref.org for Agence universitaire de la francophonie (F)

Accents and Regional Languages

French is spoken with a different accent in different parts of France. The rapid, taut Parisian accent is very different from the twangy, nasal accent in the Midi (the South of France), which—if we are to believe the southerners—reflects their jovial personality and their sunny climate. Thus, for example, *demain matin* (rhymes with *vin*, for wine) sounds more like "demeng mateng."

Outside France, many people speak French as their first language, for example in Belgium, Luxembourg, Switzerland, Quebec, Haiti, Guadeloupe, Martinique, and French Polynesia. In many countries, French is the official language, or one of the official languages, as in Senegal, the Ivory Coast, Cameroon, Mauritania, Mali, Rwanda, Congo, Zaire, Togo, and Benin. In North Africa, French is spoken in Morocco, Tunisia, and Algeria. In the United States, there are French speakers in Louisiana and Maine. Accents and vocabulary in states or countries like Quebec, Haiti, and Senegal vary greatly from one another and from what one hears in France. This diversity is a source of vitality for the continuing universal use of the French language. There are also more than a thousand French language newspapers and magazines published throughout the world, and a dynamic range of French literary works by writers in Quebec, the Caribbean, and black and North Africa. Since 1984 there has been an annual Francophonie Theatre Festival in Limoges in France.

The principal regional languages of France are Occitan, Corsican, Breton, Basque, Catalan, and Alsatian. The Occitan movement began in the 1960s as part of the cultural reunification of the areas in southern France where the "oc" language was spoken in medieval times. Occitan is closely related to Provençal. In 1999, France signed the European Charter for regional and minority languages, but it has not yet been ratified. Opponents see the charter as "a danger to the uniqueness of France and the indivisibility of the Republic." Ratification would allow the use of regional or minority languages in the administration and justice sectors, to the detriment of French. For these people, French alone is the official language of the country and remains a symbol of France, just like the national anthem, the flag, and freedom.

However, the teaching of regional languages and cultures has been recognized by law in France since 1951, and in 1997, 100,000 school students were learning them. In 2001 the French government developed a new plan for regional languages, including bilingual teaching, as part of the richness of the national heritage.

Related Web links: multimania.com/marraire /Main.htm for the origins of Occitan (F); geocities.com/CapitolHill/2057 for Occitan links (E, F); bzh.com, perso.wanadoo.fr/brezhoneg, for Breton sites (F); heimetsproch.org for Alsatian (E, F); http://corsica.net.free.fr for Corsican music, pictures, dictionary (E, F)

Protecting French

The English spoke French before the first English word entered the French language. When William the Conqueror left Normandy and conquered England in 1066, the French language (in fact, Anglo-Norman) was adopted on the other side of the Channel. It was not until 1125 that *acre* became the first English word in French. Since then the French have borrowed many English words, but their pronunciation, and often their meaning, have changed, and English speakers don't always recognize them in French conversation. The number of borrowed English words has increased greatly in recent decades as a result of the rapid expansion of American technology, computerization, pop culture, and business management practices.

The language of France has always been *une affaire d'état* (a state affair). Alarmed by the lack of precision in usage and the loss of the "purity" of the French language—a result of borrowed Anglo-American words and syntax—the government in 1966 established the Haut comité de la langue française, a commission under the prime minister's control. Its original mission was to defend French against the linguistic invasion of English by creating French equivalents for the English words, and to discourage the use of franglais, a mixture of French and English that advertising made trendy in the 1960s. This trend provoked a public outcry that French was being destroyed.

In 1992 the government inserted a new article in the constitution: "The language of the Republic is French." In 1994 the French Parliament passed the Toubon law to expand similar 1977 legislation, making it obligatory to give a translation of foreign words or phrases used in advertisements. The new law makes it mandatory to use the French language in all official circulars, public notices, and advertisements in France.

The alarmists foresee the demise of French and claim that the laxness currently exhibited in the use of the language is due, above all, to the ease with which words and expressions are borrowed from English. Expressions such as *"Top cool!"* or *"Trop bon!"* (imitating "Too much!") aren't newly invented words, they say, but instead betray a dramatic lack of rigor, even of respect, for French. According to the alarmists, people aren't interested in French anymore, in its grammatical subtleties, its finer points, its beauty, its poetry. They see in advertisements and in the directions for use of appliances, for example, an impoverished new language with deplorable syntax.

The moderates assert that French has always been able to accept outside influences and linguistic contributions as part of its evolution. For them, the survival of a language is ensured more by literature than by daily speech and international commercial exchanges. A language is best defended, they say, by making it widely known and admired, and by teaching it correctly.

Related Web links: culture.fr/culture/dglf for acceptable French technical terms (F)

LANGUAGE
Académie Française

In 1635, Cardinal Richelieu, the prime minister of King Louis XIII, established the Académie française to stabilize and perfect the French language. This body is now responsible for protecting the language, and it symbolizes the importance the state gives to the national language in promoting French culture throughout the world. The Académie meets in an imposing 17th-century domed building on the left bank of the Seine.

The 40 elected-for-life members of the Académie (*académiciens*) are popularly known as the *Immortels*, in a possibly ironic reference to the seal presented to them in 1635 by Cardinal Richelieu, which bore the motto: "To Immortality." The head of the Académie is known as the *secrétaire perpétuel* (permanent secretary). The first woman to become *secrétaire perpétuel* was Hélène Carrère d'Encausse, who was elected, unopposed, to the position in 1999. A historian and a Russian specialist, she had been a member of the Acacémie since 1990. The first woman to be elected to the Académie was the writer Marguerite Yourcenar in 1980.

The Académie française carries out its mission of defending the French language by publishing an official dictionary of French language usage (*Dictionnaire de l'Académie française*). The last edition, the eighth, was published in 1935. In 1985, when Maurice Druon became *secrétaire perpétuel*, the preparations of a new edition had only reached the letter F, so he decided to start again. But progress was slow, and negative; only the first volume of the ninth edition has come out, taking the work up to the letter E. The first dictionary of the French language was published with Latin translations by Jean Nicot in 1606. The first purely French dictionary was published by Richelet in 1680. The Académie's dictionary adopts a very conservative approach to correct usage of French. The weekly language columns in many French newspapers adopt a similar approach.

Feminists in France, as in other countries, had long demanded that titles should cease to be automatically masculine, as in "chairwoman" rather than "chairman." In 1984 the then-Socialist government recommended that titles should be feminized. But the Académie objected, and the recommendation was not followed. In the new Socialist government of 1997, several women ministers wanted to be addressed as Madame la Ministre, not Madame le Ministre, but Maurice Druon publicly protested against this scandalous innovation, and Hélène Carrère d'Encausse stated, when elected, that she wanted to be known as *Madame le secrétaire perpétuel*. This symbolizes the long-standing role of the Académie: to represent tradition and oppose innovation. However, since 1999 the battle of the titles has been won by the government, and now women ministers, at least, are called Madame la Ministre.

Related Web links: academie-francaise.fr for its history and role (F); **chass.utoronto.ca/~wulfric /academie** for the 1694 and 1835 editions of *Dictionnaire* (E); **http://gallica.bnf.fr**, see *Recherche* for dictionnaires and encyclopédies

Spelling and Dictation

Generally, the French are proud of their national language and acquire prestige from their knowledge of its syntax and spelling rules. Recent official attempts to modernize spelling (*orthographe*) have been opposed by a majority of the population.

The members of the Académie française have also been opposed to the reform of French spelling. In 1673 the *académiciens* stated that they preferred the old spelling, "which distinguishes people of letters from the ignorant and simple women." And when they brought out their first dictionary, in 1694, they said they were attached to the old spelling "because it helps understand the origin of words."

In 1805, Napoléon imposed a spelling test in all public exams, and in 1832 a spelling test was required for all public sector jobs. One result is that the rules and the exceptions of French spelling—which is made even more difficult by gender, grammatical agreements, and the three accents (acute, grave, and circumflex)—have remained horrendously complex.

In France, the spelling test, known as a dictation (*dictée*), is usually an artificial amalgam of difficult words, spelling traps, and grammatical tricks. A perfect score is 20, and since a spelling error costs a point and an accent error half a point, it is easy to score zero.

Some of these *dictées* have become famous. Probably the most famous of all the was by the 19th-century French writer Prosper Mérimée, who also became inspector of historic monuments. Mérimée wrote it in 1857, at the request of the Empress Eugénie, wife of Emperor Napoléon III, to entertain the court. Those who took part in this party piece included the novelist Alexandre Dumas (author of *The Three Musketeers*), the writer Octave Feuillet, and 84-year-old Prince Metternich, Austrian ambassador to the French court at the time. These were the mistakes scored: Napoléon III—75; Eugénie—62; Dumas—24; Feuillet—19; Metternich—3. In those days, of course, French had been the language of diplomacy since the 18th century!

In 1985, Bernard Pivot, moderator of a popular television program on books and reading, launched a World French Spelling Competition, in which viewers did the *dictée* while it was read on television. In 1986 over a million viewers entered the competition. In the first six years, only seven competitors made no spelling mistakes. In 1993 the competition changed its name to Dicos d'or (Golden Dictionaries), and today continues to attract large numbers of competitors. In 1998, when the new Stade de France near Paris opened prior to the World Soccer Cup, the national finals of the Dicos d'or were held there!

Related Web links: dicosdor.com to test yourself with audio-video dictation and games from Bernard Pivot; see *Dico franglais* for French alternatives to franglais (F)

Language and Slang

Modern French is based on the language spoken by the Gauls and the Latin spoken by the Roman invaders who conquered the Gauls in 52 B.C. and occupied their land until A.D. 406. Other contributions came from the Germanic language of the Franks, who ruled France during the 5th and 6th centuries, and from the Arabs, who invaded France and were defeated at Poitiers in 732.

The language called "Old French" was used until the 13th century. It was different depending on whether it was spoken in the North (*langue d'oïl*) or South (*langue d'oc*) of France, the *oïl* and the *oc* being the two different ways of saying "yes." The first text considered to have been written in "French" was the *Serments de Strasbourg* (*Strasbourg Oaths*) in 842.

In 1539, King François I declared the French spoken in Paris the official language of government and the justice system. Ever since the French Revolution, which made the teaching of French mandatory throughout the country, the language has continued to grow and transform. Nowadays it is heavily influenced by the media and the speech of young people, and by new words and expressions from other languages.

Colloquial expressions and slang (*argot*) are a lively part of everyday speech. It could be said that each trade, social class, or group has its own slang. Some of this slang has had colorful names in the past, like *le jargon* for criminal slang in the 15th century, for instance, or *le narquois* for beggar slang in the 17th century. Today, there is school slang, like *pion* for *surveil-lant* (supervisor) and *bahut* for *lycée* (high school), as well as military slang, sports slang, and the slang of the underworld (*le milieu*). And there's also slang formed by inverting the syllables of words, which is called *verlan*.

Slang is rich in new words and expressions, whose origins are often obscure, like those of *le pinard* (wine), and it readily transforms or deforms words, for example, Paname for Paris, Parigot for Parisian, and frometon for *fromage* (cheese). It uses metaphors that are often ironical, like *la rousse* (redhead) for the police, *le dur* (hard) for the train, and *les cognes* (from *cogner*, to strike) for "the cops."

Other examples of slang words are *frangin* (brother) and *frangine* (sister) from *frère*; *fringale* (raging hunger) from *faim*; *pieu* (bed) from *peau*; *plumard* (bed) from *plume*; and *tricoter des jambes* ("knit with the legs" for "run away").

Many slang terms have passed into everyday language, renewing it.

Related Web links: restena.Ln/cul/BABEL/T .SERMENTS.html for *Serments de Strasbourg* (F); metafort.org/rduproject/96-97/cefrans/index .html for verlan, argot (F)

Exclamations in French include words like *zut, merde,* and *bof. Zut,* which often becomes *"zut alors,"* expresses frustration and exasperation. It is a polite expression used by all social groups, whereas the somewhat equivalent *merde* (shit) is considered impolite. The exclamation *bof* expresses indifference to an idea or project. If a French person replies *"Bof!"* with a shrug of the shoulders to a proposal, you know not to expect any enthusiasm. In contrast, *"Super!" "Génial!" "Sympa!"* and, more recently, *"Top génial!"* are enthusiastic responses.

The vocabulary of teenagers has widened over the last ten years. Many expressions use *verlan,* the French slang formed by inverting the syllables of words. Some *verlan*-inspired words are:

- *beubon* (for *bombe*): a bombshell, an extremely attractive woman
- *feba* (for *baffe*): a slap (in the face)
- *meuf* (for *femme*): woman
- *ripou* (for *pourri*): rotten
- *zarbi* (for *bizarre*): strange, weird

Other words or expressions are invented, or give a new meaning to an existing word:

- *biomanes, dabs, leufs* (for *parents*): means parents
- *carbure, rebuc, keus* (for *argent*): means money
- *caviar* (*c'est*) (for *C'est génial*): means "That's fantastic!"
- *nain* (for dwarf): means child

A new edition of the *Petit Larousse* reflects the economic, social, political, technical, and cultural changes in France.

ECONOMIC
- *après-vente* (aftersale)
- *assurance-crédit* (credit insurance)
- *défiscaliser* (to exempt from taxation)
- *narcodollar*
- *sponsoriser*

SOCIAL
- *aérobic*
- *amincissant* (slimming)
- *antitabac* (antismoking)
- *dealer*
- *défonce* (high on drugs)
- IVG (termination of pregnancy)
- *jogging*
- *multiracial*
- *must* (essential item)
- *overdose*
- *pin's* (lapel badge)
- *rap*
- *sitcom*
- *skinhead*
- *top-model*
- *top niveau* (the best)

TECHNICAL
- ADN (DNA)
- *biodiversité*
- *bioéthique*
- *cliquer*
- *clonage*
- *micro-ordinateur* (microcomputer)
- *multimédia*
- *télémarché* (teleshopping)
- *télépaiement*
- *vidéo clip* (pop video)
- *zapping* (channel flicking)

Proverbs and "False Friends"

It's always interesting to compare the literal meaning of proverbs in one language with their equivalents in another. Here are some French proverbs, with their literal translation and their English equivalents:

A quelque chose malheur est bon (Misfortune is good for something): Every cloud has a silver lining.

C'est en forgeant qu'on devient forgeron (It's by using the forge that you become a blacksmith): Practice makes perfect.

Il ne faut pas vendre la peau de l'ours (avant de l'avoir tué) (You mustn't sell the bear's skin before killing it): Don't count your chickens (before they're hatched).

La raison du plus fort est toujours la meilleure (The reason of the strongest is always the best): Might is right.

Les petits ruisseaux font les grandes rivières (Little streams make big rivers): Take care of the pennies and the pounds will take care of themselves.

On n'arrive à rien quand tout le monde s'en mêle (You don't get anywhere when everybody gets into it): Too many cooks spoil the broth.

Un malheur n'arrive jamais seul (A misfortune never comes alone): It never rains but it pours.

Un point à temps en vaut cent (A stitch in time is worth a hundred): A stitch in time saves nine.

"False friends" (*faux amis*) are foreign words that look like words in one's own language but have a different meaning. For example, English and French both bor-rowed the Latin word *extra*. However, the French teenager who says "*Cette glace est extra!*" does not mean that it costs more, but that it is fantastic. *Extra* is a colloquial shortening of *extraordinaire*.

Some other "false friends" are *le foot* (soccer), *le car* (a tour bus), and *la location* (hiring or renting). The actual words for foot, car, and location are *le pied, la voiture*, and *l'endroit*.

Other "false friends":

- *achever* (to complete): to achieve (*réaliser*)
- *cave* (cellar): cave (*grotte*)
- *conducteur* (driver): conductor (*contrôleur*)
- *injurier* (to insult): injure (*blesser*)
- *libraire* (bookstore): library (*bibliothèque*)
- *monnaie* (change): money (*argent*)
- *propre* (clean): proper (*correct*)
- *regarder* (to watch): to regard (*considérer*)
- *slip* (underpants/briefs/pants): slip (*combinaison, jupon*)
- *sympathique* (nice): sympathetic (*compatissant*)
- *user* (to wear out): to use (*utiliser*)

There are also a lot of "partial false friends," like *type* (type; guy), *parent* (parent; relative), and *important* (important; considerable); and "half borrowings" like *un dancing* (dance hall) and *un parking* (parking lot).

Related Web links: proverbes-citations.com for proverbs listed by theme (F)

Abbreviations and Acronyms

Abbreviations have entered the daily vocabulary of the French. Tourists will need to recognize these:

TRANSPORTATION

- **RATP** Régie autonome des transports parisiens: Autonomous administration of Parisian transportation; the Paris Metro and bus system
- **RER** Réseau Express Régional: Paris and suburban rapid rail system
- **SNCF** Société nationale des chemins de fer français: National syndicate of railroads; the national train system
- **TEE** Trans-Europe-Express: Trans-Europe express train
- **TGV** Train à grande vitesse: High-speed train
- **VAL** *Véhicule automatique léger*: Light automatic vehicle; driverless Metro train
- **VTT** *Vélo tout-terrain*: mountain bike

FRENCH INSTITUTIONS

- **AFP** Agence France-Presse: France-Press Agency
- **ANPE** Agence nationale pour l'emploi: National unemployment agency
- **BNP** Banque nationale de Paris-Paribas: National Bank of Paris-Paribas, a major national bank
- **EDF** Electricité de France: State-owned electricity agency
- **GDF** Gaz de France: State-owned natural gas agency
- **P et T/PTT** Postes et télécommuni-cations, or Postes, télégraphes et

téléphones: French post office and telephone monopoly
- **RF** République française: French Republic

DAILY LIFE

- **BA** *Bonne action*: good deed
- **BD** *Bande dessinée*: a cartoon or comic book; literally, "drawn strip"
- **BP** *Boîte postale*: mailbox
- **CEDEX** Courrier d'entreprise à distribution exceptionnelle: Special Corporate Mail delivery
- **CRS** Compagnies républicaines de sécurité: Republican Companies of Safety; the riot police
- **FNAC** Fédération nationale des achats des cadres: discount chain of book, record, and computer stores
- **HLM** Habitations à loyer modéré: low-rent state-subsidized high-rise condominiums
- **PDG** Président-directeur général: CEO of a firm
- **PMU** Pari mutuel urbain: state horse-race betting agency
- **PV** Procès verbal (Contravention): parking fine
- **SAMU** Service d'aide médicale d'urgence: Urgent Medical Ambulance Service
- **SDF** *Sans domicile fixe*: no fixed address; homeless
- **SVP** *s'il vous plaît*: please
- **TTC** *Toutes taxes comprises*: all taxes included
- **TVA** *Taxe sur la valeur ajoutée*: value-added tax

Numbers

The French use of numbers is more than a matter of translation, and knowing about French numbering style can be useful not only for making sure you get correct change in shops and restaurants, but also to understand distance and telephone numbers, among other things.

French telephone numbers have ten digits, which are not recited singly but in pairs: for example, 01-43-12-95-06, or *zéro un, quarante-trois, douze, quatre-vingt-quinze, zéro six*. The first two digits indicate one of the five zones into which France is divided by France Télécom. In this example, it's the Paris zone, 01.

The country is officially divided into 95 administrative districts, or *départements*. Each one has a number as well as a name. The numbers correspond to the alphabetical order of the names of the *départements*. For example, the Ain *département* in the Rhône-Alpes region is 01, the city of Paris is 75, and the Val d'Oise *département* in the Paris region is 95. The numbers serve as the beginning of the *département* postal codes and terminate the license plate numbers of cars registered in the *département*. French drivers know to be aware of vehicles displaying 75 on their license plates because of the disrespect Parisian drivers display for slow drivers and for conventional safety rules in general. Parisian road behavior causes animosity in country areas.

Some handwritten French numerals look different from the corresponding American ones. A French 1 looks like a narrow capital A without the cross bar, and a French 7 is crossed with a bar to avoid confusion with a 1. To many English speakers (and writers), the French use of commas and full stops in numbers seems reversed. A comma is used to indicate decimals, as in the price F2,30 (two francs, 30 centimes; sometimes written 2F30) or 54,5 *pour cent* (54.5 per cent). A full stop sometimes separates numbers above 1,000 into groups of three digits (6.819 for 6,819), although spaces are more common: 60 082 000 *habitants* (60,082,000 inhabitants).

The street-level floor of a building is called the *rez-de-chaussée*, not the first floor (*le premier étage*), which is the floor above the street level. The French defend their logic by saying that the street level is not a story.

The French observe some conventions in counting days that can cause unwary travelers some problems. A week is *huit jours* (eight days), and two weeks is *quinze jours* (15 days). Therefore, a Eurailpass for *huit jours* is actually valid for only seven days. This can be a source of total incomprehension when a British traveler counts out the eight days for which he believes the pass is valid and an exasperated French conductor tries without success to explain the meaning of *huit jours*. Neither stiff upper lip nor *sang-froid* (cool composure) is maintained on such occasions.

Place Names and Addresses

Many place names in France go back to the time of the Gauls, or the Gallo-Roman era, or the Franks. Through these names, we can follow the major stages in the history of France. Here are some examples:

- **6th century B.C.:** Greek names recalling the Greek colonization of the Mediterranean coast, for example, Marseille and Nice (meaning "victory").

- **5th century B.C.:** Celtic names given by the Gauls to rivers (Isère, for "sacred"), mountains (Jura for "wooded height"), and towns (Paris, from the Parisii people who lived there).

- **1st century A.D.:** Gallo-Roman names, which are by far the most numerous, and reveal the extent of the urban civilization brought by the Romans. Aix (baths), Bagnères (caves), Baume (a spring), Fontenay, (a camp).

- **9th century:** Norman names, indicating natural features, as with Dieppe (deep) and Honfleur (gulf), or primitive dwellings: Yvetot (tumbledown cottage).

- **11th century:** Religious names, of monasteries—Moustiers, Montreuil—or of saints: Saint-Jean, Saint-Martin, Domrémy.

- **16th century on:** Modern names recalling famous people (Richelieu), aristocratic residences (Bellevue, Plaisance), or historic events (Malakoff).

Streets in many French cities and towns also carry the names of famous historical figures and events, as well famous writers, musicians, and artists. Some contemporary celebrities also are commemorated in street names. People may not remember a great deal about some of the events and people in the street names of their cities, but the signposts remind them of a glorious past.

Americans accustomed to the predictable grid pattern and numbering of city streets are often disoriented by French streets, which do not follow a recognizable geometric pattern and are called by names.

Some streets are named after saints. Tourists using a street directory should remember that all such names beginning with *Saint* precede those beginning with *Sainte*, which in turn precede any beginning with *Saints*. Thus, rue Saint-Thomas precedes rue Sainte-Genevieve, which precedes rue Saints-Côme-et-Damien in a directory. Another distinct feature of French addresses is the use of *bis* and *ter* to insert new addresses between adjacent numbers. In the English system two addresses between 125 and 126 would be 125A and 125B; the French call them 125 *bis* and 125 *ter*. (French concert-goers, incidentally, will cry "*Bis!*" to encourage an encore, not "Encore!" The encore performance is similarly *un bis*.)

Related Web links: ign.fr/fr/Pl/activites/ geodesie/index.html, the National Geographic Institute site, provides town and village coordinates (F)

LANGUAGE
Names and Name Days

France is a traditionally Catholic country, and so the majority of first names are taken from the Catholic calendar of saints' names. Children celebrate their birthday (*anniversaire*) and, though it has become less common, their saint's day (*fête*) for the saint after whom they are named.

Until 1992 state law recommended that children be given a name from a roster of names. Parents being parents, they sought more original names for their children by hyphenating simpler names, creating such as Marie-Françoise and Jean-Pierre. Some French names are "unisex": Camille, Claude, and Dominique, for example.

As in other countries, there are fashions in first names. The most popular names for girls given from 1970 to 1974 were Sandrine, Nathalie, Isabelle, Valérie, Karine, and Stéphanie; and for boys, Stéphane, Christophe, David, Laurent, Frédéric, Olivier, and Sébastien.

In the 1990s there were more Americanized first names chosen, especially in the families of salaried employees and working people; for example, Kevin, Anthony, Jonathan, and David. Managers gave their sons more traditional names, like Thomas, Pierre, Nicolas, and Alexandre. For girls, Elodie, Laura, Julie, Marion, and Martine were popular.

The most frequent French family names are Martin, Bernard, Moreau, Durand, Petit, Thomas, and Dubois. Dupont, frequently treated as the typical French family name, actually ranks 19th.

The oldest family names go back to the Middle Ages, when, in the 9th or 10th century, the nickname was added to the first name and became hereditary, along with property. Family names were fixed in 1539, when the register of births, marriages, and deaths was created. From then on, names had to consist of a first and a family name.

Family names evoke the many aspects of French civilization. For example:

- **Geographical terms:** Montaigne (mountain), La Fontaine (fountain), Duchesne (oak), Dumas (dwelling), Lebreton (Breton)
- **Historical terms:** Béranger (Germanic origin), Adam (biblical origin), André (Greek origin), Antoine (Latin origin)
- **Social terms:** Meunier (miller), Lemaître (master), Leneveu (nephew)
- **Lifestyle terms that are nicknames:** Legrand (tall), Bossuet (humpbacked), Lefranc (frank), Lesage (wise), Boileau (drinks water), Lamoureux (lover)

The article *de* before a family name indicates that the family belonged to the nobility or wishes to give the impression that it did. Adult members of the family usually wear a signet ring stamped with the family crest. Despite being a republic, French families with a *de* name enjoy social prestige. Those descended from noble families who lived before the Revolution in 1789 have more prestige than those whose families bought the title since then.

Related Web links: geocities.com/Paris/Louvre/ 9647/almanach.htm for a calendar of saints' days and lives of the saints (F)

Writing Letters

The greeting and farewell expressions in professional and personal letters present strictly codified levels of formality that takes some getting used to. The most formal level omits first and family names and begins with a bare "Monsieur," "Madame," or "Mademoiselle." The addition of *Cher* or *Chère* colors the formality with a shade of warmth, but this is added only when the person is well-known to the writer. The first name is used in letters between family members and close friends: "*Mon cher Pierre*," "*Ma chère Isabelle*."

When writing to a person in an important position, even if his or her name is known, the French use the person's title in their opening and closing expressions: "Monsieur le Directeur" or "Madame la Directrice." In letters to someone in the same profession it would be: "*Cher Collègue*" or "*Chère Collègue*."

In letters to a company, the form of address is "Messieurs" ("Sirs"). In general mail-outs from companies or institutions to customers or residents, both gender greetings are often found: "Madame," "Mademoiselle," "Monsieur" from the Paris Town Hall; "*Chère* Madame" or "*Cher* Monsieur" from a bank; or "*Cher Lecteur*" or "*Chère Lectrice*" ("Dear Reader") from a publishing house.

Farewell expressions in French letters strike English speakers as particularly wordy, complex, and flowery. The terse Anglo-Saxon "Yours sincerely" has many variations in French, depending on the relationship between the writer and the people receiving the letter. The form of address that appeared in the opening greet-ing reappears in the farewell at the end. Some examples ranging from very formal to relatively informal endings are:

Veuillez agréer, Monsieur, l'expression de mes sentiments les plus distingués: Please be willing to accept, sir, the expression of my most distinguished sentiments.

Je vous prie de recevoir, cher Monsieur, l'expression de mes salutations les meilleures: I beg you to accept, dear sir, the expression of my best greetings.

Je t'envoie, ma chère Isabelle, mon amical souvenir: I send you, my dear Isabelle, my friendly remembrance.

Je t'embrasse (or, more informally, *Bises*; more informally, *Grosses bises*): kisses

Adept French letter writers will construct many other variations to express the relationship precisely, but these four models will serve English speakers who have not been initiated into the subtleties of relationships from early childhood. The first example is appropriate for most business letters to customers or suppliers or when applying for information; the second to colleagues or acquaintances; the third for well-established friendships; and the fourth for close friendships. When in doubt between the last two choices, opt for the more formal of the two and observe the ending that's used in the reply to your letter.

LANGUAGE
Cards

Calling cards (*cartes de visite*) are frequently used in France. When issuing invitations and expressing New Year's wishes, for example, people send their calling cards, printed with their names and home addresses, instead of commercial greeting cards. Incidentally, it is more traditional in France to send New Year's greetings, throughout January.

People use a formal style in the messages on their calling cards, which means in part avoiding the use of *I* or *we*. For examples:

M. et Mme Jacques Beaumarchais vous souhaitent une très heureuse Nouvelle Année. (Mr. and Mrs. Jacques Beaumarchais wish you a very happy New Year.)

A *carton* is a larger card, used for a more formal invitation (*carton d'invitation*) or for an official thank you (*carton de remerciements*):

Pour les 20 ans de sa fille
Geneviève,
Madame Gérard Fontaine
recevra chez elle,
le 3 novembre à partir de 19h.
(For her daughter Geneviève's 20th birthday, Mrs. Gérard Fontaine will entertain friends at her home, on November 3 from 7:00 P.M.)

Mme Béatrice Thollet,
profondément touchée par vos
témoignages de sympathie,
les envois de fleurs et l'union de
prières à son cher défunt vous
adresse ses sincères remerciements.

(Mrs. Béatrice Thollet, deeply touched by your expressions of sympathy, the flowers sent, and your prayers for her late husband, sends you her sincere thanks.)

A *faire-part* is a different sort of card, printed as the occasion demands, to announce births, marriages, and deaths. A *faire-part* to announce a marriage is sent in the names not only of the parents of the bride, but also of all her surviving grandparents. Some examples are:

BIRTH:
Michel et Françoise Bernard ont la joie de vous annoncer la naissance de Xavier, le 4 juillet 2001 à Toulouse.
(Michel and Françoise Bernard joyfully announce the birth of Xavier, on July 4, 2001 at Toulouse.)

MARRIAGE:
Monsieur et Madame Paul Tavernier ont l'honneur de vous faire part du mariage de leur fille Marie avec M. Thomas Roussin.
(Mr. and Mrs. Paul Tavernier are honored to announce the marriage of their daughter Marie to Mr. Thomas Roussin.)

DEATH:
M. et Mme Pierre Lambert et leurs enfants ont la douleur de vous faire part du décès de Mme Charles Potet née Leblanc.
(It is with great sorrow that Mr. and Mrs. Pierre Lambert and children inform you of the death of Mrs. Charles Potet née Leblanc.)

Mobile Phone Text Messages

The mobile phone (*le portable, le mobile*) was eagerly adopted by the French, and the number of SMS (Short Message Service) messages sent from mobile to mobile has skyrocketed. Mobile phone users are sending each other millions of messages each day, and inventing a new language as they go.

According to a recent France Télécom study, most users of the service are between 15 and 25 years old. Many live with their parents, and the mini-message is a way of communicating discreetly, without their family hearing private conversations, or without being disturbed by calls.

When composing a message, being concise is essential: only 160 signs (letters or spaces) are available for each message. But this is enough for an invitation to the cinema, an angry comment on the math homework, or a word of love to a girl- or boyfriend. Most messages are sent between 10:00 and 11:00 P.M.

Literary users might eschew all simplification of language, but most users try to pack a maximum of information into a minimum of signs, and abbreviations are essential. Some examples, most of which are based on the similarity of sound, are:

TA: *tu as* (you have)
C: *C'est, ces, or ses* (It is, these/those, his/her/their)
E: *es or est* (are or is)
2: *de or deux* (of or two)
TT: *tout* (all)
NRV: *énervé(e)* (stressed, up tight)
OQP: *occupé(e)* (busy)

The use of English words is widespread, for example:
4U: *pour toi*
CU: *à bientôt*

Numbers are written in figures, and punctuation is almost non-existent. Each group has its own code. Some examples are:

SLT Y A SOFI KI VIEN ESSAY DALE LA CHERCHE:
Salut, il y a Sophie qui vient. Essai d'aller la chercher: (Hi, Sophie's coming. Try to go and meet her.)

OQP, NRV G PAL TEM:(:
Je suis occupé, énervé, je n'ai pas le temps. (I'm busy, stressed, I haven't got time.)

ALE COOL RDV 21H A LA GAR CALL ME:):
Allez cool. Rendezvous à 21 h à la gare. Appelle-moi. (OK, no problem. See you at 9:00 P.M. at the station. Call me.)

Related Web links: dourdan.com/eti/lexique.htm
for télécom dictionary (F)

Traditional Religious Holidays

All countries have traditional holidays, usually inspired by a mixture of history, religion, and paganism, and France is no exception. A large number of state holidays commemorate France's Catholic heritage. Although a majority of French people no longer attend church, and many don't know the religious significance of some of these holidays, they remain a traditional part of French social life.

The public holidays (*jours fériés*) with a religious inspiration are :

- **Easter** (Pâques): Easter Monday is a holiday. Shops sell items that commemorate the holiday's Christian origin as well as pagan symbols of fertility—chocolate bells, fish, rabbits, and eggs.
- **Ascension** (L'Ascension): Comes 40 days after Easter, usually in May and on a Thursday.
- **Pentecost** (La Pentecôte): Comes 50 days after Easter. Being a Sunday, the Monday following is set aside as a day off from work and school.
- **Assumption** (L'Assomption): August 15. The taking of Mary into heaven has been forgotten by many French people, and they treat this holiday as a bonus day attached to the beginning or end of the traditional August vacation. For this reason, the *autoroutes* are doubly crowded with vacationers on this day.
- **All Saints** (La Toussaint): November 1. On this day, the French commemorate their dead, particularly family members, by making a journey to the family cemetery and placing chrysanthemums on the graves. This tradition illustrates two facts of French life: the physical rift between generations, for many have moved away from their family's place of origin, and the desire to return to a rural past and family roots.
- **Christmas** (Noël): December 25. This holiday is very much a family holiday. On Christmas Eve religiously inclined people attend midnight mass and the whole family stays up late for the Réveillon, a lavish traditional meal with white and red wines for which no expense is spared. Traditional foods served at the Réveillon and over Christmas day are pâté de foie gras, oysters, smoked salmon, turkey with chestnuts, and the *bûche de Noël* (a chocolate-coated cake in the form of a log), with which you drink champagne. Churches display nativity crib scenes. In the South of France, live lambs are placed near the cribs during midnight mass, and the Nativity is made with *santons* (typical clay figurines). Children leave out shoes rather than stockings to receive gifts from Le Père Noël (Father Christmas). In the northeast region of France, a special celebration for St. Nicholas's day occurs on December 6.

Related Web links: frenchculture.about.com, see *Holiday* (E); **joyeuse-fete.com/joyeux-noel** recipes (F); **paques.com** for Easter traditions (F)

Other Official State Holidays

In addition to the public holidays linked to France's Catholic heritage, there are state holidays (*jours fériés*) that have a civil or historic origin:

- **New Year's** (Le Jour de l'An): January 1. New Year's Eve (la Saint-Sylvestre) is the occasion for parties and late night feasting (*le réveillon*) with friends and family. At midnight celebrating drivers herald the new year with a cacophony of car horns, and people say "*Bonne Année!*" ("Happy New Year!") and kiss in the streets. Family and friends who have not been celebrating at midnight wish each other a Happy New Year on New Year's Day or on the first occasion they see them up until January 31. If they are not going to see them in January, they send them a greeting or visiting card.
- **Labor Day** (La fête du Travail): May 1. The holiday was instituted in France in 1947. Trade union marches are organized. Sprigs of lily-of-the-valley (*muguet*) are sold at Metro exits and in the streets on that day and during the first weeks of May in flower shops. Lily-of-the-valley is a symbol of happiness and is traditionally offered to family and friends at the beginning of May with a wish for their happiness.
- **Victory Day** (La fête de la Victoire): May 8. Commemoration of the Allied victory over Nazi Germany that brought an end to World War II in 1945.
- **National Day** (La fête Nationale): July 14. Called "Bastille Day" in the United States, this holiday celebrates the storming of the Bastille in 1789 and the birth of democracy. It strikes a patriotic chord in the French. The French Revolution ousted the absolute monarchy and established a republic. This promulgated the Rights of Man and the Citizen, which was the inspiration for all Republican constitutions since. On the morning of July 14 there is a large military parade in Paris on the Champs-Elysées in the presence of the French president, and processions in the main French cities. After the parade, the president gives a nationally televised interview on the state of the nation and hosts a huge garden party on the grounds of his official residence, le Palais de l'Elysée. In the afternoon and evening there is dancing in the streets to accordion music, and at night there are fireworks displays throughout France.
- **Armistice Day** (L'armistice): November 11. This day marks the date of the armistice of World War I in 1918. The French president places a wreath on the tomb of the unknown soldier under the Arc de Triomphe at the top of the Champs-Elysées.

When the date of a public holiday is a Thursday or a Tuesday, many French people *font le pont* (have a long weekend) by taking an extra day off on the Friday or the Monday.

Related Web links: elysee.fr/instit/symb5.htm for July 14 (F)

Popular Celebrations and Festivities

These special days and festivals are not public holidays but are very popular :

- **Epiphany** (L'Epiphanie or la fête des Rois): January 6. The French celebrate the three kings by buying a special cake, *la galette des rois*, sold for several weeks around the holiday at bakers' shops and supermarkets. This cake comes with a gold paper crown and conceals a tiny ceramic figure, *la fève* (originally a bean). The cake is solemnly cut for dessert, and the person whose slice contains *la fève* is crowned king or queen and chooses a royal partner.

- **Carnival** (Le Carnaval): Between Epiphany and Mardi Gras (the last day before Lent, usually late February), many regions hold carnivals that feature costumed processions and masked parades. Nice holds the biggest carnival.

- **Candlemas** (La Chandeleur): February 2. On this feast of the Virgin, it is traditional to eat pancakes (*crêpes*) at home.

- **Valentine's Day** (La Saint Valentin): February 14. The Anglo-Saxon tradition of a special day for people in love has been introduced into France. Often, flowers are sent.

- **April Fools:** April 1. On this day, many French people indulge their mischievous side. Children cut out paper fish (*poissons d'avril*) and attach them to people's backs. When the fish or one of the other practical pranks of the day is revealed, the traditional cry is *"Poisson d'avril!"*

- **Mother's Day/Father's Day:** La fête des Mères is celebrated on a Sunday in May, and la fête des Pères, a month later, on a Sunday in June. The occasion is celebrated with gifts and family get-togethers. Mother's Day is the more widely observed. At school, children prepare small presents for their mother and father. These celebrations were begun after World War II.

- **Music Day** (La fête de la Musique): June 21. Initiated in 1982 by Jacques Lang, the Minister for Culture, this celebration of music is on the first day of summer, which is the longest day of the year. Everywhere in France, bands and musicians play in the streets, in cafés, and in concert halls. Many performances are free of charge.

- **Halloween:** Since 1997, when it was launched in France as part of a publicity campaign, Halloween, modeled on its American counterpart—with imitation pumpkins, masks, witches, and ghosts—has become a popular festivity. To counteract criticism that the French Halloween is another example of the Americanization of the French way of life, the Celtic European origins of this festivity have been highlighted. However, faced with the popularity of Halloween overshadowing the traditional celebration of Toussaint, which takes place the next day, French bishops have condemned the holiday as an example of the paganization of modern society replacing the observance of Christian festivals.

Sports

The French have traditionally stood apart for their intellectual rather than athletic achievements. This, however, is changing. The French now spend more money on sports and sports equipment than any other leisure activity (16.3 percent). One out of two people participate in athletic events from time to time, and one out of ten are regularly involved. In the 1980s, the fitness trend and aerobic exercise arrived from the United States. Since then the French have developed their own forms of fitness, which includes working out in a gym (22 percent), playing a team sport, and involvement in an individual activity like cycling. In almost every French city there are government-funded municipal swimming pools and sports centers which are used by the many local clubs. More than 6.5 percent of the French people are active members of sporting associations, whose activities include soccer, tennis, swimming, skiing, table tennis, basketball, and karate. In the 2000 Olympics, France won a total of 38 medals.

The French prefer to watch *le football* (soccer) on television and about 500 hours a year can be seen on public and private channels. In 1998 the World Cup soccer competition was played at sites throughout France. The French team, affectionately called les Bleus (the Blues), survived the grueling elimination process to emerge in the finals against heavily favored Brazil. On July 13, at the Stade de France in Paris, les Bleus won, 3–0. The next day, which happened to be France's National Day, a joyful crowd of 500,000 crammed the streets of Paris to celebrate. The hero of the match was Zinédine Zidane, a French-Algerian who is not only a magnificent soccer player, but has become a symbol of the "new France" that accepts its diversity with pride. Another team sport the French follow is rugby, which is most popular in the Southwest. The French generally see the European rugby competition, le Tournoi des six nations (England, France, Ireland, Italy, Scotland, and Wales), as a contest for national pride. There is also a World Cup of Rugby where French teams take on Australia, New Zealand, and Fiji, and the European nations.

Each summer, cycling becomes the focus of the French and the rest of Europe and the world. France's famous cycling race, the Tour de France, takes a different route around the country, but always includes difficult mountain stages in the Alps and the Pyrénées, and always concludes with a finish in Paris, down the Champs-Elysées. Occurring over three weeks in late June and two-thirds of July, it is a grueling 21-stage contest comprising over 2,000 miles, testing the best bicyclists and teams in the world. Since Bernard Hinault won the race in 1985, his fifth victory in the Tour de France, French riders have fared badly. In three successive years, 1999, 2000, and 2001, American Lance Armstrong has won the race, and become a national hero in the United States due not only to his victory in the Tour, but also his victory over cancer.

Related Web links: sports.com/fr/ for French and world sports from the French perspective (F)

Sports Activities

Each year, Paris is host to several major international sporting events, including the Paris Marathon in April and the French Open tennis tournament, held in June on the red clay courts of Roland Garros Stadium. Racing enthusiasts can attend two Formula 1 events, the 24 Hours at Le Mans, and the Monaco rally. The French driver Alain Prost (1955–) was for many years a leader of Formula 1 racing. French sailors, often from Brittany, have been among the leaders in around-the-world and transatlantic yacht races. In 1990, Florence Arthaud (1957–) became the first woman to win an ocean yachting race, and she established the record for a solo crossing of the Atlantic: 9 days and 21 hours. Since then she has competed in the Round-the-World Solo Yacht race, and had to be rescued in one attempt, in the Indian Ocean, close to the Antarctic.

A traditional sport still popular in France is *pétanque*. Created around 1910, and a particular favorite in the South of France, *pétanque* is similar to the Italian game of bocce. It's played with metal balls and a small wooden ball, which is the jack. As a form of relaxation as well as skill, it attracts men in every village and city in southern France, which has compacted areas of soil where the game is played.

A number of new sports have become popular in France, particularly with the young, such as wind-surfing, scuba diving, hang gliding, and mountain climbing (*escalade*). Sports such as roller skating, roller boarding, and skateboarding—the *sports de glisse* ("sliding" sports), along with skiing and snowboarding—have gained a huge following among the young. The high rate of accidents, about 850,00 a year among those 12 to 19 years old, has led to campaigns aimed at encouraging youth to wear helmets and other protective equipment such as knee and elbow guards.

Hunting is still considered a sport in France, and 1.5 million hunters strongly defend their right to do so. As in other countries, hunting has been criticized by animal rights and environmental groups. Currently, the French hunting season lasts seven and a half months, with around 44 million birds of 60 different species killed each year. In 1999 the government, under pressure from the Greens, released a report recommending that the hunting season be reduced to five months to protect certain endangered species. The president of the hunters' association and the political party Mouvement chasse, pêche, nature et tradition (CPNT), called the report a declaration of war against hunting. With both sides equally determined to have their way, it is an issue that will require time and skilled negotiating to resolve.

Related Web links: magnyf1.com for Nervers Magny-Cours Formula 1 (E, F); **f1.acm.mc** for Monaco Formula 1 (E, F); **prostgp.com** for Alain Prost Formula 1 team site (E, F); **24hdumans.net** for the Le Mans site (E, F); **multimania.com/ petanque** for rules and history of pétanque (E, F); **http://fr.dir.yahoo.com/sports_et_loisirs/sports/ sports_de_glisse** for a directory of "sliding" sports (F); **chassepassion.net** is a hunting site on game and legislation (F); **les-verts.org** for the Green party site (F)

Leisure Time

The French workweek is now officially 35 hours. The legal retirement age is 60, or 55 for some categories of workers. French leisure time (*le temps libre*) has increased as a result. Leisure activities can include cultural pursuits, such as reading and listening to music (on average, the French watch television and listen to the radio six hours a day); going to movies, theater, and concerts; visiting museums and art galleries; and photography. And they can include sports, forest walks, mountain climbing, fishing, hunting, playing cards, dancing in clubs, gardening, house repairs, and so on. In accordance with the precept of 16th-century philosopher Michel Montaigne (1533–92) that an active mind needs to be balanced by a healthy body, the French typically mix these two types of leisure activities.

An increasingly popular leisure activity is a visit to a theme park. There are more than 20 in France, including Parc Asterix, Sportica, Walibi Stroumpf, Futuroscope, and Disneyland Paris. *Les studios Disney*, is opening a second theme park, whose popularity as tourist destinations for the French themselves has overtaken visits to the more traditional castles and museums. Disneyland Paris, about 20 miles from the city, opened under the name Euro Disney in 1992. Its Enchanted Kingdom is the single most popular tourist destination in Europe, with 12.5 million visitors a year. Parc Asterix, opened in 1989 and aiming to capture, through the comic book hero Asterix, the spirit and essence of the French, has 2 million visitors a year. Many theme parks combine a scientific or technology theme with local attractions: Vulcania (Auvergne), Bioscope (Strasbourg), le Parc du Végétal (Angers), and Vivacity, la Cité de la vitesse et des technologies avancées (Mantes-la-Jolie). Futuroscope opened near Poitiers in 1987. Its cinema, video, and moving image displays attract the most visitors.

A more recent pastime is the weekend away, though less than 50 percent of the French go away for a weekend at least two times a year. This is no doubt because the two-day weekend is new for France. Children go to school on Saturday mornings, and adults usually spend Saturdays doing the shopping, housework, house repairs, and gardening. Sunday is often a day of rest spent with the family, although the traditional long Sunday lunch is less important now, as is Sunday mass, particularly among the young. Often, theme parks are the destination for a weekend away.

Related Web links: french-vacations.com, francevacations.net, fr-holidaystore.co.uk, frenchlife.co.uk are some of the many tour operators in France (E); ffsp-ivv.com is the site for Fédération français des sports populaires, for walking, bicycling, and so on (F)

Vacations

The Socialist Front Populaire government of 1936 introduced a law mandating two weeks of annual paid vacation (*congés payés*) for all salaried workers. The law is often cited in France as a watershed in the progress of the working class toward an improved lifestyle. The required vacation was increased to three weeks in 1956, four in 1969, and five in 1982. Many workers in special categories now receive six weeks of paid vacation each year. Germany is the only country in the world where the annual vacation is longer than in France.

Most of the French take their vacations in July and August, and many industrial plants close for the entire month of August. The first wave of vacationers leave Paris and the North of France after Bastille Day (July 14) and seek out the sun and beaches of the Mediterranean and Atlantic coasts. The second wave departs on August 1. On August 15 a third wave leaves on vacation, while those who left in mid-July throng home. In September people resume their work or school, and life returns to normal. Many people use their fifth and sixth weeks of vacation to go skiing in the winter or take other short trips.

The French are traveling more. In 1995 about 70 percent traveled on vacation at least once a year, though only 12 percent spent their vacations overseas. This percentage is growing rapidly, but when it comes to international travel, France still has a long to way to go to catch up with the Netherlands and Switzerland (66%), Germany (65%), and Belgium (56%). More than 30 percent of those French taking foreign vacations went to Spain and Portugal.

Young French people under 25 go away more frequently and for longer periods. About one-fourth go overseas. An increasing number of the French want more intelligent vacations than idle sunbathing (*le bronzage idiot*) on the beach. The Club Méditerranée, which began in 1950 with resorts in France, has expanded its village concept by building vacation sites at many exotic locations and offering a range of sports and cultural activities. One of the fastest growing activities in France is *la randonnée* (walking or trekking), with an estimated 3 million people practicing it regularly. It is most popular in the 25 to 49 age group. Making it possible to exercise close to nature, and expanding into such activities as mountain climbing and canyoning, it has become a new way of having a vacation. The Centre info rando in Paris helps people to plan their walking trips in the French countryside. Adventure holidays like kayaking and ecotourism are also fashionable, and destinations suitable for all levels of stamina and age are now marketed. The most popular winter vacation is skiing. Forty percent of those over 15 years old go to one of the many ski resorts in the Alps, the Pyrénées, or the Massif Central.

Related Web links: french-vacations.com, francevacations.net, fr-holidaystore.co.uk, frenchlife.co.uk for some of the many tour operators in France (E); ffsp-ivv.com for the Fédération français des sports populaires, for walking, bicycling, and so on (F)

Cultural Tourism

Not all the visitors who flock to France's museums, galleries, castles, cathedrals, and churches are foreign tourists; many are French. Cultural tourism is very much part of French education and socialization. Often, a family will spend part of its vacation following the itinerary in one of the Michelin guides, a cultural icon in itself. Some of the most popular cultural attractions for French tourists are the museums (there are 34 national museums, with 19 outside Paris), the Palace of Versailles, Mont Saint-Michel in Normandy, and the Chambord and Chenonceaux castles in the Loire Valley. Paris is home to more than 60 museums. Some of the favorites for the French are the Louvre, the Centre Georges Pompidou (20th-century art), the Musée d'Orsay (art of the second half of the 19th century), and the Musée Picasso. Another example of cultural tourism are the "Writers' Houses" found all over France: about 120 houses, dating from the Renaissance to modern times, which were home to some of France's most famous writers and philosophers. It is possible to visit where Voltaire, Rousseau, Georges Sand, Victor Hugo, Balzac, Emile Zola, or Proust lived. As the philosopher Gaston Bachelard said: "A house, even more than a landscape, reflects the soul."

The pleasure the French get from visiting their cultural monuments and museums is enhanced by their knowledge of the historical events and art forms that have molded their nation. These constitute the shared cultural heritage, or "cultural baggage," and serve as examples and points of reference in conversations. They are an important component of what it means to be French.

It has become a tradition of French cultural life that Presidents of the Fifth Republic leave behind a cultural monument in Paris. Georges Pompidou, who was president from 1969 to 1974, left his name on the Pompidou Center. His contemporary architecture has been described as "like a building turned inside out." President Valéry Giscard d'Estaing (1974–81) opened the Musée d'Orsay. President François Mitterrand (1981–95) left Paris with a new National Library, the Bastille Opera, and the pyramid and new entrance to the Louvre. The contribution of President Jacques Chirac (1995–) will be a new museum on the Quai Branly near the Eiffel Tower, to open in 2004. It will be called the Musée des arts et civilisations, and display African, Asian, Oceanic, and American primitive art.

Related Web links: francetourism.com for travel info, region info, vacation options (E); viamichelin.com for travel guides and maps (E, F); greatbuildings.com for Chambord, Chenonceaux, Fontainebleau, Versailles, Museé d'Orsay, Mont Saint-Michel, Pont du Gard, Louvre (E); chez.com/museesdefrance provides a list of museums by region (E, F); rmn.fr is a site for 33 national museums and exhibitions (E, F); bnf.fr for National Library website for François Mitterrand–Tolbiac site (E, F); quaibranly.fr for Musée des arts et civilisations (E, F)

LEISURE
Foreign Tourists

France is the most popular tourist destination in the world, ahead of the United States and Spain. More than 66 million tourists visit France each year. The majority come from other European countries, led by Germany and Britain, and then the Netherlands, Belgium and Luxembourg, Italy, and Spain. After the Europeans, Americans are the next most frequent visitors, and then Japanese, who are the newest major national group to visit France in large numbers.

Most tourists visit Paris, attracted by its historic and cultural monuments and the way of life. The most visited sites in the city are the Georges Pompidou Center, the Eiffel Tower, the Louvre, the Parc de la Villette, and the Musée d'Orsay. Near Paris, the Palace of Versailles and Disneyland are the most popular destinations. The regions most foreign tourists visit are Brittany, where Mont Saint-Michel is located; the Loire Valley, with its historical castles; and in the south, Provence. There, they find Roman colosseums (in Nimes and Arles); monuments dating from Julius Caesar's invasion of Gaul in 52 B.C.; and the languid pleasure of Mediterranean life in the Côte d'Azur; Corsica, and Languedoc-Roussillon. The Alps is very popular for winter skiing and summer mountain vacations. The combination of spectacular scenery and the richness of historical sites are what attract so many tourists, in addition, of course, to French food and wine. A campaign run by the government, titled "Bonjour," strives to make the French people more sensitive to cultural differences and more welcoming to foreign tourists.

In addition to enhancing France's national and cultural image overseas, tourism is an important part of the French economy. It is the second largest export industry after the automobile, and, at 700 billion francs annually (nearly $100 billion) it accounts for nearly 10 percent of the gross domestic product. Another 150 billion francs ($20 billion) are spent by French tourists every year in France, in an industry that employs more than a million French people.

Visitors to France can have many different types of vacations: from a stay in one of the luxury hotels run by French companies such as Sofitel, Concorde, Frantel, Novotel, and Méridien to camping and caravaning and staying at one of the 8,500 camping grounds. A uniquely French travel experience is staying in a *gîte*, usually an old farmhouse or house in a village which is rented out, or in a *chambre d'hôte*, which is similar to a bed and breakfast in that the tourist stays in a French home and has an experience closer to the French way of life.

Related Web links: sofitel.com, novotel.com, lemeridien-hotels.com for hotel chains (E, F); gites-de-france.fr for chambre d'hotes, gîtes, camping, chalets (E, F)

Global City

Paris is a global city, like London, New York, and Tokyo. It survived the German occupation during World War II intact, and postwar Paris saw the construction of a new *quartier* (quarter) called La Défense, as a well as a system of exterior highways that relieved the great traffic jams of central Paris. In 1962 a program to preserve the older districts of Paris such as the Marais was begun. Modern Paris has grown with its own distinct architecture. Buildings such as the Pompidou Center, the pyramid entrance to the Louvre, the Arch of La Défense, La Villette, the Opera de la Bastille, and the new National Library are all part of today's Paris, living in harmony with the historic city. It is the combination of the two that gives Paris its unique place among the cities of the world.

At the center of Europe's largest urban agglomeration, Paris is a financial center and a center for intellectual, cultural, and technological creativity. Although a policy of decentralization has given a greater role to the regions, Paris remains the economic and financial capital of France, as well as its administrative center. Most of the major French corporations have their headquarters in Paris—Total, Vivendi-Universal, France Telecom, Renault, Alcatel—as do most of the large banks: BNP, Paribas, Crédit Agricole, Société Générale, and Crédit Lyonnaise. It is also the main center for insurance companies and the stock market.

The Parisian dominance of cultural and intellectual activities includes the publishing industry and large media groups.

Of course, the nation's great cultural institutions such as the Louvre and other museums are in Paristhe Comédie-Française, the Opera House, the national opera and ballet, and the symphony orchestras. There are ten universities in Paris and the *grands écoles*. The Académie française and the headquarters of France's main scientific research organization, the CNRS, are also in Paris.

Paris is also an international capital. The embassies of 140 countries are in the city, and the headquarters of two United Nations organizations—UNESCO and the OECD—along with the General Secretariat of the Francophonie, the agency promoting French language and culture internationally.

History of Paris

When the Romans conquered Paris in 55 B.C. it was a small Celtic fishing village inhabited by the Parisii tribe, on the Ile de la Cité, an island in the middle of the Seine River. In this area, known as Lutetia, a Roman settlement soon flourished and spread to the left bank of the river. Around 360, Lutetia changed its name to Paris. In 451 Sainte Geneviève galvanized the people of Paris to repel the attack of Attila the Hun. Clovis (481–511), leader of the Franks, defeated the Romans, and Paris became Christian and the center of their kingdom. During the Middle Ages the city flourished due to its position on a river crossing. It became an important center of political power and learning, focused on the Church, which dominated intellectual and spiritual life. Sorbonne University was created during this period, and architectural masterpieces such as Sainte-Chapelle were erected. Most people still lived on the left bank and the Ile de la Cité until the marshes (*marais*) were drained in the 12th century, allowing Paris to expand.

At the end of the Hundred Years War in 1453, Paris, which had been occupied by the English, lay in ruins. King Louis XI (1423–1483) brought back prosperity and a new interest in art and architecture, which continued in the 16th century under the influence of the Renaissance. The initial attempts at town planning were made with the construction of elegant buildings and open urban spaces such as the Place des Vosges, Renaissance churches, and the first bridges across the Seine, among them the Pont Notre Dame and the Pont Neuf (1589). In 1546 work commenced on the great palace of the Louvre, and the face of Paris continued to change through the 17th century, during the period of absolute monarchy. Louis XIV constructed his glittering palace at Versailles, and in Paris, imposing buildings, squares, theaters, and aristocratic hotels, such as the Hôtel des Invalides, were built. Paris in the Age of the Enlightenment (18th century) grew in population to about 650,000. The catacombs were established in 1785 as a more hygienic alternative to the cemeteries of Paris.

The streets of Paris saw the blood of the French Revolution, but Paris itself did not change much until Napoléon Bonaparte seized control in 1799. Napoléon left the city with two triumphal arches, the Arc de Triomphe and the Arc de Triomphe du Carrousel. His nephew, Napoléon III, in power from 1852 to 1870, was responsible for the transformation of Paris into the city that exists today. He entrusted the task of modernization to Baron Haussmann, who replaced the medieval slums with elegant avenues and boulevards. Haussmann improved the water supply, laid an underground sewerage system, and created large parks. The end of the century saw the construction of another great Paris landmark, the Eiffel Tower (1889).

Related Web links: paris.org, see *Maps of Paris* for historic maps (E); http://gallica.bnf.fr, see *Recherche* for documents including a photographic collection of Parisian monuments (F); oir.ucf.edu/wm/paris/hist for a history of key buildings (E); multimania.com/houze for Paris catacombs (E, F)

The Quarters of Paris

Although Paris can be geographically divided between its more well-known densely populated eastern *quartiers* and its more affluent western ones, it is more common to view the city according to the left and right banks of the Seine. Paris is divided into twenty *arrondissements*, or districts, which are identified by their number; for example, the 18th or the 6th. For Parisians, this immediately provides not only a geographical location, but the locale's features as well.

1. The right bank (*la rive droite*) comprises the *quartiers* of Chaillot, Champs-Elysées, Opera, Tuileries, Beaubourg and Les Halles, and the Marais. The *arrondissements* are 1 through 4, 8 through 12, and 16 through 20. The islands, Ile de la Cité and Ile Saint Louis, are considered to be part of the right bank.

2. The left bank (*la rive gauche*) comprises the *quartiers* of the Invalides and the Eiffel Tower, St.-Germain-des-Prés, the Latin Quarter, Luxembourg, Montparnasse, and the Jardin des Plantes. The *arrondissements* are 5, 6, 7, 13, 14, and 15.

The Right Bank

There is no older part of Paris than the boat-shaped islands of the Ile de la Cité and the Ile Saint Louis, which are connected to both the right and left banks by the famous Pont Neuf and other bridges. The islands were formerly the center of political and religious power. Today one can see the imposing architecture of the Palais de Justice and the glorious Gothic masterpieces of Notre Dame Cathedral and Sainte Chapelle.

The more affluent *quartiers* of Paris can be found on the right bank, as well as *les grands boulevards*, department stores, banks, and the Bourse (stock exchange). The Champs-Elysées, which links the Place de la Concorde and the Arc de Triomphe, is a major tourist location, lined with restaurants, cinemas, and luxury shops. It is also where the famous July 14 parade is held. To the north, on the heights on Montmartre, is the impressive white basilica of Sacré Coeur. The Montmartre *quartier* is still home to many artists.

The *quartier* around Place de la Bastille has become a notable recreation area for young people, boasting a large number of cafés, bars, and restaurants. The Marais is also in the 4th arrondissement. The *quartier* was officially declared an historical monument by de Gaulle in 1962, and restoration of the area was begun. Today it is extremely chic, full of galleries, boutiques, and gay bars, though it still has a Jewish presence from the garment industry. Two modern shopping districts are located in the Beaubourg and Les Halles *quartiers*, where the Pompidou Center completes the atmosphere of modernity.

Related Web links: allocine.fr/live for webcam of Champs-Elysées; pariserve.tm.fr, see *Paris vu du ciel* for an aerial view of city by quarter (E, F); proloc.com, see map of Paris by quarters; paris-france.org for plan of Paris (E); monum.fr for Arc de Triomphe (E, F)

The Left Bank

The left bank (*la rive gauche*) has traditionally had a bohemian reputation, which has attracted artists and musicians. Students are drawn to the area by the universities, libraries, galleries, bookshops, and art cinemas. Although such leading postwar intellectuals as Jean-Paul Sartre and Simone de Beauvoir no longer frequent its famous cafés, such as Les Deux Maggots and the Flore, St-Germain-des-Prés is still lively. It's the major publishing district of Paris, a center for interior design, and the location of many trendy fashion boutiques and antique shops. The Musée d'Orsay, originally a railway station, is now one of the most visited museums in Paris.

Next door to Saint Germain is the Latin Quarter, situated between the Seine and the Luxembourg Gardens. Since the Middle Ages this *quartier*, where the Sorbonne is located, has been a meeting place for students, intellectuals, and artists. It has also been the center for much of the city's political unrest. In 1871 the Place Saint Michel was the scene of the Paris Commune, and the May 1968 student uprisings began in the Sorbonne.

Many of France's national heroes are buried in the Panthéon near the Sorbonne, including Voltaire, Rousseau, Victor Hugo, Emile Zola, Jean Moulin, and Pierre and Marie Curie. Behind the Panthéon is one of Paris's oldest streets, the winding rue Mouffetard, where François Villon (1431–63) lived in the 15th century. Close by are the Luxembourg Gardens. On warm days it is filled with people walking or playing chess or *pétanque* under the chestnut trees. Bordering the park, to the south, is Mont-

parnasse. Its dominating—many would say obtrusive—architectural feature is the tallest modern office tower in Paris, the Tour Montparnasse, constructed in 1973. Formerly the haunt of artists and writers such as Picasso, Hemingway, Cocteau, Giacometti, Matisse, and Modigliani, the *quartier* still has a reputation for art and high living. Many famous French have chosen the Montparnasse cemetery as their final resting place. Maupassant, Baudelaire, Saint-Saëns, Sartre, Simone de Beauvoir, and Serge Gainsbourg are buried there.

One of the more tranquil *quartiers* of Paris is the Jardin des Plantes, named after the botanical gardens that were established there in the 18th century by the naturalist Count Buffon. Two renovated left bank *quartiers* are Masséna and Tolbiac, in the 13th arrondissement near the new National Library. Still under construction, apartments, office buildings, shops, schools, and a university are part of a controversial development known as the ZAC Rive Gauche, which aims to create a completely new urban area in an old part of Paris.

Related Web links: musee-orsay.fr is the official museum site (E, F); **smartweb.fr/fr/orsay/index .html** for Museé d'Orsay with 360-degree panoramas (F); **monum.fr** for Panthéon (E, F); **tourmontparnasse56.com** for Tour Montparnasse (E, F)

La Seine

In September 1998, for the first time in its history, Paris celebrated the river that is part of its unique identity. The fête de la Seine highlighted historic monuments and the river's value for relaxation and recreation, as well as its continuing use for transport and commerce. The Seine is the essential point of reference to the city: distances are measured from it, street numbers determined by it, and it divides the city into two distinct areas, the right bank on the northern side of the river, and the left bank on the southern side. Twenty-one miles of the Seine flows through Paris. Highways have been built along it, but one-third of its banks is reserved for pedestrians. Thirty-one bridges span the Seine. Most have a unique character of their own, from the oldest—the Pont Neuf (1589)—to the most ornate—the Pont Alexandre III (1900)—to the Pont des Arts, the first cast-iron bridge in Paris, built in 1904.

Practically every building or monument worth visiting in Paris is accessible via the Seine. The embankments (*quais*) are lined with elegant apartment buildings, great museums such as the Louvre and the Musée d'Orsay, and, on the Ile de la Cité, the cathedral of Notre Dame. The *quais* are a great place to stroll, to be a *flâneur* (stroller of the streets), and enjoy the beauty of Paris or browse for books at the many *bouquinists* (bookstalls) that line the parapets of the river wall.

Above all, the Seine is a living river, used as a means of transportation by Parisians. About 200,000 people a year use the *batobus* to move around Paris. For tourists, the *bateaux-mouches* or the *bateaux-vedettes* are the most famous sightseeing boats. Around 5 million tourists see the city from the river, making Paris the world's foremost tourist port.

The Seine is also still a working river, with barges loading and unloading millions of tons of cargo, removing garbage, and transporting construction materials. The quays and banks of the Seine were classified by UNESCO in 1991 as part of France's national heritage, and great effort has been put into conserving and giving back to the people of Paris this crucial aspect of their city.

Related Web links: smartweb.fr/fr/paris.index seine.html for 360-degree panoramas, history, bridges; batobus.com for an aerial view (E, F); bateaux-mouches.fr (E, F); jellesen.dk/webcrea/ places/paris/parismap.htm for photos, including Paris bridges (E)

PARIS
Four Monuments

Paris is a city of intense architectural variety and beauty, and some monuments in particular have come to symbolize it. The Eiffel Tower, of course, has become an icon not only of Paris, but also of France. Its image can be found on nearly every tourist brochure or advertisement. In fact, the tower was built as a temporary addition to the Paris skyline, to impress visitors to the Universal Exhibition of 1889. Designed by the engineer Gustave Eiffel (1832–1923), it was the world's tallest human-built structure until 1931, when New York's Empire State Building was completed. The complex pattern of pig-iron girders came from the need to stabilize the 1,050-foot tower in strong winds, but the overall design is aesthetically pleasing. From on high, on a clear day, it is possible to see 45 miles.

Overlooking Paris in Montmartre in the 18th arrondissement is the Sacré Coeur. Construction began on the basilica in 1875 after two Catholic businessman kept their vow to build a church dedicated to the Sacred Heart of Christ should Paris be spared from the Prussian attack that brought down the Second Empire in 1870. The architecture is inspired by the Romanesque church of Saint Front in Périgueux, in the Dordogne region of France. The basilica was completed in 1914, but not consecrated until 1919. The dome is the second-highest point in Paris.

On the island in the Seine stands a smaller replica of New York's Statue of Liberty, given to the people of Paris in 1885, the same year that the original, designed by Frédéric Bartholdi (1834–1904), departed in crates for New York. Not far away, on the bank of the Seine near the Place de l'Alma, is the Liberty Flame, an exact replica of the flame of the Statue of Liberty, a symbol of Franco-American friendship to celebrate the centennial (1887–1987) of the *International Herald Tribune* newspaper. Since the death of Princess Diana in 1997 in a high-speed car accident in the tunnel of the Pont de l'Alma, mourners have left messages and flowers on the Liberty Flame.

Not far from the Eiffel Tower, the Hôtel des Invalides and the église du Dôme (Dome Church) are impressive masterpieces of French classical architecture. Established by Louis XIV as a hospital and accommodation for military veterans, the Invalides, with its majestic 650-foot facade facing the Seine, was completed in 1676. Today it also houses an impressive War Museum. The church behind it, with its gilded towering dome, was designed by Jules Hardouin-Mansart. Originally intended to receive the tomb of the royal family, it became the final resting place of Napoléon, his son, his brothers, and other prominent military figures. In 1861, Napoléon's body, brought back from exile to the Invalides in 1840, was placed in an imposing red porphyry marble tomb in a monumental sunken crypt under the dome.

Related Web links: greatbuildings.com, see *Eiffel Tower* (E); **montmartrenet.com** for Sacré Coeur (E, F); **invalides.org** for Musée de l'Armée, Napoléon, Tomb (E, F)

The Villages of Paris

In the stressful world of Parisian apartment life, traffic jams, the crowded Metro, and city regulations, are small oases that have survived from another century: the villages of Paris. These *"mini-quartiers"* often surround a square or a market, and share a strong community spirit and the pleasures of secret gardens and specialist shops. Located all over Paris, each has its own character, but all hark back to another way of life, one that focused on the countryside village. The rising cost of housing in Paris has forced most of the original residents who gave the villages their character to move to less expensive places in the suburbs. But the new, more well-to-do residents have preserved the village atmosphere that attracted them to move there.

In the 3rd *arrondissement*, close to the Marais, there's a village located around a small square (Le Square du Temple). The people of this village watch the ducks on the small lake in the center of the square or chat with each other. Early in the morning the Chinese do their gymnastics. Later, mothers with their children—Africans, Moroccans, Yugoslavs, Portuguese, and Indians—arrive to play. Teenagers kick a soccer ball, and on sunny days people sun themselves or picnic. Hidden in the 13th is la Butte-aux-Cailles, a village of workers' houses with small vegetable gardens and paved streets. Called "little Montmartre," The workers themselves are gone, having been replaced in the last 20 years by professionals and artists, and at night this village comes alive as they fill its bars and restaurants. The Butte's historic swimming pool still survives, as well as bistros that put on puppet shows for the local children.

Auteil, in the 16th *arrondissement*, was a village outside Paris until the transformation of the city by Baron Haussmann. The southern section of this *quartier* has two types of houses. Company executives live in large houses (*maisons de campagne*) surrounded by private gardens, and the former houses of the Renault factory workers, with their small gardens, have become homes for office workers. They all meet and shop at the open air market on the Avenue de Versailles. Nearby, ultramodern buildings house the TV stations TF1, Canal, and France 2.

On the other side of Paris, to the east, in the 20th *arrondissement* and close to the highway (*boulevard périphérique*) that encircles Paris, is an oasis perched on top of a hill. It consists of only a few streets, with red brick houses built by workers after World War I and small gardens. This corner of Paris has also become the address of well-known artists and stage performers.

Related Web links: infres.enst.fr/~premiere /butte for a virtual game around la Butte-aux-Cailles (F)

Parisians

Parisians have a reputation for believing they are superior to all non-Parisians, in France and throughout the world. Their candid opinions about the virtues of life in Paris strike many outsiders as undisguised arrogance. The stereotypical Parisian sees the entire world as revolving around Paris and awaiting its judgments before adopting new fashions and attitudes. The beautiful atmosphere of light that bathes the city in spring and fall, and the elegant nightly illumination of Parisian monuments and historic facades, have given birth to the expression *la ville lumière* (City of Light); non-Parisians scoff that Parisians commonly misinterpret the expression as referring to the intellectual and cultural enlightenment that Paris bestows on the world.

Many Parisians maintain strong links with country regions from which their families came. The wealthy of the *beaux quartiers* (upper-class neighborhoods) can escape to their weekend country houses, but the working and middle classes must content themselves with Sunday afternoons walking the streets, sitting in cafés, and using the public parks or the two huge forest and garden areas, situated on either side of Paris: the bois de Boulogne in the west and the bois de Vincennes in the southeast. There is a growing trend for some couples with children to leave the stress of the capital to work in large regional towns, which offer a higher quality of family life. However, Parisians, like the French in general, make career moves to other cities and regions less readily than Americans. There is more social mobility

today among "chic" Parisians, with the old distinction between the affluent *quartiers* and the poorer ones rapidly fading as people search for affordable housing that can be renovated to modern tastes.

Paris is home to many immigrant groups, mostly from its former colonies. The largest is the North African community, consisting of people from Algeria, Tunisia, and Morocco. There is also a strong black African community from Mali, Senegal, Zaire, the Ivory Coast, and Mauritius. Many immigrants have come from the former colonies of Cambodia and Vietnam in Indochina. In addition, the open borders between European Union countries have brought residents from other European countries to Paris. Some *quartiers*, or even streets, have come to be identified with the culture of particular national groups: part of the 18th, on the southeastern side of Montmartre and called *la goutte d'or*, is North African and African; in the 9th, the rue des Martyrs is described as the "new Athens"; Indians and Pakistanis have their corner in the 10th, particularly in an arcade called the Passage Brady; while for the Indochinese, it is the 13th, around the Porte d'Italie. The presence of these different communities enriches Paris and strengthens its cosmopolitan appeal. While the French believe strongly in assimilation into the French way of life, they also appreciate the riches of other cultures.

Shopping

The image of Paris in the world is often that of a leader in fashion and taste, in cuisine, clothes, perfumes, accessories, and interior design. Luxury shops in historic surroundings, and colorful food and flea markets selling the unusual or the bizarre, come to mind when people think about shopping in Paris.

Shopping as a pastime and commercial activity began in Paris in the early 19th century with the shopping arcades (*galeries* or *passages*). Many have survived, the most famous being the Passage des Panoramas, located between Boulevard Montmartre and the rue Saint Marc. In the 20th century the arcades fell into disuse but were revamped in the 1970s. They now house an eclectic mixture of boutique shops. In the second half of the 19th century the first department stores (*grands magasins*) opened in Paris; on the right bank of the Seine in 1855, Bazar de l'Hôtel de Ville (BHV); in 1865, Au Printemps; in 1870, Samaritaine; and in 1898, Les Galeries Lafayette. On the left bank, Au Bon Marché opened in 1852. They are all still trading today. Au Bon Marché was the first store to give customers open access to the merchandise, to set fixed prices, and to offer home delivery. Its innovations in retail trading and display inspired Emile Zola's popular novel *Au Bonheur des Dames* (1883). For today's bargain shoppers there is the Tati chain of department stores, and for cultural purchases there's FNAC, specializing in books, music, and information technology.

Certain areas of Paris have become famous for fashion, like the rue du Faubourg Saint-Honoré and the avenue Montaigne, with stores such as Fauchon and, for gourmet food shopping, Hediard, behind the Madelaine Church. For bread, chocolate, charcuterie, cheeses, and wine there are specialty shops all over Paris. Parisians will often shop daily at their local open-air food market, in order to get the freshest possible produce. These markets, full of colors and tempting smells, contribute to making the streets of Paris full of life and interest. The city is also well-known for its flea markets, which sell a range of secondhand clothes, objets d'art, and antiques. Buyers are expected to haggle over the price, and treasures are still to be found. The most famous Paris flea market is the marché aux Puces de Saint-Ouen, in the 18th arrondissement.

Chain stores such as Monoprix and Prisunic flourish in most towns. Shopping centers (*grandes surfaces*) and supermarkets (*hypermarchés*) like Carrefour, Géant, and Auchan on the outskirts of larger cities are increasingly popular. Because of their huge selections, cheaper prices, and ample parking they have led to the demise of small shops in nearby areas.

Related Web links: les-puces.com for a description of *marchés* and goods at *aux Puces* (E, F); printemps.fr (F), glparis.com (Galeries Lafayette) (F), bhv.fr (Bazar de Hôtel de Ville) (F), lasamaritaine.com (E, F), monoprix.fr, carrefour.fr, auchan.fr (F); fnac.fr (F); frenchfashion.com for a directory of designs and outlets; paris.org/Shops is a shopping guide (E)

PHILOSOPHY
Analytical Skills

French philosopher René Descartes (1596–1650) postulated that intellect is humanity's distinguishing characteristic. This could serve as a definition of what the French, who take pride in being universal in their thinking and rational in their behavior, think of themselves. *Je pense, donc je suis* (I think, therefore I am): Descartes's use of reasoning to discover the basic truth of man's existence began the analytical tradition known as Cartesian logic, which established the principles of the search for truth, objectivity, and the principle of noncontradiction. Voltaire (1694–1778) and other 18th-century philosophers of the Age of Enlightenment subjected all fields of social and political endeavor to critical inquiry based on Cartesian principles.

This form of rationalism, known as the *esprit géometrique* (geometric mind) has been the dominant strand in French intellectual traditions. In contrast to the "geometric mind" is the "subtle mind" (*l'esprit de finesse*), first posed by the French philosopher and mathematician Blaise Pascal (1623–62), who proclaimed the relativity of all truth and privileged the idea of experimentation. More recently, a unique amalgam of the analytical rigor of the scientific method and intuition was made by the eminent intellectual and philosopher, Paul Valéry (1871–1945), who spent his life reflecting on the functioning of the human mind. He filled 30,000 pages with his observations in his *Cahiers* (*Notebooks*).

The Cartesian influence can be seen in many aspects of French life. A young child who misbehaves is told to be *raisonnable* (reasonable). Schools practice a rational approach to learning and stress the ability to memorize, think clearly, and discuss abstract ideas. High intellectual performance is valued above sporting or civic achievements. The final high school examination, *le baccalauréat*, includes philosophy as a subject and emphasizes rhetorical skills and deductive reasoning.

It has been said that the French prefer the exchange of ideas and lengthy discussion about the theoretical principles of a project before acting upon them. Reflected in the educational system, this characteristic is criticized as favoring the intellectual over the practical approach. Taken further, critics say it has restricted France's development in industry, commerce, and technology; that more pragmatic peoples achieve consensus more efficiently, because French discussions bring about ideological conflicts that delay decision making. In response, it's argued that by daring to be different, and by challenging solutions based on mere expediency, the French have a positive influence on the way the world thinks. In fact, the French are proud of *la clarté française* (French clear thinking) that infiltrates all aspects of their lives. Combined with their insistence on the liberty and dignity of all mankind, it produces an *art de vivre* (way of living) that is uniquely French.

Philosophical Heritage

Many of the modern founders of Western philosophical traditions are French. René Descartes, in his *Discourse de la méthode*, presented the principles of scientific thinking, asserting that the only truths are based on free intellectual inquiry and reason and not on the authority of dogma or tradition. In his ethical works, he stressed the concept of *le libre arbitre* (moral freedom), stating that the mind can think as it chooses, make decisions, and exercise unlimited willpower.

Blaise Pascal was a child prodigy who became a brilliant mathematician and physicist and then gave up his scientific career to devote himself to religion. In *Pensées*, his religious meditations, he contrasts the insignificance of man with the limitless world of the stars and galaxies. But man has one quality, he says, which is denied to the whole physical universe: man alone knows that he exists and is capable of reflecting on the meaning of his life.

The rationalism of Descartes flowered during the 18th century, known as the Age of Enlightenment. The philosophers of this *siècle des lumières* developed and employed the scientific method to call into question traditional assumptions about religion, morality, and the monarchy. From this was born their optimism in the progress of freedom, tolerance, and social justice. Baron de Montesquieu in *L'Esprit des lois* (*The Spirit of the Laws*) concluded that dividing political power among the legislature, the executive, and the judiciary, each acting as a check on the others, is the best guarantor of freedom for a nation's citizens. This "separation of power" had a powerful influence on the framing of the American constitution.

Voltaire (1694–1778) was a poet, playwright, popularizer of science, political theorist, and a brilliant propagandist. A passionate believer in freedom, he hated tyranny, all forms of religious intolerance and fanaticism, and all manifestations of man's inhumanity to man, among them slavery, torture, and imprisonment without a just trial. Denis Diderot (1713–84) edited the vast *Encyclopédie* that summarized the discoveries resulting from the use of the new scientific method in the fields of science and technology, philosophy, politics, economics, history, literature, and the arts. His purpose was to develop a new freedom of thought in its readers.

Jean-Jacques Rousseau (1712–78) went against this grain of French rationalism. He rejected the absolute belief in reason, saying it had stifled man's instinct and emotions. In *Le Contrat Social* he proposed the model of democracy in which freedom and democracy were the fundamental rights of every individual, and in which society was governed by the general will of the people. Rousseau's model was the basis of the democratic principles of the French Revolution.

Related Web links: culture.com.au/brain_proj /descarte.htm for Descartes (E); http://plato .stanford.edu/entries/descartes-epistemology for Descartes's epistemology (E); wabash.edu /rousseau presents Rousseau links, including his works (E); http://abu.cnam.fr/BIB/auteurs/ for works by Diderot, Pascal, Rousseau, Voltaire (F)

Modern Philosophy

Philosophy in the second half of the 19th century remained under the influence of Auguste Comte (1798–1857), who is also considered the founder of sociology. Comte developed his science of "positivism" in *Cours de philosophie positive* (1830–42), which provided an ethical and moral basis for predicting and evaluating social progress. Hippolyte Taine (1828–93) and Ernest Renan (1823–92) became the advocates of a variation of rationalism called *scientisme*.

It was also in the 19th century that socialism developed from a philosophy into a political ideology. The first socialist thinkers included Saint-Simon (1760–1825) and Pierre-Joseph Proudhon (1809–65), whose *What Is Property?* states that only free credit and the disappearance of capitalist profit will put an end to social injustice. Frédéric Blanqui (1805–81) was one of the leaders of the Revolution of 1848, and Flora Tristan (1803–44) spoke out for women. Toward the end of the century the philosopher Henry Bergson (1859–1941) opposed positivism by examining the process of thought and concluding that perception was a more immediate and basic source of understanding. He attempted to prove that all evolution and progress are due to the action of *l'élan vital* (the life force).

The debate between rationalism and science, on the one hand, and spirituality and humanism, on the other, continued in the 20th century. The Catholic philosopher Emmanuel Mounier (1905–50) edited the journal *Esprit* (*Spirit*), which emphasized the "engagement" of the human being. Existentialism and its most persuasive proponent, Jean-Paul Sartre, had immense influence after World War II. A reaction against classical rationalism and Bergson, existentialism rejected the idea of God and absolute moral values and painted a picture of man living in an absurd world. The only genuine values, the existentialists said, were those created by each individual exercising freedom of choice and action. In this philosophy, human life in itself has no "higher" meaning. Michel Foucault (1926–84) rejected existentialism and developed his philosophy, often labeled "structural," by an historical analysis of power: how human thought and behavior is constructed by social institutions and ideologies. In the late 1970s the *nouveaux philosophes* (new philosophers) like Bernard-Henri Levy (1948–) attacked Communist ideology. Modern France has a rich intellectual life in diverse domains such as anthropology (Claude Lévi-Strauss), psychoanalysis and linguistics (Jacques Lacan), semiotics (Roland Barthes), social sciences (Pierre Bourdieu), literary analysis (Jacques Derrida), and the history of science (Michel Serres).

Related Web links: multimania.com/clotilde on Comte and Positivism (F); **france.diplomatie.fr/ culture/france/biblio/** see *Auteurs* for Descartes, Saint-Simon, Lévi-Strauss (F); **http://perso .wanadoo.fr/jean-pierre.proudhon** for Pierre-Joseph Proudhon (F); **thecry.com/existentialism /sartre** for an overview and links to Sartre (E); **theory.org.uk/foucault** is a guide to Foucault (E)

The Skeleton of France

France is a tightly organized nation with three levels of administration. The smallest administrative unit is the *commune*, of which there are 36,000 in France. Each *commune* has a municipal council, which elects a mayor (*le maire*). In June 2000, in response to the under-representation of women in politics, the French Parliament adopted la Loi sur la parité. It requires *communes* with more than 3,500 inhabitants to present equal numbers of male and female candidates in municipal elections. Today, women make up 47.5 present of the councilors in France but only 6.93 percent of the mayors. As a result of the law aimed at ensuring greater parity, the 2001 municipal elections generated 3,956 female mayoral candidates from across the 36,680 communes, which resulted in 1,010 more female mayors than in 1995, the date of the previous elections.

The *communes* are grouped in 96 *départements*, whose head is a *préfet* (or *préfète*, if a woman)—a commissioner appointed by the national government. The chief city (*chef-lieu*) of each *département* houses the *préfet* and the administrative offices.

The *département*, a product of the Revolution, has been an important administrative unit since then. The division of the France into *départements* of approximately equal size made it easier for Paris to manage the nation and impose a uniform culture on the people. This was the beginning of the special feature of the French administrative system: its centralization in Paris.

In 1960 the 95 *départements* were grouped into 21 *régions*, because it was thought that the larger grouping was limiting the development of broader economic policies. This number was increased to 22 in 1976 with the creation of the Ile-de-France region around Paris. The administrative head of the region is a *préfet* (or *préfète*) *de région*, also appointed from Paris. Each region has an elected Conseil régional (Regional Council) whose offices are in the *ville principale*, or chief city. In 1982 a law enhancing regionalization was passed granting these councils greater independence in implementing policies for regional development.

The regional grouping of *départements* brought together areas that share cultural, linguistic, or historical backgrounds. The names of the regions correspond to those of the provinces that covered similar areas before the 1789 Revolution; for example, Picardie, Bourgogne (Burgundy), Auvergne, Provence-Alpes–Côte d'Azur.

When it comes to identity, studies show that roughly 40 percent of the French identify most strongly with France, another 25 percent identify primarily with their region, 20 percent with their town, and 15 percent with Europe. The increasing economic unification of the member countries of the European Union has created economic bonds across Europe. Regions such as the Rhône-Alpes and Lyon, for example, have ties to Barcelona and Spain.

Related Web links: lesservices.service-public.fr for national and local office holders (F)

Decentralization

If the *communes*, *départements*, and *régions* make up the skeleton of France, then Paris is the pulsating heart of the nation. The constitution states that France is a republic "United and Indivisible," a tenet that has ensured the supremacy of the national legislature and a highly centralized administration. All major decisions are made in the capital. Attempts by militants in Brittany or Occitanie to develop autonomous local institutions, for example, were viewed by the government as an attack on the founding principles of the Republic. Paris dominates the country, and the Parisians, with less and less justification, consider themselves superior to the "provincials."

The revolts and strikes of May 1968 infused the nation with a spirit of liberation and calls for social reform, including greater decentralization. In 1982 the Socialist government of François Mitterrand put into effect a reformist program that introduced direct universal suffrage for regional councils. The program also and gave the regions power to make certain financial and local policy decisions without authorization from Paris or the government appointed *préfet de région*. But despite the reforms, Paris continues to exert a strong influence on all aspects of French life; the centralizing attitude that established its administrative, political, economic, and cultural preeminence has been entrenched for centuries.

Among the most fervent supporters of decentralization are Bretons, Basques, Occitans, Alsatians, and those regions that share their border with neighboring European regions. Their objective is to preserve their regional culture.

The violent actions of Corsican nationalists in the late 1990s put decentralization back on the political agenda. In 1999 the government of Lionel Jospin set up a "commission for decentralization" in an attempt to put in place a more legitimate, effective, and coherent program. In 2000 the Jospin government granted Corsica a limited degree of self-determination. This decision was strongly criticized by opponents, including President Chirac, who claimed that it would destroy the indivisibility of the French Republic.

In spite of these steps toward decentralization, a long road lies ahead to implement effectively regional policies and to overcome two centuries of centralized traditions. Parisian centralists can point to the many national benefits that have resulted from state planning and control, such as the Euro Tunnel under the English Channel, the nuclear power grid, and the Train à grande vitesse (TGV).

> **Related Web links: dgcl.interieur.gouv.fr/ index.html** is a Ministry of Interior site for decentralization (F); **manca-naziunale.org** (F) and **corsica-nazione.com** (E, F) for Corsica independence groups

Government Institutions

France is currently in its Fifth Republic, founded in 1958 by Charles de Gaulle (1890–1970). It is a presidential regime in which voters elect the president in a direct national vote, elect a National Assembly for five-year terms, and vote at other times for councils of their region and locality and for French representatives in the European Parliament. An electoral college elects a Senate for nine-year terms. In a referendum in 2000 the French voted to reduce the presidential term from seven to five years, the same duration for both the executive and legislative powers.

The prime minister is selected from the majority party in the National Assembly by the president. The prime minister then appoints a government (a set of ministers) with the president's approval and runs the country according to the political program of the majority in the National Assembly. The members of the government don't have to be elected members of the National Assembly or even belong to the prime minister's party. When the president and the prime minister are from different parties, they must agree to cooperate according to the functions of their office as defined in the constitution. This arrangement is called *cohabitation*. As head of state, the president has considerable powers, in addition to responsibility for foreign policy and defense, but is expected to leave the day-to-day running of the country to the prime minister and the government.

The first president of the Fifth Republic, Charles de Gaulle, held office from 1958 to 1969. His mission was to restore the grandeur of France, and his office was marked by the liberation of the French colonies of Africa and the student revolts of May 1968. The next president was Georges Pompidou (1969–74), and he mainly followed in de Gaulle's footsteps but gave more attention to economic policy and was more open to the construction of Europe. The third president, Valéry Giscard d'Estaing (1974–81), was more of a reformist. The oil crisis of 1973 introduced a period of economic austerity during his term. The first Socialist to be elected president was François Mitterrand, who held office for two terms, from 1981 to 1995. In his first term, Mitterrand undertook many social reforms, but unemployment continued to increase and further economic austerity was necessary. Mitterrand's second term focused on foreign policy and, in particular, the construction of the European Union. In 1995 the Gaullist Jacques Chirac was elected president. After his seven-year term concludes in 2002, future presidents will serve five-year terms.

The official residence of the president in Paris is le palais de l'Elysée and the prime minister's is l'Hôtel Matignon. The National Assembly sits at le Palais Bourbon and the Senate at le Palais de Luxembourg. The press often refers to elected officials by the names of their official residences.

Related Web links: elysee.fr is the official president site, including a virtual visit, gallery of presidents, presidential residences (E, F); **premier-ministre.gouv.fr**, **assemblee-nationale .fr**, **senat.fr** are the official sites for the prime minister, National Assembly, and Senate (E, F)

Political Life

French political life is structured around the opposition between right and left. This opposition originates from as far back as the Revolution of 1789, when the aristocracy and the clergy of the Ancien Régime opposed the revolutionaries who stood for liberty, equality, and fraternity.

The right has traditionally been composed of conservative parties concerned with security, stability, and protecting the French identity. The two main parties of the right are the Rassemblement pour la République (Rally for the Republic)—the descendant of the Gaullist party—and the Union pour la démocratie française (Union for French democracy), which is an alliance of parties of the center-right.

The left has traditionally comprised parties concerned with social reform. The two main parties of the left are the Parti socialiste (Socialist party), which has an agenda of social justice and the defense of liberties, and the Parti communiste français (French Communist party), which until the 1980s aligned itself with Soviet communism and the class struggle. The general improvement in the living standards of the diminishing working class led to the decline of the PCF in the 1990s.

Despite the firm foundations of the left-right axis in France, in recent years the barriers between the two have begun to dissolve. In 1986, French politics entered a period of *cohabitation*. President François Mitterrand was Socialist, but the majority of his newly elected parliament was right-leaning. This was to happen again in 1993 and also in 1997, this time with a right president (Jacques Chirac) and a left prime minister (Lionel Jospin). The cycle of *cohabitation* and the diminishment of traditional right-left ideologies in favor of pragmatic economic policies have made French politics increasingly centrist.

In response to the trend toward centrism, two radical parties emerged: the ultranationalist and racist Front National, led by Jean-Marie Le Pen; and the left-leaning Greens movement, les Verts. Both parties enjoyed great popularity in the 1990s, with the FN receiving 15 percent of the votes in the presidential elections of 1995 and 18 percent in 2002, and the Greens getting close to 15 percent in the regional elections of 1992. Since then, the Greens joined with the main parties of the left to form a coalition government, *la gauche plurielle* (the plural left), with the Socialists after the National Assembly elections in 1997.

The political behavior of the French has also changed. Since the mid-1980s the passion for political ideas that has always characterized the French has apparently cooled. The number of people who do not to vote has soared, and political participation has plummeted. Social and cultural developments have left the public disenchanted with outdated debates between the traditional parties of the right and left.

Related Web links: pcf.fr (Communist party), parti-socialiste.fr, rpr.asso.fr, udf.org (Nouvelle Union pour la démocratie française), front-national.com, les-verts.org (Greens), are political party sites (F)

The Green Movement

The Green movement did not develop a social base in France until the late 1980s. It grew out of the student revolt of May 1968 as a protest movement, but the 1974 oil crisis and the resulting economic crisis of the late 1970s and 1980s relegated the movement to a minor role in the French political dialogue. Part of the government's response to France's energy crisis and lack of oil and other natural energy resources was to develop nuclear energy, and the strategy enjoyed wide public support, further weakening the Green movement's appeal.

Several events of the late 1980s galvanized French concern over environmental issues, and French attitudes shifted dramatically. In 1986 the Chernobyl nuclear reactor disaster threatened Europe with nuclear fallout. French media, like media around the world, also focused attention on the recently discovered gap in the ozone layer, the greenhouse effect, acid rain, and the destruction of the Amazon rain forest. And a number of oil tanker accidents polluted stretches of the French coastline. These brought the Greens and their environmental program to the forefront. The Green parties polled 14.4 percent of the votes in the 1992 regional elections, but at least some of that total could be attributed to public disillusionment with the traditional political parties. In the 1995 presidential elections, the Green candidate, Dominique Voynet, polled 3.3 percent of the votes. Since the Parliamentary elections in 1996, the Green party, led by Voynet, has been an influential part of the governing coalition with the Socialist and Communist parties.

Young people, senior managers, and the self-employed are the most concerned about the environment in France. To varying degrees, the French feel that action must be taken concerning air pollution (59%), water pollution (39%), waste management and nuclear risk (20%), safeguarding plants and animals (17%), protecting the countryside (13%), and noise pollution (12%). Two-thirds of the French oppose continued construction of nuclear power plants, and 48 percent believe that drinkable water will one day be unavailable.

To combat pollution of their cities an overwhelming number of the French favor the development of public transportation (96%), creation of obligatory parking at the entry to towns, with a shuttle bus service (93%), reduction of space reserved for cars at the expense of other modes of transportation (90%), and creation of collective taxi services (75%). Sixty percent favor banning diesel-engine cars in town centers, 45 percent want alternate traffic circulation all year, 41 percent want all cars banned from town centers, and 9 percent favor installation of a toll (*péage*) at the entry to towns.

Related Web links: **les-verts.org** for the Greens (F); **environnement.gouv.fr**, see *Dossiers* on battle against pollution, water, nature, the countryside, and so on (F); **onf.fr** for the National Forestry Office (F)

Taking to the Streets

Social change in France is often the end product of collective action. The most common course is to take to the streets to express one's grievances, known in French as *le ras-le-bol*. The expression *Ras-le-bol!* means "Enough is enough!" The rallying cry before a demonstration is *Descendons dans la rue!* (Take to the streets!).

The French attach great importance to the right of citizens to voice their opinions and be heard by the authorities. Social protest lies at the heart of revolutionary ideology, and as such it has become a tradition. It was collective action that ended the Ancien Régime and thus paved the way for the founding of the French Republic. The legacy of this revolutionary past is the general belief that demonstrations (*manifestations*) enliven and enrich democratic life. The causes of demonstrations (*manifs*) are countless. Some are organized by political parties expressing opposition or support for a government proposal. Others are led by workers demanding change. Still others are expressions of solidarity with particular social groups, such as the unemployed, or third world countries.

Demonstrations have allowed students to gain political leverage. In May 1968 university students took to the streets and set up revolutionary barricades to protest overcrowded classes and an antiquated education system. Violent clashes erupted between the riot police and the students. The demonstrations turned into a national strike when workers joined the students in sympathy. The nation remained in turmoil for three weeks, until the government finally capitulated to the protesters' demands. Since then, governments have often preferred to give in to student demands.

Despite low membership, French trade unions are still capable of seriously disrupting and even paralyzing the nation with strikes (*les grèves*). The start of the new working year in September, after the summer vacation, has become an annual hot spot on the political calendar for conflict between unions and the government. The end of 1995 has become a reference date for successful union action. A national strike by rail workers, to protect their social benefits, was supported by other public sector employees. For more than three weeks the French had to survive without trains, and the national economy deteriorated because so many people could not get to work. The government was forced to give in to the unions to get France back to work.

In France, in contrast to the United States, the farmers have unions too. In fact, the farmers' unions are among the most active in organizing demonstrations, usually against the agricultural policy of the European Union.

Related Web links: lesgreves.com for reports on current strikes (F); **confederationpaysanne.fr** and **fnsea.fr** are farmer union sites (F)

Women Leaders

The first woman prime minister of France, Edith Cresson, appointed by the Socialist president, François Mitterrand, only held the position for 11 months (1991–92), failing to win popular support for her policies. Previously, the only woman who had a high national profile was the conservative politician Simone Veil, a survivor of the Nazi concentration camps. As Minister for Health, she persuaded a male-dominated Parliament to vote for the legalization of abortion in 1975. She later became the first President of the European Parliament (1979–82).

Women took a much higher profile in public life with the election of the left-wing government in 1997. In Prime Minister Jospin's 1997 cabinet, eight of the 27 ministers were women. Martine Aubry, Minister of Employment and Solidarity, was number two in the cabinet; Elisabeth Guigou, Minister of Justice, was number three; and Dominique Voynet, leader of the Greens, was Minister for Regional Development. In 1999 the Jospin government had the French constitution modified to include the principle of parity (*la parité*): an equal number of men and women in the lists of candidates proposed by political parties for municipal and national elections.

In 1999 the largest conservative party, the neo-Gaullist RPR, elected a woman, Michèle Alliot-Marie, as its president. In 1999, a French woman, Nicole Fontaine, was elected president of the European Parliament. Nicole Notat became the first woman to lead a union when she was elected leader of the CFDT in 1992, the second largest trade union.

Women have not had the same success in being appointed to top management positions. In 1999 only eight women (2 percent) were CEOs of the 400 largest French companies, and three of them were CEOs for branches of American companies (Coca-Cola, Colgate Palmolive, and General Electric).

Annette Roux was the head of the boat-building family company Bénéteau, the largest of its type in the world, and Philipine de Rothschild was the head of the Rothschild wine company. The first woman appointed to direct a French state industrial company, Cogema, was Anne Lauvergeon. And in 1999 a married mother of two, Christine Lagarde, 43 years old, became the first woman president of the largest American international legal firm, Baker and McKenzie.

Marianne Grunberg-Manago, a molecular biologist, was the first woman elected president of the Academy of Sciences in 1995. Claudie André-Deshays was the first French woman astronaut in 1996, on board the Russian *Mir* space station. In 1999, Catherine Cesarsky was appointed to head the European Space Agency.

Nathalie Sarraute (1900–99) was the fifth women writer, after Colette (1873–1954), George Sand (1804–76), Madame de Sévigné (1626–1696), and Marguerite Yourcenar (1903–87), to be given the ultimate distinction of having her collected works published in the prestigious Gallimard edition La Pléiade.

A Woman's Lot

The traditional French role for the man was as the breadwinner and the one with the power and authority to make all family decisions. In the working classes many women have always worked. (Traditionally, their husbands gave them their pay packets and they were responsible for the family budget.) In all classes, women were responsible for supervising the children's education.

On average, French women still do 80 percent of the housework, and men only 20 percent. But the increased number of women in the workforce, combined with greater financial and reproductive independence, has influenced family life, and the role of men is changing. Household and family duties are now shared more often, despite the fact that French men, like those of Mediterranean Europe, have been slower than men in Northern Europe to share these chores with their wives.

A recent survey revealed that on weekdays 76 percent of mothers and 14 percent of fathers did the cooking, and during the weekend 65 percent of mothers and 24 percent of fathers. In another survey, 40 percent of the respondents cited ironing as the most unpleasant household chore, followed by vacuuming (14%), meal preparation (13%), dishwashing (12%), and doing laundry (6%).

To balance their working life and their family life, 67 percent of the women in the Paris region with two or more children have no personal leisure time. Among proposals for making this "double life" easier to manage, the most popular are to adapt the system of part-time work to the requirements of family life and to increase the availability of child-care centers, as well as operating child-care centers with more flexible hours. Almost one-third of French children under 11 have some form of paid child care, and the government reimburses parents for part of this expense in generous family subsidies to increase the birthrate.

The need to help women who want to work is likely to be even more pressing in the future. An increasing percentage of upper-class women continue their studies with an eye toward a career in management, like men. In 1972 a law established equal salaries for men and women, and in 1974 a ministerial post for women's affairs (Secrétariat d'état de la condition féminine). Françoise Giroud assumed the post and proposed that for biological reasons women should seek equivalent rather than identical status with men.

Interestingly, French women, in winning equal status with men as far as employment is concerned, have not suffered from the stigma attached to many successful Anglo-Saxon businesswomen, who are often viewed as less feminine and more aggressive. Indeed, French women, at least to foreign observers, seem to have maintained their reputation for femininity and fashionable appearance.

Male chauvinist attitudes that are slower to change in many aspects of daily life are not as evident in intellectual discussions in France, where women's opinions receive the same respect as men's. Men and women from the same social class treat each other as intellectually equal, and discussions are mutual.

The PACS

The Pacte civil de solidarité (PACS) confers a legal status on nonmarried couples, giving them many of the rights and obligations that were previously only available to married couples. The PACS law was passed on November 15, 1999, after almost 13 months of political deliberation. Like all major social changes, the new law was the result of the influence of lobby groups, a complicated political process, and a passionate and sometimes violent public debate. Many people in favor of the law thought that their opponents' reaction was excessive, especially since PACS is essentially a fiscal document. But the symbolic aspect of the law recognizing unmarried couples was the real controversy.

Practically speaking, the PACS law provides for the creation of a pact between two people. This pact can be established between two friends, by a homosexual or heterosexual couple, or even between the members of a family (under certain conditions). After concluding this pact, two signatories—the *pacsé(e)s*—have access to certain rights and benefits previously only accorded to married couples.

In effect, PACS modified several legislative instruments (particularly the Civil Code, the Social Security Code, the Taxation Code, and the Employment Code) to extend the rights that these laws provide to those who have entered a PACS agreement. It relates mostly to financial arrangements such as taxation, inheritance, and succession and was not intended to accord parenting rights to its signatories.

In addition to the rights that PACS confers upon its signatories, it also includes obligations with which they must comply. The statute explains that members of a PACS agreement owe each other "practical and mutual assistance and support."

In essence, PACS accords legal recognition to couples previously denied such recognition. This is perhaps most significant for homosexual couples, whose relationship status was formerly ignored by the state, thus limiting their access to various rights and services.

The opponents of this law claimed that the institution of marriage and the moral standards of the nation were being dealt a fatal blow. However, statistics produced on the first anniversary of PACS showed that the number of PACS agreements signed was much lower than expected.

According to the recently amended Code du Travail, it is illegal in France to discriminate against someone in the workplace because of his or her sexuality. PACS was a further legislative achievement relating to homosexual rights.

The Gay Pride march held in June each year in Paris is a major event. In 2001, 500,000 people participated. The election in 2001 of the new mayor of Paris, Bertrand Delanoe, who had publicly declared his homosexuality during his electoral campaign, signaled a greater acceptance of homosexuals in France.

Related Web links: chez.com/obspacs is a pro-PACs site (F); **http://vpacs.ooups.net** for online virtual PACs agreement (F); **generations-famille.com** is an anti-PACs site (F)

Early Scientific Thinkers

The relationship between science and philosophical thought among the French ensured that scientific and arithmetic discovery in France would be firmly rooted in what came to be known as Cartesian logic. The French tradition of scientific research was formally established in 1666 when the Académie des Sciences was founded by Louis XIV.

Seventeenth-century France produced three great mathematicians: René Descartes (1596–1650), Blaise Pascal (1623–62), and Pierre de Fermat (1601–65). By expressing geometric form in terms of algebraic equations, Descartes established algebraic geometry. Pascal and Fermat did fundamental work on differential calculus and on the theory of probability.

In the 18th century Adrian Legendre (1752–1833) worked on partial differential equations and elliptic functions, and Louis de Lagrange (1736–1813) discovered the calculus of variations. Joseph Fourier (1768–1830) invented a method of analysis applicable to wave motions used in the study of electricity, light, sound, and heat. A committee of the Académie des Sciences established the metric system in 1790. Augustin Cauchy (1789–1857) developed the theory of functions of a complex variable. The great mathematician of the late 19th century was Jules Henri Poincaré (1854–1912), one of the pioneers of the relativity of space and time.

Blaise Pascal also made an important contribution to physics. "Pascal's Principle" is one of the basic laws concerning the equilibrium of liquids, and Pascal discovered the principle of the hydraulic press.

André-Marie Ampère (1775–1836) established the laws of force between a magnet and a constant electric current, thus founding the science of electrodynamics. And Nicolas Sadi Carnot (1796–1832) laid the foundations of thermodynamics through his research on the steam engine.

Two well-known names in French chemistry are Antoine Lavoisier (1743–94), who founded modern chemistry as we know it today, and Joseph Gay-Lussac (1778–1850), who discovered the law of expansion of gases by heat.

In the Renaissance period, Jean Fernel (1497–1558) made one of the earliest attempts to classify diseases, and Ambroise Paré (1510–90) was a pioneer in surgery. René Laënnec (1781–1826) was the first to develop the technique of auscultation to diagnose internal disorders, and he invented the stethoscope. The physiologist Claude Bernard (1813–78), who founded experimental medicine, demonstrated that indigestion is not restricted to the stomach. Around the same time, Louis Pasteur (1822–95), chemist and microbiologist, discovered that fermentation is caused by microorganisms. He also developed a vaccine for rabies, which led to the foundation of the Pasteur Institute in Paris in 1888. Pasteur made many other important discoveries and inspired his pupil, the English surgeon Joseph Lister, in his work on antiseptic surgery.

Related Web links: ambafrance-ca.org/
HYPERLAB for famous French scientists (E, F)

Modern Scientific Thinkers

The early 20th century in France was a time of great scientific advances. Pierre and Marie Curie had been investigating the nature of radioactivity and by 1902 isolated the pure elements of polonium and radium. Together with Henri Becquerel, whose investigation into radioactivity was also seminal, they were awarded the Nobel Prize for Physics in 1903. After the accidental death of her husband, Marie Curie continued with the research they had begun, and in 1910 published a *Treatise on Radioactivity*. In 1911 she was awarded another Nobel Prize, this time for Chemistry. Theoretical physicist Louis de Broglie laid the foundations of wave mechanics and was awarded the Nobel Prize in 1929. Other French scientists who have won the Nobel Prize are Professors F. Jacob A. Lwoff and J. Monod, for their work in molecular genetics and in showing how the production of proteins from DNA is controlled (1965). Professor Kastler won the Nobel Prize for the discovery of optical pumping (1966). Louis Néel won for his work in the field of magnetism (1966), chemist Jean-Marie Lehn for discovering cryptands (1987), physicist Pierre-Gilles de Jennes for molecular physics and physiochemistry (1991), and Georges Charpak for inventing a highly sensitive electronic detector for particle accelerators (1992).

The French school of mathematics, built on the work done by the Bourbaki group early in the 19th century, has been awarded the prestigious Fields medal seven times, including two in 1994. It is an international leader in the areas of fractal geometry, equations with partial derivatives, and chaos dynamics.

In the field of life sciences, particularly in biology, French researchers at the Pasteur Institute and the National Institute for Health and Medical Research (INSERM), including Luc Montagnier and Pierre Chambon, have made significant progress in molecular genetics, immunology, and endocrinology. The HIV virus that causes AIDS was first isolated at the Pasteur Institute. French biologists have been successful in mapping the human genome. In 1992, Daniel Cohen drew up the first complete physical map of Chromosome 21, and Jean Weissenbach announced the 1,400 genetic markers for 22 chromosomes.

Since 1939 the French government has strongly supported scientific research in France through the Centre national de la recherche scientifique, which coordinates 1,300 laboratories and more than 26,000 researchers throughout France. In order to "bring science to the people," the government built an immense science and technology museum, La Villette: Cité des Sciences. Officially opened in 1986, the museum, located near the 19th arrondissement in Paris, covers seven acres.

Related Web links: ambafrance-ca.org/ HYPERLAB/PEOPLE/_marie.html for the life of Marie Cure (E, F); bourbaki.ens.fr for Bourbaki group site (F); inserm.fr is the National Institute for Health and Medical Research site (E, F); cite-sciences.fr for La Villette history, exhibitions, science magazine (E, F)

High Technology

Recent French governments have assertively supported high-technology industries. France is the second-largest exporter of services after the United States, and biotechnology is a fast-growing export market. Within France, nuclear technology supplies three-fourths of the country's electric power, but because of safety and environmental concerns, the government is looking at other technologies to gradually replace nuclear energy as a power source.

The French have always been fascinated by technical inventions and adopted new electronic and computerized aids at home and at work. In 1983, the Minitel, a French-invented home computer service linked through telephone lines, was introduced, and it can still be found in more than one-fourth of French homes today. It also serves a large number of administrative and commercial offices and offers satellite hookups abroad. The French attachment to the Minitel, however, turned out to be a disadvantage in the rapidly changing world of computer high technology that was to explode. It made the French slower than other Western countries to use the Internet, for example. Today, 82 percent of French homes are not connected to the Internet, a result partly of the number of families that own personal computers. It is estimated that only 1 percent of French workers are *télétravailleurs* (telecommuters). In business, however, Internet use has grown rapidly. Between 1996 and 1997 the value of transactions for products and services increased by 850 percent.

In 2000 the French government launched a huge three-year program aimed at educating the French public about the Internet and creating 4,000 new jobs for young people in the field of multimedia. French universities are gradually launching education programs on the Internet, and many of France's libraries have enthusiastically embraced the new technology. The (National Library) in Paris uses high technology in all its operations, and through its Internet site you can access their catalogue. Through the Gallica part of its site, the most important books from the 16th through the 20th centuries can be downloaded.

The *carte à puce* (smart card) was invented in 1967 by Parisian Roland Moreno (1945–). This ingenious electronic device has a memory, serves as a personal identification, and can pay for banking, shopping, and telephone services. The French have also enthusiastically adopted the mobile telephone (*le portable*). One in four people now own one, and more than half belong to people under 30.

Related Web links: **minitel.tm.fr** for a guide to Minitel services from France Télécom (payment required for access) (F); **adminet.com/minitel** for information on Minitel (E, F); **bnf.fr** for the National Library (F); **http://gallica.bnf.fr** for downloadable literature (F); **multimania.com /dbon/somie.htm** for a history and future of the smart card (F); **raymanworld.com** (E, F)

Population

The population in France reached 60 million in 1999. But the average growth rate of 0.38 percent was lower than in 1982–90, when it was 0.55 percent. Although the annual number of births still exceeds the number of deaths, the overall birth rate in France continues to decline. The average is currently 1.8 children per couple. Women are having their first child at a later age. In 1980 the average age was 27. Today it is 30.

Reasons cited for the declining birth rate are the use of contraceptive methods, which makes having children a personal choice; the high proportion of professional women; and the trend among couples to favor a comfortable lifestyle over the material sacrifices that would be required to raise a large number of children. To encourage people to have more children, the government promotes a policy of generous child benefits, family allowances, housing grants, and tax incentives.

Immigrants make up 6.5 percent of the French, and there has been a dramatic change in the origin of this population. The percentage of immigrants from European countries was 84 percent in 1954; today it's 41 percent. Immigrants from former French territories in Africa, especially from Maghreb (Morocco, Algeria, and Tunisia), have risen from 13 percent of the total in 1954 to 47 percent today. Asian immigrants have risen from 2.5 percent in 1954 to 12 percent today. Immigrants from former French territories in Africa generally have more children than French-born couples and they live mainly in high-rise housing estates in the suburbs.

There are more women than men in France. The average life expectancy of a woman is 82, the highest in European record; it was 69 in 1970. A man can expect to live until he is 74; up from 63.5 in 1950. Jeanne Calmet, who died in 1997 at the age of 122, was the oldest woman in the world at the time of her death.

France has the 20th largest population in size (the United States ranks third) and is the 47th largest in relation to its land size (212,360 square miles), approximately equivalent in size to Texas. The French population is the fourth largest in Europe, after Germany, the United Kingdom, and Italy. In terms of population density in Europe, France has a relatively low rate of 259 inhabitants per square mile, compared to Germany's 610 and Belgium's 866.

Within France, the four largest regions of population density are: Ile-de-France (which includes Paris), where one-sixth of the total population lives; Lyon-Rhône-Alps; Lille-Calais region; and Provence–Côte d'Azur region. In 40 percent of France, the population density is fewer than 15.5 inhabitants per square mile. This large, sparsely inhabited region makes France particularly attractive to nature lovers in a densely populated Europe.

Related Web links: recensement.insee.fr for 1999 census data, search by theme: nationality, immigration, family, employment, residence, household size (F); **http://sref.free.fr** for national and local census data (F)

From the Baby Boom to the Papy Boom

Following World War II there was a sudden, large increase in the French birthrate. This so-called baby boom significantly changed the proportion of young people in the population and, in the 1960s and 1970s, generated a dominant youth culture. Today, however, with a decline in the birthrate and the increase in life expectancy, France finds itself with an aging population. One-fifth is older than 60, the official retirement age for salaried workers. The average retirement age in France is 57 (the lowest in the world, incidently). There are now less than two young people younger than 20 for each person older than 65.

From 1970 to 1998 the number of people under 20 fell from 33.2 to 25.8 percent of the total population. In the same period, the number of those older than 60 rose from 18 to 20.4 percent. It is estimated that by 2010 the over 60s will outnumber the under 20s. The first baby boomers reach retirement age in the year 2005. Among those over 75, there are twice as many women as men.

Social attitudes toward the older generation have changed. During the youth culture decades the elderly were called *les vieux* ("old people"). This expression was often a pejorative and was replaced by *le troisième âge* ("the third age"). The current ion for the elderly is *les seniors*. Attitudes have changed not only because of the growing number of seniors but also because of their disposable income. The average income of today's retirees is 8 percent higher than the average income for workers; in 1970 it was 20 percent lower.

Today's retirees possess 40 percent of the national wealth.

With their money, seniors have become a powerful force in the consumer market, in addition to being important contributors to their families. Thirty-five percent of French seniors help their children and grandchildren financially. This help has had a stabilizing economic effect during period of high youth unemployment in the 1990s, and at a time when young people stayed in educational institutions on longer in the hope that an advanced degree would help their future employment possibilities. The role of retirees has thus turned around completely. Previously, children expected that they would have to take care of their parents in their old age. Today it's the parents who are taking care of the younger generations.

Not that all seniors are wealthy. There are many who survive on limited resources and lead lonely lives if they don't have a family. Increasingly, young people help provide company for these older people. Solidarity within the family and between young and older generations has become a feature of French life. In addition, the government helps seniors through pension payments and programs such as price reductions for seniors using public services; for instance, the *carte senior* for train travel.

Related Web links: ined.fr for population tree and causes of death since 1925 (E, F)

Marriage and Divorce

French couples often celebrate two separate marriage ceremonies because of the separation of Church and state that has existed since 1905. The civil ceremony is obligatory, which gives the marriage legal status, and takes place at the city hall (*mairie*). The mayor records it in the *livret de famille* (family booklet) given to the newlyweds. The couple's children will be recorded in the *livret*, giving the children legal status. If the couple wants a church marriage, it will come after the civil ceremony.

France has the lowest per capita marriage rate in Europe; it decreased by half between 1972 and 1987 and has increased only slightly since. From 1980 to 1996 the average age of marriage rose from 23 to 27.5 for women and from 25 to 29 for men. Over a quarter of French women have never married by the age of 35. Today, an estimated 15 percent of couples living together are unmarried, and they are living together longer. If they decide to get married, it is often to legitimize the children they've had and to qualify for the tax advantages unmarried couples with children lost in 1996. The proportion of marriages between partners who have already had several children is now 32 percent, compared to 19 percent in 1980. Forty percent of children are currently born to unmarried parents, compared to 10 percent in 1980. Over 60 percent of couples who marry lived together as an unmarried couple before their marriage.

The marriages in which at least one partner is not French has declined to 10.1 percent today from 13.6 percent in 1990.

A high proportion of marriage partners come from similar social backgrounds and have lived in the same locality.

Even though the marriage rate has declined, the divorce rate has increased. There are four times more divorces today than there were in 1960. In 1975 a law was passed recognizing divorce by mutual consent, but a change in attitude toward marriage has also helped increase the divorce rate. Partners expect to be happy in a marriage. If they aren't, they divorce. Seventy percent of the French believe that partners divorce for insufficient reasons, and a similar percentage believe it should be harder to get a divorce. Forty-six percent feel that unfaithfulness is a sufficient reason for divorce, and of these, 48 percent are women and 44 percent are men. According to current trends, more than a third of French marriages will end in divorce.

Marriage is no longer seen by many French people as a religious and social institution but as a personal decision. Despite the lower marriage rate, the growing divorce rate, the growing number of unmarried couples cohabiting, and the increase in single-parent families, a majority still agree that "the family is the place where you can feel comfortable and relaxed," and only a small minority think that "people should no longer get married."

Related Web links: **mariageweb.com** for preparation for marriage, history, ceremony, procedures (F); **divorce-famille.net** for legal advice on divorce and separation (F)

The Upbringing of Children

From the time French children can walk and talk, their parents begin training them to become civilized, responsible citizens and to conform to the rules of French society. A combination of strong discipline and tender affection is used during this early apprenticeship for adult life. They learn early the social courtesies of adults, such as shaking hands, which the French call *éducation*, as distinct from *instruction* (what is learned at school). Young children who disobey their parents are reprimanded in public verbally or even with a slap. This differs from the lack of such reprimands by some American parents, who believe it will inhibit the natural development of the child's personality. American children are generally encouraged to freely express their individual personality, even if this disrupts the life of the adults around them. French children are trained to be young adults.

And though French parents are authoritarian with their children, they also openly show their love. They kiss and hug them in public, and at home children kiss their parents and other family members when they get up in the morning and before bed at night. No child would dare object to this ritual. Of all Europeans, the French spend the most on gifts for their children, 60 percent of it on Christmas presents.

French parents set high standards of behavior and have high academic expectations for their children. During their daily routine, children are pushed to perform better ("That's not good enough, you can do better" with a stern face) whereas the American way is to reward what they have done ("Good for you" and applause). At meals, bad behavior and thoughtless remarks are criticized and children are told that if they're going to say something, it has to be either intelligent or witty or both. And parents closely monitor their children's school progress and their homework. At school, children are taught that knowledge is important. Their homework can take several hours each night. Consequently, few children have part-time jobs, and parents provide pocket money as well as finance them during their university studies.

French children live at home much longer than American children and usually attend the university closest to their home. Seventy-three percent of children 15 to 24 years old live with their parents. In fact, they usually stay close to their parents all their life. They have learned at an early age that the nuclear family is not an independent unit but rather a part of a network of relatives of various generations. Because French people don't like moving to a different location, parents, their married children, and members of the extended family often live near each other. Grandparents help with minding their grandchildren, and on Sundays there is frequently an extended family gathering. Mutual support by family members is a strong feature of French life.

Related Web links: bac2002.fr.st and lebac.com for *baccalauréat* study aid (F); firstcampus.com, click French flag for student's guide to *grandes écoles*, medical schools, and other options (F)

French parents have a constant preoccupation with the education of their children. Children who achieve top grades in the national education system can expect the financial and social benefits of a rewarding career. However, though in principle intellectually gifted children from the French working class benefit from this democratic principle, the success rate of children from wealthy families is higher.

The primary and secondary schools are administered nationally, which means that course content and final exams are the same for all students. The state subsidizes private schools, which make up 14 percent of primary schools and 21 percent of secondary schools.

French pupils soon become accustomed to long hours at school and lots of homework. Primary school classes start between 8:00 and 8:30 A.M. There is a two-hour break for lunch, and classes end after 4:30. Children then come home, have a snack, and do their homework, which is often supervised by their mothers.

Students end their final secondary school year (at around the age of 18) with the *baccalauréat* exam. They are under pressure to achieve good grades because it determines their future study and career possibilities. A perfect score on the *bac* is 20; students who score above 10 are entitled to enroll in one of the universities, all of which are state-financed. Because this allows a tremendous number of students to enroll in first-year classes, French students receive far less guidance and personal assistance from their instructors than American students. Most assessment is done by intellectually demanding formal exams that prevent a large proportion of students from progressing to their senior year.

Students with the highest grades on the *baccalauréat* may apply to a two-year preparatory class for one of the entrance examinations to the *grandes écoles*, which are also state-financed. These schools prepare students for specialist professions such as engineering and finance. Only the best students pass the competitive entrance examinations to these *écoles*, whose diplomas often guarantee a high-ranking position in a particular profession.

The two most prestigious *grandes écoles* are the école polytechnique, founded by Napoléon in 1804 and colloquially called X because of its courses in advanced mathematics and physics, and the Ecole nationale d'administration (ENA), established in 1945 to train top public servants. Its graduates, called *énarques*, have a virtual monopoly on all significant government administration positions and include two presidents, Valéry Giscard d'Estaing and Jacques Chirac, and most prime ministers since the 1980s.

Attempts to reform this rigid educational system provoke controversy among parents who want their children to benefit from its hierarchy, and from secondary and university students, who are quick to organize street demonstrations.

Related Web links: education.gouv.fr is an extensive Ministry of Education site (F); students-life.com for student culture (F); mgel.fr is a student guide to finance and housing (F)

Religion

Sixty-seven percent of the French say they are Catholic (81% in 1986), but only 10 percent go to church every week (29% in 1975), and just 7 percent of 18- to 24-year-olds. Twenty-three percent of the French say they are nonbelievers. Much of French history and tradition, however, are closely bound up with a Catholic identity.

Since Clovis (465–511), the king of the Franks, converted to Catholicism in A.D. 496 and made Paris the royal capital, the Catholic tradition has been glorified throughout France in abbeys and churches and the magnificent medieval Gothic cathedrals. France was called the eldest daughter of the Church of Rome. Each year, more than 5 million pilgrims visit the grotto of Sainte Bernadette (1844–79) in Lourdes (Pyrénées).

The Protestant Reformation in France, and opposition to it, brought about the conflicts characterized as the Wars of Religion (1562–98). The fierce battles between the French Protestants (Huguenots) and Catholics were culminated by the Edict of Nantes (1598), in which Henri IV (1553–1610) gave Protestants the legal right to practice their religion and granted them certain cities as safe havens. But Louis XIV (1638–1715) revoked the edict in 1685, and more than 250,000 French Protestants emigrated to the Netherlands, Germany, and Switzerland. Today, 2 percent of the French population are Protestants.

The French Revolution of 1789 attacked the privileges and wealth of the Catholic Church, and the Church and the Republic became adversaries. In 1905 the Third Republic separated Church and state by law, enshrining the lay tradition (*la laïcité*). Since then, France has been constitutionally secular, and no reference to God or religion is made in state ceremonies. Government financial aid to private schools, most of which are Catholic, is a subject of controversy.

The second-largest religion after Catholicism in France today is not Protestantism, but Islam. The large number of practicing Muslims among North African immigrants and their families account for more than 900 mosques in France, over a fourth of which are in the vicinity of Paris.

Jews make up 1 percent of the total French population, the highest percentage in Western Europe. More than half live in Paris. Not that France has been a congenial haven for Jews. Ultranationalist sentiments at the close of the 19th century contributed to the acclaimed trial of Jewish army officer Alfred Dreyfus (1859–1935) in 1894. Dreyfus was falsely convicted of espionage, and it became a cause célèbre throughout France, rallying intellectuals and Republicans. Dreyfus was finally cleared in 1906. Half a century later, many French Jews died in Nazi concentration camps during the German occupation of 1940–44, often with the complicity of the Vichy government.

Related Web links: cef.fr for Catholic Church in France(F); **lourdes-france.com** for Lourdes site with webcam (E, F); **mosquee-de-paris.com** for Paris Grand Mosque (F); **topj.net** is a Jewish community website (F); **bnf.fr/pages/pedagos /dreyfus** for the Dreyfus case (F)

Urban and Rural Life

France is one of the least densely populated countries in Europe, with 259 inhabitants per square mile in 1999. Because 90 percent of the French population live in urban or semiurban areas, and 20 percent in the Ile-de-France region around Paris, large areas of the country offer unspoiled vistas.

After World War II the population shifted rapidly from the country to urban agglomerations because of the mass exodus of farming families. The suburbs (*la banlieue*) of major cities grew as the countryside emptied. Today, many contemporary Parisians identify themselves with the region from which their family came; for example, as Bretons or Normands, rather than Parisians.To house the new urban dwellers, including immigrant workers' families, subsidized low-cost apartment buildings, *habitations à loyer modéré* (HLMs), were erected in the suburbs with government financing. HLMs are now often concentrations of a socially deprived population suffering high unemployment, especially among the young and immigrants. In contrast to the United States, the pattern in France is for high-income earners to live in the city center and low-income earners in the suburbs. Thus, low-income workers from the city have moved to the suburbs, to join the immigrant families, as their old neighborhoods were gentrified and rents were raised. In the 1980s government reforms gave greater power to regional councils, and as a result, provincial cities began a new growth cycle. Regional economic growth was also stimulated by managers and other workers who abandoned the stress of Paris in search of a higher quality of life. The TGV network has reduced the isolation of provincial cities by making travel between them and Paris faster. Thirty-five urban agglomerations outside Paris each hold more than 100,000 people. The five largest, in order, are Lyon, Marseille, Lille, Bordeaux, and Toulouse.

Until recently, agriculture made the greatest contribution to France's wealth, and a large proportion of the farming community lived in villages, where conservatism and respect for tradition shaped attitudes and values. Today, the traditional rural society has been displaced by an urban one, and the rural sector has had to accept the modernization brought about by French membership in the European Union. Farmers' demonstrations against the PAC (the European Union's common agricultural policy) have received widespread popular support, even though only 5 percent of France's current economy was at stake. The nationalist and conservative values of the rural sector continue to exert an influence on the national psyche, an influence out of proportion to the economic importance of farming. The administrative division of France into 36,000 *communes*—more than in the rest of the European Union nations out together—has helped maintain these rural attitudes.

Related Web links: union-hlm.org for a history of HLMs (F); **tgv.com**, see *Decouvert le reseau* for interactive map of TGV network (E, F)

Housing

Most inhabitants of French cities live in apartment buildings. The population explosion led by the post–World War II baby boomers led to a rapid expansion of the suburbs around the cities and, somewhat illogically, a sudden increase in the construction of individual houses. Today 58 percent of the housing units in France are houses rather than apartments. However, a recent poll asking city dwellers whether they would prefer to live in an apartment near the city center or a house in the suburbs revealed that 51 percent prefer an apartment.

The *concierge*—guardian of the entrance to the apartment building and a French institution—is disappearing. Modern buildings have replaced the concierge with *le gardien* or *la gardienne*, or else no one at all is performing surveillance and mail distribution duties. The mail carrier (*le facteur*) puts the mail in personal letter boxes at the entrance to the building, and visitors gain entrance through an intercom. To increase security against robberies, many buildings have installed a number-code lock on the street entrance door. This *code de la porte* is changed from time to time, and residents and visitors must know the code in order to enter the building after 8:00 P.M.

The number of people living alone has increased greatly. The percentages in major cities are: Paris (50%), Bordeaux (46%), Lyon (42%), Toulouse (41%), Strasbourg and Nice (38%), and Marseille (32%).

The government began constructing the cheap high-rise housing condominiums known as HLMs on the periphery of cities and towns after 1948. Today more than 3 million families live in these unattractive tower blocks, many of which are immigrant and working-class families with high rates of unemployment.

At the moment, more people in France own a vacation home (*une résidence secondaire*) than anywhere else in the world: 13 percent. Most of these families belong to the upper class, live in a city, and use the home for weekends and vacations. Many country houses that have gone up for sale, as much of France's previously large rural population migrated to the city, have met the demand for such homes.

The economic recession of the 1980s and its resulting unemployment created a phenomenon to which France had been unaccustomed: the *sans domicile fixe* (SDF); the homeless. Paris had always had *clochards* (tramps) who slept under the city's bridges and were a picturesque and not unsettling part of the tourist's view of the romantic Seine, but the increase in people begging on the streets has not been charming.

Charitable institutions like the Emmaüs hostels founded by abbé Pierre, and the Restaurants of the Heart, started by Coluche, provide shelter and meals to the poor and homeless.

Related Web links: caf.fr for interactive calculation of housing assistance (F); **emmaus-international.org** for the hostel organization (E, F)

Forms and Bureaucracy

A French citizen becomes a legal adult at 18, and from that age he or she may vote in national elections. All citizens carry their *carte d'identité nationale* (national identity card), which shows the citizen's name, birth date, physical characteristics, address, and photograph (head shot), and bears an official stamp. Until adulthood, a child's name and date of birth is officially recorded in the *livret de famille* (family booklet), which is given to the new husband and wife at their civil marriage ceremony.

Identity documents must be produced when requested by the police or public administration offices. Of course, for visitors, passports serve in the place of national identity cards.

Other important personal documents are the French passport (whose cover is identical throughout the European Union); the *carte de securité sociale*, demonstrating entitlement to national health benefits; and the *carte d'allocations familiales* (governmental grants are given to families with children as part of a policy to increase the national birthrate). In addition, all drivers must have a *permis de conduire* (driver's license) and a *carte grise* with registration details of the car.

The large number and frequent use of these documents in daily life reflects the influence of the state in France. A French citizen goes to the *mairie* (city hall) when the documents need to be changed and to other administrative offices when documents are required to be stamped to satisfy the numerous state regulations. Getting the appropriate approval is usually time-consuming because long lines of impatient French citizens are a feature of public agencies. Civil servants (*les fonctionnaires*) have a reputation for strictly applying the letter of the law. The excessive bureaucratic attitudes and the number of forms to be filled in frequently provoke frustration and annoyance.

The lower ranks of civil servants (*les petits fonctionnaires*), who have no power except to implement the instructions passed down from the superiors—but assured permanence as state employees—stand between the bureaucracy and clients. They are the first officials the public encounters, and they characteristically permit no variations to the prescribed procedures. The counter where they meet and deal with the public is called *le guichet*. While the civil servant verifies that all the required forms are present and correctly filled out, the client line in front of the *guichet*, whether at the city hall, the tax collector's office, or in a post office, is prone to long delays. If the forms are missing or filled out improperly, the client, despite his or her protestations, will be told to come back when everything is in order. The unhelpful French bureaucracy, obsessed with regulations and forms, has been an object of satire since Georges Courteline's (1858–1929) popular plays at the end of the 19th century.

Related Web links: securité-sociale.fr for history of social security; entitlements for family, unemployment, illness, retirement; links to other bodies (E, F)

Public Servants (Fonctionnaires)

With more than 5 million employees working for the state, France has the largest proportion of public servants among the countries of the European Union. This number represents 28 percent of the working population, excluding those employed on a casual basis.

Public servants are employees of state ministries, service departments, agencies, and local government. They include teachers and employees in state schools as well as teachers in private schools under state contract, and employees in the public health system, the postal and telecommunications sector, public transportation, policing and the administration of justice, and defense. As a result of the nationalization of key economic sectors (energy, transportation, banking) following World War II, and then further nationalization of industry in 1982 after the Socialists came to power, state employment more than tripled in France in the past century. In the last two decades alone, state employment rose by 20 percent, despite the privatization of some nationalized companies when right-wing governments regained power. Over the same period in the Netherlands and the United Kingdom, state employment dropped by 25 percent.

Public servants have an important advantage over private sector employees: they have guaranteed employment even during times of economic crisis. Certain liberal professions, as well as employees and managers of businesses in protected sectors, also do not fear unemployment. Together with retired public servants, they number 17 to 20 million. A recent survey suggests that the French public has a favorable attitude toward public sector employment: 91 percent think public servants are useful. However, 80 percent consider them privileged, compared to workers in the private sector. The groups with the most positive image are teachers (27%), postal workers (15%t), hospital staff (10%), and police (7%).

In an era when unemployment is a permanent threat, the advantages of state employment are attractive: 86 percent of the population would be happy if one of their children became a public servant.

Public Servants in Europe
Public employment as a percentage of the total employment

	PUBLIC SECTOR (1)	PUBLIC SECTOR (2)	GUARANTEE OF JOB FOR LIFE
	(IN % OF STATE EMPLOYMENT)		
Germany	14.1%	15.4%	25%
Spain	15.1	18.0	NA
France	20.2	27.0	89
Italy	18.2	23.2	0
United Kingdom	11.9	16.9	0

(1) Central or federal government + regional or state governments + local government.
(2) All of (1) above + public enterprises.

Throughout the European zone, the trend is toward a decrease in the number of state employees and, with the rise in contract work, the weakening of the notion of a state-paid job for life. France and Spain are the exceptions. Moreover, France is one of the rare countries to recruit its public servants by competitive examination, which makes any modification of their current status more difficult.

Previously, workers were separated into the categories blue-collar workers (*les cols bleus*) in factories and white-collar workers (*les cols blancs*) in offices. Today, however, white-collar workers have joined the middle classes, which also include CEOs and managers (*les cadres*), public servants, and the liberal professions (doctors and lawyers, for example). At the other end of the pay scale, factory workers have been joined by immigrant workers in poorly paid jobs in industry and in agriculture.

Profession is no longer a sufficient criterion for the identification of social category. More of the French people are categorizing themselves according to their income and level of education. In addition, new professions have emerged, and established professions have become less homogenized. Membership in a particular social group today depends more on personal than professional criteria, which has reduced the class consciousness that has traditionally characterized French society.

Women's roles in social and professional life have increased significantly, with a greater number of women than men undertaking post-graduate study. Most women are now involved in some professional activity, and as a result of gaining a measure of financial and personal autonomy, have enhanced their position in both family and society.

With a lower percentage of farmers and factory workers in the working population, the traditional social hierarchy is changing. Employees and members of intermediate professions such as technicians, foremen, and supervisors account for half the working population. The number of managers and tertiary-educated professionals has also increased. In contrast, the traditional occupations of law, medicine, and teaching have lost some of their privileges. Managers are feeling the pressures resulting from globalization and a need for greater efficiency. Employment in the service industry, which may be undertaken independently and profitably, has become more highly regarded.

A new "knowledge" elite, including senior executives, the liberal professions, politicians, unionists, experts, and journalists, is expanding. What sets them apart is their possession and use of essential information. The gap between this elite and the social groups that do not possess this "knowledge" is widening and creating a two-tier society.

Middle Classes

Since the beginning of the consumer society, the French middle class has grown exponentially. With increasing prosperity, social groups that were once not considered middle class are able to adopt to a middle-class lifestyle. Thus, the two main socioeconomic groupings in France are the middle classes (*les classes moyennes*) and the lower classes (*les classes populaires*).

Within *les classes moyennes* the rigid barriers have disappeared, but distinctions based on wealth, power, and privilege remain, and there is far less social mobility than in the United States. The upper middle class remains successful in keeping out the nouveau riche by dominating the higher rungs of the educational ladder. Intellectually gifted children in working-class homes will find work in positions usually filled by the lower middle class. Only a tiny percentage will aspire to a liberal profession, such as doctor or lawyer, and to join that level of the middle classes. It is estimated that only 3 percent of the most famous and powerful people in France today come from working-class homes. Even when they can afford it, those from the lower middle and working classes rarely venture into the public world of the upper middle classes.

The conflicts between the working class and the middle class in French history have formalized the place allocated to each group, despite the concept of Republican equality (*égalité*) that treats all individuals as citizens rather than as members of a social class. Members of the working class may drive the same cars and dress similarly to those in the middle class, but they are separated by family background.

The traditional concerns of the middle class were purchasing power, career advancement, and social welfare. Contemporary concerns include employment security, financing retirement, education for their children, and tax reform. In a survey of areas in which the middle classes think the French government should act, the highest priority was alleviating unemployment (75%), followed by lower taxes (55%), reduction of social inequality (53%), financing retirement (49%), protection of the environment (48%), educational reform (46%), and security (41%).

How the Middle Classes Spend Their Money

	WORKERS	EMPLOYEES	MANAGERS	SELF-EMPLOYED	RETIREES
Housing	46%	35%	60%	67%	69%
Second home	4	5	17	15	13
Car	90	79	92	94	68
Freezer	56	40	48	62	48
Dishwasher	30	28	62	59	27
Video	74	63	75	76	35
Home computer	9	12	39	21	3

The Bourgeoisie

The bourgeoisie—the urban middle class—grew in power and importance during the 19th century as a result of the Revolution of 1789, which ended the privileges of the nobility, who had dominated French society. Because membership in the true nobility depended solely on birth, not on personal merit or achievement, the revolutionaries considered the nobility's privileges unjust.

The power of the nobility was shattered by the Revolution. The bourgeoisie was the new wealthy class, providing the bankers, traders, and shopkeepers for the economic growth of post-Revolutionary France. They increased the political power they had won in the Revolution by supplying the educated workforce needed to expand the administrative bureaucracy. In addition to their wealth, the bourgeoisie achieved social prestige by marrying members of the impoverished nobility. The Industrial Revolution further increased their wealth and influence.

The vast French middle class has imposed its values on 21st-century France despite opposition from two groups: the working class, which became more politically organized through trade unions and the Socialist and Communist parties, and the intellectual class, which expressed contempt for the bourgeois obsession with money and materialistic goals. The growth of the liberal professions and of senior management in industry and commerce expanded the top echelons of the bourgeoisie during *les trente glorieuses*—the thirty years of rapid economic growth in France after World War II. During this period, the ethos of the consumer society altered the traditional bourgeois attitude of spending little and saving as much money as possible. A generation of affluent, professionally successful men and women emerged—the "new bourgeoisie." Unlike preceding generations, they were not afraid to use credit to purchase consumer and luxury goods that were not essential but enhanced their lifestyle. The glossy magazine sold with the newspaper *Le Figaro* on Saturdays reflects the tastes and aspirations of these new trendsetters.

It has been said that in today's France the old aristocracy has been replaced by a new one that controls the political, economic, intellectual, and social power of the nation. This new elite is made up of the leaders in politics, industry, management, public administration, and the liberal professions. Their power is based on family connections, success, and wealth. They are *les gens bien* (the admirable people), whose attitudes, fashions, and lifestyles are copied by the lower social classes. Two centuries after the Revolution, a strong social hierarchy remains, with the upper levels of the bourgeoisie having replaced the nobility at the top of the hierarchy, controlling the power and the wealth in a state-dominated society.

The New Poor

In France, the new poor, a social group excluded from professional, cultural, and social life, forms what has been called an "ectocracy" (the prefix "ecto" from the Greek "ektos," meaning outside) of some 6 or 7 million people. High levels of unemployment have caused a huge increase in their number. The new poor receive government welfare benefits but tend to be overlooked by the rest of French society, even though it is clear that the spiral of exclusion can affect anyone.

The "poverty threshold" is generally defined as half of the median income (dividing the population in two halves). The poverty threshold in France is approximately 3,500 francs per month (about $485) by unit of consumption (one unit for the first adult, 0.7 for the second, and 0.5 per child). Accordingly, 12 percent of the French population may be considered poor, twice as many as in the Netherlands.

State agencies have been under pressure to satisfy welfare demands. The regional offices for family benefits, Caisse d'allocations familiales (CAF), have been faced with a sharp rise in both borderline poverty and in the number of beneficiaries of social welfare. In the past decade, the number of recipients claiming the minimum benefit has doubled. This benefit, the *revenu moyen d'insertion* (RMI), was introduced by the government in 1988 and is payable to all people over 25 living below the poverty threshold. Further, the number of people requiring rent assistance has grown from around 1 million to more than 6 million, or one household in three. Among the 10 million beneficiaries of social welfare, a third have a monthly income below 4,200 francs ($585), and one-half (approximately 5 million) have an income below 6,300 francs ($880).

During the years of economic crisis it has become apparent that not even employment protects the individual from poverty. The minimum salary, *le salaire minimum de croissance* (SMIC), guarantees a basic wage to full-time employees, the majority of whom are found in the private sector (1.5 million), including the hotel and restaurant industries (40%), service industries (29%), and the leisure industry (17.6%). However, with the rise of part-time employment, a new social group consisting of those who lack the opportunity to earn even the minimum salary, *travailleurs pauvres* (the working poor), has emerged. The standard of living of the *travailleurs pauvres* has been eroded by the low wages paid for short-term, part-time, or casual work, and this population finds itself worse off than people living wholly on social welfare (family benefits, rent assistance, and RMI). A recent survey found that the average income derived from social welfare (3,829 francs, or $530, per month,) was slightly higher than that of households with a low work-derived income (3,649 francs, or $504, per month). This adversely affects the attractiveness of state programs aimed at getting the unemployed back to work.

Related Web links: tripalium.com/chiffres/smic
/chiffre2.htm, insee.fr/fr/indicateur/smic.htm
for SMIC wage levels (F)

Benevolent Associations

High unemployment has placed strains on the welfare state, which has long been an accepted role of the French Republic. Benevolent associations have been called upon to help the victims of poverty and exclusion from normal social life, and a new public solidarity has emerged to support the underprivileged. Membership of associations has increased in France, though it is still the lowest in Europe.

THE IMPORTANCE OF BENEVOLENT WORK

French	17%
Austrians	22%
Irish	23%
Dutch	25%
British	28%
Swedish	33%
Italian	34%
German	35%
Spanish	51%
Greek	54%

Associations present a level of social support different than that offered by the public and private sectors. They present a more manageable, human face to those they help. Those who belong to these benevolent associations are generally more well off than the population at large. They include managers (61%), retirees (40%), and housewives (36%), as well as workers (35%).

One of the best known and most popular benevolent associations in France is Restos du coeur (Restaurants of the Heart). Started in 1985 by the comic actor Coluche, who died the following year, the 36,000 volunteers of Restos du coeur help collect, prepare, and serve food in the association's 2,000 soup kitchens throughout France. The association provides 18 percent of the food aid nationally, doing much of its good work during winter. In the winter of 1997–98, for example, an estimated 59 million meals were served (seven times more than in 1985) and over 400,000 people gave money to Restos du coeur. The association also distributes books, clothing, and other nonperishables, which are donated and collected at the various distribution centers. The group Relais du coeur assists the excluded to reenter the work force, requiring teams of voluntary teachers and trainers throughout the country.

Another well-known benevolent association is Emmaüs France, founded in 1945 by a priest, Abbé Pierre (1912–), who has become a popular folk hero through his work for the poor and homeless. Emmaüs runs hostels for the homeless, and its volunteers raise money by collecting and recycling clothing and discarded furniture and other items that would otherwise be thrown away. In a 1999 poll, Abbé Pierre and General de Gaulle topped the list of people the French admired most.

Related Web links: restosducoeur.org for the benevolent association (F)

Money

As of January 2002, the euro became the currency of most countries in the European Union, replacing the franc, mark, peseta, lira, florin, schilling, and escudo. An easy way to convert francs to euros is to take the price in francs, add to it half the price in francs and then divide by ten. For example, if the price in francs is 20, it's 20 + 10 ÷ 10 = 3 (euros).

English speakers should remember that *la monnaie* means change or small coins and not money, which is *l'argent.* "Cash" is *argent liquide* or *espèces.*

The French are generally conservative about money and consider it distasteful to flaunt wealth. The wealthy acquire respect and status among the bourgeoisie by investing discreetly in property and cultural artifacts, such as antiques, old paintings, and tapestries. Until the 1980s money was a taboo topic of conversation. During that decade the fortunes amassed by flamboyant entrepreneurs like Bernard Tapie (1945–) inspired media coverage. Such entrepreneurs were called the "golden boys" because of the success of their stock raids and takeovers. Their ostentation shocked the French. The recession of the 1990s brought collapse to the fortunes of the golden boys, but the general French attitude toward money had by then changed. Amassing wealth with good money had become acceptable, though flaunting it is still distasteful. Wages in France depend mainly on profession and the level of qualification within the profession. A graduate from one of the prestigious *grandes écoles*, for example, earns on average 30 percent more for the same work than someone not from the same academic background. In general, men earn around a third more than their female counterparts. Wages also vary with the type of industry. Workers in the automobile and chemical industries, for instance, are paid more than metal workers and employees in the transportation sector.

France has a wider disparity in income between rich and poor than most other European countries. Five percent of the population has 50 percent of the nation's private wealth and the bottom 10 percent have 0.1 percent. However, the wage difference between a senior manager and an unskilled worker, which was 13 to 1 in the 1970s, is now approximately 7 to 1. Approximately 8 percent of workers receive the basic wage, the SMIC.

The French have altered their spending patterns over the years to become more selective consumers, paying attention to prices instead of remaining faithful to certain shops and tradesmen. Although purchasing power continues to increase in France, spending on leisure and clothing has been falling. The French prefer to limit themselves to a few high-quality garments that are worn longer and replaced less often. Another trend can be seen in the growing number who are saving their money as insurance against unemployment.

Related Web links: euro.gouv.fr for Ministry of Economy, Finance, and Industry on euro currency (F); **ecb.int** for European Central Bank site (E, F)

Gambling

Napoléon Bonaparte (1769–1821) outlawed gambling, and it has been illegal continuously since—except for state-run gambling activities, whose revenues account for a great deal of government income, over 20 billion francs ($3 billion) in 1997. More than half of the French participate, hoping their luck will win them some money and change their lives.

One such source of state income is Pari mutuel urbain (PMU), which controls off-track betting on horse racing. Bettors line up in cafés on Sundays to bet on *le tiercé* (choosing the first through third place finishers), *le quarté* (choosing first though fourth place), or *le quinté* (choosing first through fifth). Eighty percent of PMU gamblers are men, and by far the largest proportion of them come from the working classes. In 1995 the PMU had a turnover of 33 billion francs ($5 billion).

The same amount of income now flows from La Française des jeux, another state-run gambling group, dealing in Loto and instant lotteries. Loto has superseded the National Lottery and attracts many more gamblers than the PMU. Scratch lottery tickets such as Banco, Tac-O-Tac, and Bingo are growing in popularity, but the favorite among the French is Millionnaire, which includes the extra chance of adding to one's winnings on a television show. French television, in fact, has many quiz shows that attract large audiences.

On average, the French spend approximately 1,200 francs ($170) per person a year on instant lottery games. Gambling is especially popular in Corsica, and in Normandy, the Ile-de-France, and the Rhône-Alpes. It's least popular in the Auvergne, which is among the most religious regions in the country.

The law authorizes gambling casinos in sea and lakeside resorts only, but there are few of them and they are patronized largely by the upper class and wealthy tourists. The casinos contribute only a small percentage of the government's overall income from gambling, and most of this comes from slot machines (*bandits manchots*).

Based on surveys, winning Loto was at the top of the nation's wish list in 1999. When asked how they would spend their winnings, the top two responses from the French were a world tour and a vacation home.

Related Web links: pmu.fr for horse-racing calendar, results, courses (E, F); **fdjeux.com**, see *Museum* for posters and history, *Cinema* for television ads, *Café des sports* for games (E, F)

Road Transportation and Drivers

France has an extensive system of roads and highways that are based on the centralized road system used in Renaissance France, and consists of national, departmental, and rural roads. In 1955 the government adopted a policy of building highways or national autoroutes, and has completed 4,800 miles. 8,000 kilometers of them, Most of these are toll roads (*péages*), connecting Paris and the major cities of France in a star-shaped network. Traffic on the autoroutes is very heavy at the beginning and end of weekends and during the July and August summer vacation period. Drivers can use the national roads to avoid paying the tolls, but many French prefer to save time over money and take the *péages*.

Contemporary French bridges and tunnels have been used as symbols of French engineering prowess to project an international image of modern industrial France. Examples are the Pont de Tancarville (1959), suspended 155 feet above the Seine in Normandy; the Pont de Normandie (1995), at the mouth of the Seine between Le Havre and Honfleur, which is as long as the Champs-Elysées in Paris and is one of the longest bridges in the world; the tunnel under the Mont Blanc in the Alps (1965), linking France and Italy; and the Euro Tunnel, under the English Channel (1994) between Calais and Folkestone, which is used by the super-fast Eurostar train.

A common French motoring expression is *conduire comme un fou* (to drive like a madman). Dealing with other drivers brings out the impatient, aggressive, and argumentative side of the French nature.

As a people, the French have not developed an ethic of considerate driving, and they do not hesitate to honk insultingly or make gestures and scream abuse at other drivers. However, there are some signs of road courtesy in the provinces. French drivers dislike paying in underground parking lots, and so, in congested Paris, they often leave their cars parked on the sidewalk or across building entrances. The Parisian driving experience provides further challenges, what with trucks and cars often double-parked for deliveries or for shopping. Abuse of parking regulations and failure to pay parking fines is not discouraged by the genial practice of a general amnesty on parking tickets by each new President of the Republic.

French drivers generally drive faster than the speed limits, irrespective of whether driving conditions are clear or foggy; 30 miles per hour in urban areas, 50 on the Paris beltway, 55 on average roads, 65 on national roads, and 80 on the autoroutes. They also are notorious for tailgating. France has an extremely high traffic accident rate, despite the use of speeding fines, radar, and warning signs.

Related Web links: autoroutes.fr for tolls, regional expressway networks, maps (E, F); **havre .cci.fr/Chap_Ponts.stm** for information on Pont de Tancarville and Pont de Normandie (F); **atmb .net** for the Mont Blanc tunnel, including safety issues (E); **route.equipement.gouv.fr**, see *Le trafic* for *Carte du trafic* (map of France), data on traffic, future projects, bison futé road routes (F)

Individualized Transportation

France is a country that has loved cycling, an affection that gave birth in 1903 to the world's most famous cycling race, the Tour de France. Cycling (*faire du vélo*) is an extremely popular pastime in France, particularly in the provinces. Cycling in the cities is a much more dangerous activity due to a lack of bike lanes, the heavy traffic, and a lack of respect for cyclists from drivers. Nevertheless it is still popular, and locals and tourists can rent bikes in many rail stations. In Paris, the RATP offers a bicycle rental service called *roue libre* (freewheeling), and there are even guided bike rides around Paris for the adventurous.

In the cities, motorized bicycles (*cyclomoteurs*), scooters, and motorbikes (*motos*) are popular means of transportation, particularly for the young; there are more than 200,000 motorbike registrations a year. The motorbike market is the third largest in the world, behind the United States and Germany. Since 1996 those who have a driver's license are automatically entitled to hold a motorbike or scooter license, provided the motorbike is less than 125cc in capacity. This has spurred renewed interest in motorbikes, mainly among the middle-aged. Those who intend to ride motorbikes larger than 125cc must pass a rigorous practical and theoretical test in order to obtain a rider's license.

The newest and most popular forms of getting around in French cities are roller blading and skateboarding. *Le roller* and *le skateboard* have become not only the number one means of getting around since the French discovered their use during the transportation strikes of 1995, but also a social activity for an enormous group that has invaded the footpaths of French cities. This includes girls and boys and men and women of all ages, who roll and skate as couples, in small groups of friends, or as a family. Although an individual sport, it is an extremely sociable one. There are three types of roller bladers: those who do acrobatics, usually between 12 and 18 years old; those who do it for fitness, between 7 and 77 years old; and the largest group, between 20 and 35 years old, who use it as a means of commuting. Estimates put the number of roller bladers at more than 2 million. In Paris the past few years, the *randonnée à rollers* (blade excursion) has become a popular Friday night event in different areas of the city. With the assistance of the police, special routes are organized for the excursion, traffic is stopped, and even residents cannot park outside their homes from 10:30 P.M. until 1:00 in the morning. This reclaiming of the streets and squares of Paris has engendered some complaints from those who are not bladers, but it appears to be an activity that will not go away.

Related Web links: http://chappy50.free.fr for a history of cyclomoteur (E, F); **promoto.net** is a motorbike site (F); **webmoto.com** for links to motorbike dealers, accessories, manufacturers (F); **rollernet.com** for a magazine, advice for roller bladers (F)

Urban Transportation

French cities have efficient mass transit systems, which are extensively used. All cities in France try to minimize traffic congestion, and the resulting air pollution, by encouraging residents to use the public transportation systems.

There's an underground rail system, the Metro, in six major French cities: Paris, Lille, Lyon, Marseille, Toulouse, Rouen, and Rennes. These operate in conjunction with city bus services. In Paris, the Metro and the buses are part of the RATP network (Régie autonome des transports parisiens), which carries 9 million people a day. The Metro is the fastest and cheapest way to move around Paris. It consists of 14 lines in a 120-mile network, has 297 stations in Paris and nearby suburbs, and operates between the hours of 5:30 and 12:30 A.M. Trains run every two minutes during peak hours and every ten minutes at other times.

In July 2000 the Paris Metro celebrated its 100th anniversary. The first line had been constructed for the Universal Exhibition of 1900, making Paris the third city in the world to have such a train system, after London (1863) and Budapest (1896). The newest line of the Paris Metro, the Meteor line (number 14), whose name stands for Metro est-ouest rapide, was opened in 1998. It has been described as the Metro of the future, "clean, welcoming, and modern," and is unique in that it is completely automatic, with no driver and no conductor. It has been popular with Parisians, particularly because of its 99.5 percent rate of punctuality. The Meteor travels from Madeleine to the Bibliothèque de France

Metro station in 11 minutes. It is connected to the other major component of the Paris transportation system, the RER (Réseau express régional), which is a "super Metro" linking Paris to its suburbs. There are four main RER lines, and the RER and Metro systems overlap in central Paris, where some stations serve both systems.

The Paris bus system is also run by the RATP, and the same tickets can be used for both bus and Metro. There are 58 bus routes in Paris and over 2,000 buses in daily circulation. Buses are an excellent way to see the city, but they can get caught in the heavy rush-hour traffic. A special bus service, the Noctambus, operates between 1:30 and 5:30 A.M., when the Metro doesn't run.

As part of a comprehensive network of transportation, four French cities have installed tramways: Grenoble, Saint-Etienne, Strasbourg, and Nantes.

Related Web links: ratp.fr for Paris bus and Metro route finder, maps, travel guides, listings, history (E, F); **ina.fr**, see *Archives* then *Voir et revoir* for television news footage on 100 years of the Metro (E, F); **transpole.fr** for Lille transportation network (F); **http://www2.tcl.fr** for the Lyon transportation network (F); **subwaynavigator.com** for Metro maps and route finder for nine French cities (E, F)

Rail Transportation

French trains, renowned for their speed, comfort, and punctuality, are a popular means of transportation. The first railway line was constructed in 1825, and in 1842 a law was passed that established a rail network similar to the road network.

Since 1937 the Société nationale des chemins de fer français (SNCF) has been responsible for running the rail network, which has been likened to a spiderweb with its center in Paris, where all the *grandes lignes* (main lines) start.

In 1981 the French government put one of the fastest trains in the world into service: the TGV (Train à grande vitesse) between Paris and Lyon. The TGV Atlantic began operation at the end of 1989, and today TGV trains serve most major destinations in France. TGV technology has been sold around the world, and was used for the Houston-Dallas–San Antonio line in the United States.

In 2001 the TGV Méditerranée, which travels 540 miles from Paris to Marseille in three hours, was initiated. At 185 miles an hour, it provides real competition for the domestic airline services. New stations have been built at Valence-en-Provence, Avignon, and Aix-en-Provence. The TGV Méditerranée has revolutionized train travel in France by improved connections: with the Paris region; and Northeast/South and West/South connections between regional centers without having to change at Paris. TGV lines carry 48 percent of train travelers, with the other 52 percent using the *grandes lignes*. Those cities on the TGV routes are seen to hold an advantage over cities still serviced by traditional trains, because the TGV brings them closer to Paris. The Massif Central region, with no TGV, appears as a great empty space in France's train network, further adding to its economic and social isolation.

Since November 1994, France has also been linked to England by the Chunnel and the Eurostar train from Paris to London. It also travels at a speed of 185 miles an hour, although it slows to 100 kilometers in the tunnel. Eurostar offers direct services to Disneyland near Paris as well as to ski stations in the French Alps. By December 1998, 20 million passengers had been transported on the Eurostar train service. The SNCF transports goods as well as passengers. The goods sector has been growing fast and includes the movement of trucks by train.

Related Web links: sncf.com for French railways route planner, reservations (E, F); **tgv.com** for TGV network map and tickets (E, F)

TRANSPORTATION
Water Tourism and Transportation

France has a particularly rich and extensive network of navigable canals and rivers, comprising 5,100 miles. Some of the canals date from the 17th century—the Canal de Briare and the Canal du Midi, for example, which have a World Heritage listing. This system has a dual function: the transport of goods by barge (*péniches*), and tourism. A series of canals linking the main rivers allows barges to transport goods throughout France. A constant succession of barges can be seen on the Seine in Paris, which is a very busy river port. Tourism is by houseboat—or *pénichette*, as it is sometimes called—which has become a growing industry in France. More than 200,000 tourists a year, of whom 80 percent are foreign, choose to see France from the water. This relaxed way of touring, at about five miles per hour, attracts tourists who enjoy the peace and freedom of canal travel. It is possible to travel all over France, in Alsace, Burgundy, or Brittany, but the center of this type of tourism is the South of France along the famous Canal du Midi. Nearly 150 miles long, the Canal du Midi links the Atlantic Ocean to the Mediterranean via the Garonne River, and passes through Toulouse and Béziers. Canal tourism is also possible in Paris, on the Canal Saint Martin and the Canal de l'Ourcq. The Saint Martin was the former industrial canal for Paris, and has nine locks, two swing bridges, and eight romantic footbridges. The Canal d'Ourcq extends more than 60 miles into the French countryside. Both canals are now used principally for tourism.

Travel to and from France by ferry is not uncommon. Ferries to England operate from Normandy or Brittany, and may be traditional ferries or Hovercraft. Ferries departing from the Mediterranean ports of Marseille, Toulon, and Nice link France with Corsica, Sardinia, and mainland Italy. It is also possible to travel to Algeria, Morocco, and Tunisia by boat from Marseille. This route is well-patronized by French immigrants from these former colonies, returning home each summer to see their families. Usually these ferries accommodate both passengers and cars, enabling a great many families to make the trip laden with gifts and goods from France.

Related Web links: peniche.com/2sommaire 2.htm for maps of navigable rivers (F); **vnf.fr**, see *Tourisme fluvial* for interactive map from French waterways (F); **rive-de-france.tm.fr** for river vacations (E, F); **canal-du-midi.org** for Canal du Midi history, navigation, tourism (F); **seafrance .com, hoverspeed.co.uk, brittany-ferries.fr** for cross-Channel ferries (E, F); **corsicaferries.com** for ferries to Corsica (E, F)

Air Transportation

The first airborne crossing of the English Channel was made by a French scientist, Jean-Pierre-François Blanchard (1753–1809) and an American doctor, John Jeffries. After the pioneering experiments of the Montgolfier brothers, who invented the "hot air" balloon for air transport (the Montgolfière) in 1783, Blanchard made his own trial flights in England and North America. In January 1785 he and Jeffries set off from Dover and made it to Calais after throwing all their baggage overboard to gain height. Blanchard, who also made the world's first parachute descent, was killed in a fall from his balloon over Holland.

France was one of the first countries in the world to organize international flights: Paris-London and Paris-Prague in 1920, and Paris–South America in 1936. The Air and Space Museum at Le Bourget Airport, north of Paris, which recently celebrated its 80th anniversary, traces the history of commercial aviation in France. Today, Paris holds the ninth position in the world for air traffic, and the second position in Europe, after London. This is due to the capacity of Roissy–Charles de Gaulle Airport, 19 miles north of the city. In operation since 1974, it has two main terminals: CDG1 is used for long-haul international flights, while CDG2 is used for domestic and short international flights. Another terminal, T9, is used for charter flights. Paris has a second airport at Orly, nine miles south of the city. Its two terminals, Orly Sud and Orly Ouest, were 40 and 30 years old, respectively, in 2000. Both airports have train and bus links to Paris, and Roissy has a TGV link to other parts of France. Most American airlines transit either through Roissy or Orly airports. Marseille, Lyon, Bordeaux, and Nice are also used by international airlines.

Air France, the national airline, was created in 1933 from different private companies, and was nationalized in 1948. It is the world's third-largest airline in the transportation of international passengers, and completely dominates the domestic market. Air France and Delta Airlines formed an alliance in 1999, and in 2000 were joined by Korean Air, to form the "Sky Team." In the same year, however, Air France suffered a major setback when one of its supersonic Concorde aircraft, which first flew from Paris to Rio de Janeiro in 1976, crashed just outside the Roissy airport, killing all 100 passengers and the crew. Air France had six Concorde planes, and British Airways seven. As a result of the crash, Air France Concordes remained grounded until 2001, when service from Paris to New York resumed.

Related Web links: airfrance.fr for flight schedules and offers (F); adp.fr for a guide to Charles de Gaulle and Orly airports (E, F); http://montgolfiere.ifrance.com for ballooning in France, including Montgolfière photo history (F)

France in the World

Internationally, the French are held in great esteem for their achievements in the arts, their democratic values established by the Revolution of 1789, and their universal advocacy of human rights. Paris is widely considered the heart of high culture and the epitome of cultivated sophistication. French luxury products, food, and wine are renowned. But France is an uneasy player on the world stage, struggling to maintain her position among the world leaders.

The prestige attributed to French culture no longer extends to the political power of France, despite pretensions otherwise. Two superpowers, the United States and the Soviet Union, emerged from the ruins of World War II, and General de Gaulle wanted France to be a third. De Gaulle's resentment of America's heroic role in the war, however, sparked many years of diplomatic antagonism between France and the United States. And when the Soviet Union collapsed, the role of France as interlocutor between the two on the world stage diminished. Presidents since de Gaulle have forged a closer association with the United States, although France does not hesitate to oppose American foreign policy. Out of this "anti-Anglo" stance taken by France emerged the term "the French exception," which refers to the French tendency to take an alternative path.

During the cold war, France channeled her ambitions of international grandeur into other fields. The development of nuclear technology became a priority for French governments. Believing that a nuclear arsenal was the only guarantee of national sovereignty, France began testing nuclear weapons prior to 1975 in the Sahara desert, and then in French Polynesia, at Mururoa atoll in the Pacific, flexing French muscle on the world stage.

France also sought to increase her international power by maintaining a strong economic, military, and cultural presence in the former French colonies of Africa, which gained independence in the 1950s. Agreements of cooperation were based upon France providing aid in return for strategic access to raw materials and markets. Peacekeeping was another area in which the French exercised influence. Over the years, France has had a significant presence in the United Nations Protection Force.

From the outset, France has always struggled to play the leading role in the New Europe as a means of competing more effectively with the United States and controlling the ambitions of Germany. However, since the collapse of the Berlin Wall in 1989, a reunified Germany has challenged French supremacy in Europe.

In a recent French survey about the role of France in the world, the most frequent response was that French influence had become stronger. Nevertheless, France is now generally considered a medium-sized power on the world stage.

Related Web links: diplomatie.fr, see *Foreign Policy* in Ministry of Foreign Affairs site (E, F); **expatries.org/repdipet.asp** for French embassies abroad (F)

The Concept of Europe

France was a founding member of the European Union (EU). To integrate more fully, French politics and their economy have undergone considerable change. Many young French people now consider themselves European. However, when the idea of a united Europe was first proposed, it was a radical concept for postwar France.

Two Frenchmen, Robert Schumann (1886–1963) and Jean Monnet (1888–1979), are often referred to as the fathers of modern Europe. They envisaged an institutional structure of cooperation between European nations that would ensure lasting peace between Germany and France after two disastrous world wars.

The first step in unifying Europe was the creation of the European Coal and Steel Community, established in 1951 by the Treaty of Paris. The goal was to achieve a political reconciliation between federal Germany, Belgium, France, Italy, Luxembourg, and the Netherlands by creating a common market in coal and steel.

In 1957 these six countries signed the Rome Treaty to create the European Economic Community (EEC), popularly called the Common Market. The objective was to create a customs union among the six nations, allowing the free circulation of capital, goods, and people, and to implement common policies regarding agriculture, trade, energy, and transportation. In 1962 "the Six" agreed upon a common agricultural policy (CAP), which guaranteed the free exchange of agricultural produce and a standard price for producers.

France and Germany were the most powerful players in the EEC. Although de Gaulle twice vetoed British entry into the community, Great Britain finally entered the EEC in 1973, along with Denmark and Ireland. Greece became a member in 1981, and Spain and Portugal in 1986. Austria, Finland, and Sweden became members in 1995.

The European Community developed a number of unique institutions to coordinate the activities of the member states. The oldest is the European Commission, created in 1967 and located in Brussels, Belgium. A Frenchman, Jacques Delors, was president of the commission from 1985 to 1995, and in 1986 it was Delors who proposed the creation of a single market in Europe.

In 1974 government leaders of the countries within the European Community organized regular meetings, a practice that was to lead to the European Council, which eventually became the main decision-making body in the community. The European Parliament, formed in 1979, is located in Strasbourg, France, where it meets monthly. Its members are elected for five-year terms in national elections.

The development of a unified Europe has added some terms of Euro-jargon to the French vocabulary, including *Eurocrate*, *Europhile*, *Eurosceptique*, and Europol (the police force).

Related Web links: lib.berkeley.edu/GSSI /eu.html for links to EU documents (E); **europa** .eu.int/abc/obj/chrono/40years/7days/en.htm for the main steps toward Union (E); **ina.fr/Dossiers /Europe/index.fr.html** for archives on EU (F)

The European Union

By the end of the 1980s, Monnet and Schumann's dream of European cooperation had become a reality, yet the community was basically only an economic one. But changes were about to take place on the European landscape that increased the importance of a more encompassing community. The collapse of the Iron Curtain, the reunification of Germany, and the civil wars in Yugoslavia made it clear that to fulfill its mission of peace, the European Community would need to acquire a political role. As a result, the Treaty of Maastricht came about, signed by the 12 member states in 1992.

The Maastricht treaty was a revolutionary step in the construction of a united Europe. It proposed a tighter economic union with a single currency, the euro (which fully came into effect in 2002), and a central European Bank. It outlined a political union, including the creation of a European citizenship, a common defense and security policy, and cooperation between judiciaries and law enforcement services. Maastricht also took important steps to make the European institutions more democratic. The European Parliament's powers had been mostly advisory until the treaty gave it the power to approve the European Commission's budget and amend its decisions, block agreements with outside countries, and veto appointments to European executive agencies. These changes were aimed at giving the elected body representing the citizens of Europe more control over the European Commission bureaucracy in Brussels, and involving them more closely in the formulation of European policy. It was Maastricht that transformed the European Community into the European Union, entailing a closer partnership between the member states and unifying some of the rights of national sovereignty.

The French, deeply divided over the implications of the Maastricht treaty, only narrowly ratified it, with a slim 51 percent in favor, in a 1992 referendum. Wealthy, urban, educated France was eager for the opportunities within the EU. Poor, rural, uneducated France viewed further integration into Europe as another source of alienation from the protection of the French state. Like de Gaulle 30 years earlier, many feared a loss of French identity in a Europe that was *too* unified, and wanted an independent France within Europe.

With Austria, Finland, and Sweden joining in 1995, the European Union grew to 15 member states. Meanwhile, the French economy has become increasingly integrated with that of the rest of Europe. The French now carry European passports and use the euro, and their lives are influenced by the decisions of the European institutions. However, French enthusiasm about Europe has increased little since Maastricht, and many see only the negative consequences of European integration. In contrast, Germany wants greater integration, a stronger executive, and a strengthened European Parliament.

Related Web links: diplomatie.gouv.fr/europe /index.gb.html for French policy in Europe (E, F)

Regional Europe

In the European Union, sandwiched between France and Germany on the left bank of the Rhine, is a region that has often been dubbed the heart of Europe. This is the French region of Alsace. It is unlike other French regions because its cultural roots are German, and through much of history this has placed Alsace in the middle of a bitter custody battle between France and Germany.

Originally belonging to the German Holy Roman Empire, Alsace and part of the neighboring region of Lorraine became part of France in 1648 as a trophy for the military victory of Louis XIV. The defeat of Napoleon III in 1871 by the invading Prussian army saw the regions pass to the new German Empire, to become Elsass-Lothringen. France, as the victor at the end of World War I, reclaimed Alsace-Lorraine in 1918. With World War II, however, the region was invaded and annexed by Hitler, and become part of the German Reich in 1940. When this second world war ended, Alsace-Lorraine was returned to France, thus changing nationality for the fourth time in the 75 years between 1871 and 1945.

This tormented history deeply affected the population of the region. The Alsatians were often viewed as traitors by France and Germany and denied rights enjoyed by other members of the Republic and the Reich. It also bequeathed the Alsatians a dual culture. The Alsatian language is a German dialect, but Alsatians also speak French. The Alsatian culture values discipline and the German work ethic, yet it also attaches great importance to the revolutionary ideals of the Republic. Surnames are Germanic, first names are French.

The cultural, historical, and geographical duality between France and Germany made Alsace the ideal place to begin the process of European unification, which was essentially a guarantee of peace between France and Germany. It was in the Alsatian capital of Strasbourg, whose name means "ancient crossroads," that the first step in the construction of the New Europe was made with the establishment of the Council of Europe in 1949. Since then, the European dimension of Strasbourg has expanded. Other European and international institutions, including the European Parliament, the European Court of the Rights of Man, and Eurocorps, the Franco-German army corps, are now located in the Alsatian city.

Over the years, Alsace has developed a strong network of cooperation with its neighboring regions: Baden-Württemburg and the Palatinate in Germany, and Basel, Switzerland. As a result of the economic, political, and cultural interaction between the border regions, the area along the Rhine has been called a "Euroregion." Given the transnational past and present of Alsace, it is not surprising that this region was the most enthusiastic within France about the Treaty of Maastricht in 1992, recording a 66 percent vote in favor of the treaty at the referendum.

Related Web links: nfel.freeservers.com is a site for nationalist Alsace-Lorraine (F)

Daily Disharmony

France and Germany are partners in an increasingly integrated European Union. The French and the Germans are now both Europeans. However, daily life proceeds at a different pace on either side of the border, and both the French and the Germans have discovered a certain disharmony in their customs.

The Germans work more hours per week than the French: 40.1 compared to 35. The French have more strike days and engage in more part-time work than their neighbors, who have more public holidays but less paid leave.

Germany has some of the most restrictive laws concerning commercial trading. Until 1996 all shops (*Läden*) had to close by 6:00 P.M. during the week and 2:00 P.M. on Saturdays. These hours have since been changed to 8:00 P.M. and 4:00 P.M. respectively but on Sundays only those shops that sell tourist and travel goods are allowed to open. French shops, in contrast, trade all day Saturday but not on Sundays.

Championship *Fussball* matches take place at 7:30 or 8:00 P.M. during the week and 3:30 P.M. on weekends. In France, *football* matches tend to be later and more varied.

Concerning theater and the opera, the performances in the *Theater* and the *Opernhäuser* start between 7:00 and 8:00 P.M., and in France performances start between 8:00 and 8:30 P.M.

German children at primary school start class at 7:00 A.M. and finish at 1:00 P.M. Many other European schoolchildren envy this system, but it forces many mothers to stay at home. German children also spend less time at primary school and more time at high school than their French counterparts. And religious education takes up 6 percent of the curriculum in Germany and none at all in France, which, as a secular state, does not permit religious instruction in state schools.

Some things, however, are similar on both sides of the Rhine. Church in Germany begins at 10:00 A.M. for Lutherans, Calvinists, and Catholics. Museums and exhibitions open for the same hours, with a day off on Monday or Tuesday and extended hours in the middle of the week. In both countries the post office opens and closes at the same time. Similarly, there is no difference between the German *Kinos* and French *cinémas*. The first show starts at 1:30 P.M. and the last one begins around 10:00 P.M.

When it comes to eating and drinking, the French and Germans have different favorite dishes, and the Germans prefer beer to wine. However, when President Chirac and Chancellor Schroeder met in Alsace to demonstrate greater cooperation between their countries, their official dinner of *choucroute* (sauerkraut) and beer was a meal often enjoyed in both French and German homes.

Vive la Différence!

The French have for a long time been fascinated by the skyscrapers of New York, Hollywood westerns, and American business schools, whose methods were seen as the key to new economic prosperity. The older generation also remembers with gratitude the bravery of the soldiers who helped liberate France at the end of the World War II. The GIs however, also brought with them American customs, like jazz music and chewing gum. More recently, the proliferation of fast food outlets such as McDonald's ("McDo" in colloquial French) has provoked hostile criticism of a perceived takeover of French life by American values. Nonetheless, fast food chains, including French fast food chains such as La Brioche Dorée and Hippopotamus, have become popular among young people.

The opening of the Euro Disney theme park in 1992 near Paris focused the debate on the survival of French cultural traditions against the threat of international American culture. The Disney corporate culture disallows the serving of alcoholic drinks, but in response to lukewarm reception to its theme park, Disney permitted alcoholic drinks, to satisfy the French tradition of serving wine with meals. The name of the park was changed to Disneyland Paris, admission prices were decreased, and in 1996 the park finally turned a profit.

Anti-Americanism became strident in 1993. American pop and rock music, television programs, and movies came under attack by the French for stifling the expression of French values and the growth of France's own creative industries. Eighty percent of French movie houses are controlled by American film distributors, and the state-owned radio stations play a 40 percent minimum of French songs only because the government mandates it. In the final round of talks on the 1993 General Agreement on Tariffs and Trade (GATT), France successfully led opposition to the American proposal to include those industries in the agreement, arguing against unwelcome colonization by American culture and for continuing to subsidize its film and television industries. The minimum quotas on the number of French songs heard on French radio is evidence of the seriousness of this argument.

The French often use the term "Anglo-Saxon" pejoratively, as a collective description of all English speakers from countries historically influenced by British culture. The centuries of rivalry between France and Great Britain for world supremacy explains the negative attitudes toward the Brits, who the French consider cold and aloof. In comparison, the Latin temperament of the French is thought to be far superior. Americans are distinguished as a separate group among Anglo-Saxons, but the French often see Americans as childlike, uncivilized, and without taste.

Related Web links: disneylandparis.com for Disneyland Paris (E, F)

General Web Links

Many of the articles in this book provide related Web links to enable the reader to read further, view related images, and research in more detail. These sites are designated (E) for English, (F) for French, and (E, F) where both options are available. Unless otherwise stated, each site is prefaced **http://www**. Sites are selected for their interest and stability, but inevitably some addresses will have become dead links since publication. In addition to the Web addresses suggested for specific topics, the following sites are resources that provide information spanning a broad spectrum.

Government Sites
- **http://lessites.service-public.fr** for links to the wealth of French national Internet sites; search by topic or name of governmental organization (E, F)
- **insee.fr**, see *La France en Faits et Chiffres* for statistics and articles on population, work, health, education, the economy, social life. Articles and figures can be selected by region; see *Le Portrait de Votre Région* for data, maps (F)
- **france.diplomatie.fr/culture/france/biblio**, see *Thèmes* for contemporary art, comics, international relations, philosophy, photography, soccer; see *Textes* for literary works; see *Poesie* for a poetry anthology; see *Revues* for journal descriptions (F)

City Guides
In addition to official city sites, these guides cover multiple cities.
- **bestofcity.fr** guides for 90 cities (F)
- **viamichelin.fr** travel for itineraries, maps, hotels, restaurants (E, F)
- **voyager-en-france.com** for guide to 31 cities (E, F)
- **viapolis.com** for 12 city guides (F)

French Search Engines
- francite.com
- ifrance.com
- lycos.fr
- mageos.com
- nomade.fr
- voonoo.net
- wanadoo.fr
- fr.yahoo.com

Educational Sites
- **utm.edu/departments/french/french.html#history** for Tennessee Bob Peckham's Globe-Gate project, with extensive links to history, education, books, maps, culture, media, language, and daily life (E, F)

- **web-guide-fr.com/France/index.html** for links to sites for government bodies, media, shopping, and services (F)
- **about.com** is a network of guides that include *France for Visitors, French Language,* and *French Cuisine,* as well as French-related material within general topics such as *Art History, Architecture,* and so forth (E)
- **aatf.utsa.edu/surfing.htm** for links proposed by the American Association of Teachers of French (E)
- **britannica.com** for search articles from the encyclopedia and best website selections (E)
- **republique-des-lettres.com**, see *Prix littéraires* for Prix Goncourt and Prix Femina (F)
- **motorlegend.com/new/histoire/salonauto** for history of the Motor Show (F)
- **totalrugby.com**, see *6 Nations* (F)
- **parismarathon.com** (E, F)
- **festival-cannes.fr** for Cannes Film Festival (F)
- **rolandgarros.org** for the French Tennis Open (E, F)
- **letour.fr** is the official Tour de France site (E, F)
- **salon-du-bourget.fr** for the International Air Show (E, F)

Quizlink Answers

Do as the French Do
1b, 2b, 3b, 4c, 5c, 6a, 7b, 8b, 9a, 10c, 11a, 12c, 13c, 14c, 15b

What's the Number?
1b, 2c, 3a, 4b, 5c, 6a, 7a, 8b, 9b, 10b, 11a, 12b, 13c, 14b, 15c, 16a, 17b, 18c

Who's Who?
1c, 2b, 3c, 4a, 5b, 6b

Famous French
1b, 2b, 3b, 4b, 5a, 6c, 7b, 8b, 9a, 10c, 11b, 12c, 13a

What's My Line?
1a, 2a, 3a, 4c, 5a, 6b, 7c, 8a

Organizations and Companies
1a, 2b, 3a, 4a, 5b, 6c, 7c

France and Beyond
1c, 2a, 3b, 4a, 5a, 6a, 7a, 8c, 9a, 10a, 11c, 12b, 13c, 14c, 15b, 16b, 17b, 18b, 19c, 20a, 21c, 22b, 23b, 24c, 25c, 26a

Know Your Way Around Paris
1a, 2b, 3c, 4b, 5b, 6c, 7a, 8c, 9b, 10b, 11c, 12c, 13b, 14b

Dates
1b, 2c, 3c, 4b, 5b, 6c, 7b, 8c, 9c

A Question of Time
1c, 2c, 3b, 4a, 5c, 6c, 7c, 8a, 9b, 10b, 11c, 12a

The Order of Things
1cab, 2bca, 3cab, 4bac, 5bac, 6abc, 7bac, 8cba

Identify This
1a, 2c, 3abc (all three—this is a trick question!), 4a, 5b, 6c, 7b

Know What the French Know

1b, 2a, 3c, 4b, 5b, 6c, 7b, 8b, 9a, 10b, 11a, 12c, 13a, 14b, 15a, 16c, 17a, 18c, 19b, 20b, 21b, 22a, 23a, 24c, 25a, 26c, 27a, 28b, 29a, 30c, 31a, 32b, 33c, 34c

Index

INDEX

INDEX

INDEX

Mitterrand, President François, 16, 56, 87, 114, 137, 152, 153, 154, 157
Mnouchkine, Ariane, 26
Modigliani, Amedeo, 142
Moliére, Jean-Baptiste, 26, 28, 35, 74
Monet, Claude, 21, 87
Money, 178
Monnet, Jean, 187, 188
Monod, J., 161
Montagnier, Luc, 96, 161
Montaigne, Michel de, 35, 135
Montand, Yves, 30
Montesquieu, Baron de, 35, 149
Montgolfier brothers, 185
Moreau, Jeanne, 25
Moreno, Roland, 162
Moulin, Jean, 107, 114, 142
Mounier, Emmanuel, 150
Movie industry, 24–25
Museums, 16, 100, 137, 139, 143, 161, 185, 190
Music, 28–31
Music Day, 17, 132
Musset, Alfred de, 36

Nadar, Gaspard, 23
Names, 126
Napoléon I, 20, 103, 104, 105, 109, 111, 114, 119, 140, 144, 167, 178
Napoléon III, 18, 105, 109, 119, 140, 189
Néel, Louis, 161
Newspapers, 33
Nicot, Jean, 118
Niépce, Nicéphore, 23
Noiret, Philippe, 25
Normandy, 90, 108
North Africans, 110, 146
Notat, Nicole, 157
Nôtre, André le, 18, 87
Notre Dame cathedral, 18, 114, 141, 143
Nougaro, Claude, 30
Nouvelthe, Jean, 19
Numbers, 124

Odo of Bayeux, Bishop, 100
Offenbach, Jacques, 23, 28
Ophuls, Marcel, 25

Pagnol, Marcel, 25
Painting, 20–21
Paré, Ambroise, 160

Paris
  bus system, 182
  as global city, 139
  as heart of nation, 152
  history of, 140
  Ile-de-France, 89
  left bank, 142
  Metro, 182
  monuments, 144
  right bank, 141
  the Seine, 86, 143
  shopping, 147
  villages of, 145
Parisians, 146
Parks, national, 87
Pascal, Blaise, 148, 149, 160
Passard, Alain, 77
Pasteur, Louis, 79, 96, 160
Pastries, 81
Pathé, Charles, 24
Pei, Ieoh Ming, 19
Perfume, 92, 98, 147
Perrault, Dominique, 19
Perse, St. John, 37
Pétain, Marshal, 106, 108, 112
Pétanque, 134
Petit, Roland, 27
Petit, Zizi Jeanmarie, 27
Pets, 73
Philosophy, 148–50
Phone numbers, 124
Phones, mobile, 129
Photography, 23
Piaf, Edith, 30
Piano, Renzo, 19
Picasso, Pablo, 21, 142
Piccoli, Michel, 25
Pierre, Abbé, 170, 177
Pietragalla, Marie-Claude, 27
Pilon, Germain, 22
Pivot, Bernard, 17, 119
Planchon, Roger, 26
Poincaré, Jules Henri, 160
Politeness, 63. See also Customs; Etiquette
Politics. See also History; World stage
  decentralization, 152
  government institutions, 153
  Green movement, 155
  PACS, 159
  political life, 154
  skeleton of France, 151
  taking to the streets, 156

INDEX